Environment and Citizenship in Latin America

Environment and Citizenship in Latin America

Natures, Subjects and Struggles

Edited by

Alex Latta
& Hannah Wittman

berghahn
NEW YORK · OXFORD
www.berghahnbooks.com

Published in 2012 by
Berghahn Books
www.berghahnbooks.com

Library of Congress Cataloging-in-Publication Data

Environment and citizenship in Latin America: natures, subjects and struggles
/ edited by Alex Latta & Hannah Wittman. — 1st ed.
    p. cm. — (CEDLA Latin American studies (CLAS); 101)
Includes index.
    ISBN 978-0-85745-747-9 (hardback) — ISBN 978-1-78238-909-5 (paper-
back) — ISBN 978-0-85745-748-6 (ebook)
    1. Political ecology—Latin America. 2. Citizenship—Latin America.
3. Environmental policy—Citizen participation—Latin America.
4. Environmental protection—Citizen participation—Latin America.
5. Sustainable development—Latin America. 6. Nature and civilization—
Latin America. I. Latta, Alex, 1973– II. Wittman, Hannah, 1973–
    JA75.8.E57 2012
    304.20973—dc23
                                                                    2012001642

British Library Cataloguing in Publication Data

A catalogue record for this book is available from the British Library

Printed on acid-free paper

ISBN 978-0-85745-747-9 hardback
ISBN 978-1-78238-909-5 paperback
ISBN 978-0-85745-748-6 ebook

Contents

Acknowledgements

We are grateful for the generous support of the Social Sciences and Humanities Research Council of Canada, along with Simon Fraser University and Wilfrid Laurier University, for funding the 2010 workshop that first brought our contributors together in Vancouver, BC, for a critical and stimulating discussion on the evolving linkages between nature, society and citizenship in Latin America. Revised versions of many of the chapters were presented at the 2010 meeting of the Latin American Studies Association in Toronto.

Participants in both events offered invaluable commentaries on the chapters as they evolved into their present form. We would particularly like to thank Ian Angus, Alain Boutet, John Brohman, Megan Cotton-Kinch, Conny Davidson, Andrés Dimitriu, Maria Isabel du Monceau, Leila Harris, Michael Hathaway, Duncan Knowler, Tim McNeill, Gerardo Otero, Piya Pangsapa, Gabriela Pechlaner, Patricia Rodriguez, Mark Smith, Susan Spronk and Anna Zalik.

This project could not have been completed without the efficient contributions of several SFU graduate students, Christina Bielek, Amie McLean and Jennifer Thomas, who provided vital support in workshop organization, note-taking, translation and manuscript editing. We would also like to thank the anonymous reviewers and the editorial board of the CEDLA Latin American Studies series, both for their enthusiasm for the project and for their insightful comments and suggestions. We are particularly indebted to Kathleen Willingham at CEDLA and Melissa Spinelli at Berghahn Books for their roles in seeing this project through to final publication.

1 Citizens, Society and Nature

Sites of Inquiry, Points of Departure

Alex Latta and Hannah Wittman

'What science has identified as the ancestor of corn is a grass: teosintle. It is a grass from which corn emerged only as a result of an exchange between this grass and humans. In this respect, corn is the product of a dialogue between the human and the vegetable worlds ... corn could not have been created unless humans started to converse with teosintle. To understand this is to understand the world in a very different way. ... In the past, corn taught us to be humans. Today, at a time when the market rules, what we believe is that corn can help us once again to recuperate our humanity.'

—Amado Ramírez Leyva, Mixtec restaurant owner and food activist in Oaxaca, Mexico (quoted in Poole and Alonso Rascón 2009, 32–33)

'If they want to begin to pay us a little of the debt that the winka have with us mapuche, if they insist on giving me something of their modernity, I will wait for it here on my land, and I will see what parts of it are useful to me, what I will take from it, but I will not in exchange abandon the spirits of my landscape.'

—Nicolasa Quintremán Kalpán, Mapuche-Pewenche elder speaking of her resistance to the Ralco hydroelectric project on the Bío Bío River, in Southern Chile (quoted in Chihuailaf 1999, 143, our translation)

'Bebo agua, luego existo, luego voto.' (I drink water, therefore I exist, therefore I vote.)

—Graffiti in Cochabamba, Bolivia (Perreault 2010)

These words from Latin American activists remind us of something fundamental about the politics of the environment. They reaffirm that nature is not only an object of social struggle, but is also inextricably intertwined with the very voices that render the environment political. This book explores that intertwining, examining the way that socio-political subjects are mutually constituted with the ecological practices and institutions that they create, defend and reshape over time. To do so it draws on the concept of citizenship – a category of being that rests at the centre of modern forms of political order. Debates about environmental citizenship have taken on strategic importance for scholars, policy makers and civil society actors as they rethink individual and collective engagement with ecological challenges. This volume in part aims to build on these debates, but we also invite readers to revisit dominant conceptions of what it means to study environmental questions through the lens of citizenship. In particular, the chapters in this collection demonstrate that addressing socio-ecological relationships and struggles in the Global South requires nuanced attention to the ways citizenship itself is constituted and contested. As such, our premise is not simply that the lens of citizenship can shed new light on the politics of nature, but also that debates and conflicts over the fate of nature can help us better understand what is at stake in the politics of citizenship in Latin America and beyond.

Latin American Articulations of Citizenship and Environment

Latin America provides a rich context for research on the environmental dimensions of citizenship: its cultural diversity, its shared histories of conflict, and the multiplicity of specific ecological and territorial landscapes as exemplified in an array of indigenous cosmovisions. With a fraught and uneven history of conquest, imperialism, ethnic conflict and resource-related economic development, Latin America presents a complex field of socio-ecological relations. It is home to political cultures informed by a range of influences, including European traditions, such as republicanism, liberalism and Marxism; social and political traditions specific to the settler societies of the region, such as the Bolivarian revolution and Paulo Freire's pedagogy of the oppressed; and, principally, a long heritage of indigenous socio-political institutions, from the Mayan *usos y costumbres* to the Mapuche *admapu*. Each of these various political traditions is embedded in specific visions of socio-ecological relations, from the Quichua's social organization of cultivation linked to reverence for the *pachamama* to liberalism's institutions of private property. These political-ecological inheritances are constantly being reinvented and recombined, as witnessed in the Zapatista autonomous municipalities of Mexico, the Brazilian landless workers movement and the indigenous recuperation of the state in Bolivia.

During the latter part of the twentieth century, Latin American societies emerged from an era of authoritarian regimes and began processes of democratic renewal, with the environment becoming one of the first issues around which civil society movements coalesced. As a reflection of the ecological pressures associated with rapid modernization and globalization, based largely on the export of agricultural products and natural resources, the environment has remained an enduring theme of public debate and popular protest. This political ferment around environmental issues has made important contributions to new characterizations of the rights, responsibilities and relations of citizenship in Latin America, bridging the concerns of environmental justice, democratic participation and livelihoods (Latta and Wittman 2010).

Constitutional changes in Brazil, Argentina, Colombia, Peru and Venezuela have variously reconsidered rights related to access to land and a healthy environment (Gudynas 2009), while Ecuador's 2008 constitution goes so far as to provide rights to nature itself. Articulating these changes to the global scale, in 2004 the United Nations Environment Program (UNEP) launched a Latin America Global Environmental Citizenship Project (Unep/Pnuma 2006). This has been followed by other formal recognitions of the relationship between environment and citizenship, including the Peruvian Ministry of Environment's 2009 Environmental Citizenship Prize, Brazil's Secretariat of Institutional Articulation and Environmental Citizenship and Chile's Youth National Environmental Citizenship Day.

Reflecting these trends, scholarship related to environmental questions in Latin America has increasingly incorporated themes related to citizenship. Researchers working with rural and indigenous peoples have probed relationships that link the politics of land, livelihood and identity, often in the context of struggles for political recognition and agency (see, for example, Yashar 2005; Latta 2007a; Postero 2007; Nuijten and Lorenzo 2009; Wittman 2009, 2010); others studying democratization and institutional reform in the environmental sector have looked to citizen participation processes as key facets in new modes of governance (Menegat 2002; Palerm and Aceves 2004; Bachmann, Delgado and Marín 2007; Walker et al. 2007); an emerging literature on environmental justice in the region also crosses into questions of democracy and participation (Hochstetler and Keck 2007; Carruthers 2008); and efforts to historicize the political ecology of specific resources, such as water or fossil fuels, have linked struggles over these resources to the evolution of citizenship and popular imaginaries of the nation (Castro 2006; Perreault and Valdivia 2010).

In the current Latin American conjuncture a period of formal democratic consolidation has been more-or-less completed in a series of countries that experienced dictatorial regimes during the second half of the twentieth century. Nevertheless, the depth of the democratic transition in many of these nations remains in flux, not least because democracy returned under market conditions that have produced profound cultural shifts away from collective modes of popular mobilization, along with a simultaneous narrowing of the ideological spectrum among members of the political class. In this context the increasing linkage of environment and citizenship in Latin America, both within a top-down policy discourse of environmental rights and obligations and as an empirical dimension of socio-political conflicts reshaping citizenship from the bottom up, poses a new series of questions for scholars and practitioners alike.

Environmental Citizenship: A Contested Concept

Over the past decade, debates about environmental citizenship have risen to prominence in the field of environmental politics, with some crossover into interdisciplinary scholarship rooted in other areas of the social sciences. These debates have rejuvenated perennial discussions about the links between ecology and democracy, as well as the socio-political conditions required to cultivate sustainable development. There are a number of key insights and conversations within the literature that serve as important points of reference as we orient ourselves to the task of building a research agenda around environment and citizenship in Latin America. The first of these points is related to alternate philosophical frameworks for citizenship. There are several traditions that vie for precedence in the way that the ecological dimension is integrated into the institutions and practices of citizenship, most strongly evident as a debate between liberalism, with its emphasis on rights (see Hayward 2002; Bell 2005; Hailwood 2005) and republicanism, which places a much stronger accent on obligations or virtues (see Smith 1998; Dobson 2003). As social actors draw on the language of citizenship to shape their identities and political projects they draw alternately or simultaneously on these overarching traditions, with different implications for the way that nature is articulated to the political sphere.

A second important dimension of the literature on environmental citizenship deals with issues of scale and the territoriality of formal political communities within the modern nation-state. A series of scholars have argued that there is a problematic disconnect between the spatial characteristics of ecological problems and conflicts, on the one hand, and the traditional containers of political community, on the other (see Newby 1996; Jelin 2000; Valencia Sáis 2005). In an example of one widely cited response to this disjuncture, Andrew Dobson (2003) has argued that the notion of the ecological footprint promises a new way of constituting citizenship obligations, where political community is reimagined according to the material relationships that link together human communities across vast distances. For Dobson this is a powerful way of linking citizenship to justice. He is particularly concerned that consumers in the Global North recognize and act to reduce the size of their ecological footprint on ecological systems and human communities in the Global South. We can equally see how rethinking the territorial basis for citizenship helps make sense of the growth of transnational activist networks, as a response in the political sphere to the tremendous deterritorialisation of economic and commodity flows.

A third strand of scholarship on environmental citizenship has focussed on deliberation as a core tenet of democratic citizenship, emphasizing the way that deliberative approaches to education and political contest can advance the incorporation of ecological questions into public consciousness and offer more scope for broadly participatory decision making on environmental questions (see Barry 1999; Carlsson and Jensen 2006; Schlosberg, Shulman and Zavestoski 2006). Though it currently comprises a more limited piece of the scholarship on environmental citizenship, this approach has affinities with a broader literature on deliberative theories of green democracy (see Barns 1995; Dryzek 2000).

While the literature on environmental citizenship offers many insights relevant to the issues and cases addressed by the contributors to this book, three key limitations are worth highlighting. First, environmental citizenship emerged most strongly as a normative theoretical project aimed at rethinking citizenship according to the imperative of responding to ecological crisis. As a result of this orientation, academic debates on environmental citizenship are often significantly removed from the lived experience of 'actually existing' citizenly agency vis-à-vis environmental questions. In a second related problem, some of the strongest voices in the existing literature are those linked to the republican project of cultivating responsible environmental citizens. An obligations approach to citizenship can risk depoliticizing ecological questions by locating citizen action in the context of individual behavioural change, rather than political debate and collective struggle. Recent empirical work on environmental citizenship bears out our concern about this risk, as an increasing number of researchers go in search of 'good' environmental citizens, as part of efforts to test whether increased knowledge of ecological problems actually prompts individuals to change their attitudes and behaviours (see Flynn, Bellaby and Ricci 2008; Jagers 2009; Wolf, Brown and Conway 2009).

The final limitation of existing conceptions of environmental citizenship is linked to a geographical bias in the literature, which has thus far paid little attention to empirical contexts in Latin America and other regions of the Global South. Preoccupied with the cultivation of 'green' behaviour among rapaciously consuming citizens in the North, researchers have generally failed to probe the interface of environment and citizenship from the perspective of political subjects whose relationship to the environment is defined instead by the ecological dimensions of socio-economic marginalization. As we approach this interface in the Latin American context it is crucial to be aware that the history of socio-ecological struggle in the region is markedly different from the environmentalism of North America or Europe. Characterizing the Brazilian environmental movement, Angus Wright (2008) observes that in the face of extreme inequality, a lack of state accountability and a culture of impunity for the economic elite, there is a certain urgency to the question of citizenship itself that colours popular ecological struggles in the region (see also Hochstetler and Keck 2007). In Brazil and elsewhere in Latin America, the politics of nature closely link struggles for recognition and inclusion in the political collective with simultaneous struggles for economic and ecological survival. In this sense, it is important to heed the call from political ecologists to pay attention to how unequal power relations take shape across multiple fields, conflicts and territorial spaces (see Bryant and Bailey 1997; Díez and Dwivedi 2008).

The research agenda that we propose in response to these limitations is broadly framed by our attempt to remedy the theoretical and geographical biases of current debates, proposing Latin America as a new site of empirical exploration. We assert that Latin America provides a host of experiences that can help engender theoretical and methodological innovation to address the conceptual limitations of environmental citizenship described above, while a focus on citizenship can help us better understand what is at stake in the environmentalism of the South. The chapters in this collection remind us that environmental questions are almost always already tangled with struggles over the shape of citizenship identities, institutions and practices. In seeking to tease apart these relationships we draw on immanent critiques of environmental citizenship, including some of our own existing contributions, emphasizing two key points of departure. First, as Liette Gilbert and Catherine Phillips (2003) sustain, citizenship constitutes not a set of static rights and duties but rather a dynamic space of struggle, within which rights can be claimed. In other words, even as nature is politicized by citizens enacting their political and ecological subjectivities, such enactment in turn involves an active reshaping of those subjectivities. This is particularly true when subaltern political subjects are the ones to bring environmental questions into political debate, since their efforts to politicize nature are simultaneously encapsulated in demands that their voices be heard by the broader political community – that their full citizenship in that community be recognized and honoured.

The second key point of departure for conceptual innovation has to do with the way that the dynamic relationship between environment and citizenship is also bound up with other dimensions of social life. Sherilyn MacGregor (2006a, 2006b), for instance, argues that the new responsibilities invoked by the notion of environmental citizenship do not play evenly across different fields of social experience. In particular, she highlights the particularity of women's experiences of both participatory democracy and citizen responsibility in a world characterized by gender inequality. In this light, she proposes an understanding of citizenship where nature and gender are simultaneously contested. We might equally insert race, identity or class into the equation, as dimensions of socio-political life that have an undeniable bearing on the way citizenship's articulation with environment is experienced and contested by different actors. These and other contributions to the debate (see Jelin 2000; Latta 2007b; Gabrielson 2008; Wittman 2010) begin to take us beyond the scope of citizenship that is merely environmental (in the sense of being 'green') and into an analytical domain where citizenship instead serves as a node or crucible where ecological questions become politicized together with an array of other issues fundamental to the very shape of the polities, ecologies, societies and conflicts that citizens inhabit. This treatment of citizenship thus sheds new light on the convergent politicization of nature and human marginality in response to the hegemonic projects of development, modernization and globalization (Díez and Dwivedi 2008).

Sites of Inquiry

While the contributions to this collection are characterized by a series of crosscutting empirical concerns and analytical orientations, we have grouped them according to the way in which particular chapters foreground three central thematic elements. The first section draws out the co-construction of nature and social subjectivity around questions of citizenship. The chapters in part two analyse dynamics of marginalization and the struggles for recognition and justice that rise in response. The final selection of chapters takes a closer look at the relationships between citizens and states in shifting regimes of environmental governance. In what follows we offer a preliminary orientation to each of these three sections of the book.

Assembling Nature's Citizens

The literature on environmental citizenship is mostly based on the assumption that citizenship needs to be *made* environmental in various ways, implying an original ontological separation of nature and society. Instead, we assert that nature and socio-political subjectivity are mutually constitutive nodes in complex networked assemblages of actors, discourses and biophysical flows. To put this another way, rather than understanding environment and citizenship as separate categories, which interact through human practices of public debate, resource extraction and environmental management, we take the ontological mingling of natures and socio-political subjects as our starting point. From this perspective, the crucial analytical task becomes one of identifying the ways in which particular citizen/nature amalgams are assembled, contested, dissolved and reassembled within historically dynamic and geographically specific socio-natural contexts.

The chapters in this section offer four different windows on the way that emergent citizen subjectivities are assembled and contested along with specific biophysical and discursive natures. First, Andrew Baldwin and Judy Meltzer present a disconcerting exploration of a particular kind of environmental citizen that is taking shape as an integral component within a set of discourses and policies that anchor a new biopolitical approach to global security. As the risks associated with global warming are reconfigured within the geopolitical considerations of major world powers, the carbon locked in tropical forests is mobilized as a key strategic resource. An emerging knowledge and management regime aimed at reduced emissions from deforestation and degradation (REDD), enables both the protection of forest carbon reserves and the conversion of that reserved carbon (as carbon credits) into flows of capital. Anchoring the securitization and commodification of rainforest carbon are the Amazonian communities recruited as custodians of the carbon resource, even as this redefinition of the forest potentially represents a new form of restriction on their own land-use rights. In a further paradox, Baldwin and Meltzer's analysis of recent events in Peru demonstrates that these same citizens have often simultaneously become targets of more traditional state security apparatuses, where in the name of national development the government has defended the property rights of transnational oil and gas companies with concessions over indigenous territory.

Where Baldwin and Meltzer give us a view onto the way that citizens and natures are assembled from above, Analiese Richard's chapter on food sovereignty in Mexico demonstrates that popular movements are also agents in the ongoing co-construction of environments and political subjectivities. Calling upon the cultural symbolism of maize as a link between land and society, the diverse and broad-based food sovereignty movement in Mexico reinvents the ties between nature and nation as a response to the transformations wrought by neoliberal globalization. As Richard's account demonstrates, the slogan 'Sin maíz no hay país' speaks volumes of the way that socio-political subjectivity and agro-ecological relationships are bound together in struggles around the intertwined issues of land tenure, agricultural technology and trade policy. Though clearly linked to a nationalist imaginary, Mexico's nascent environmental citizens are also projected as defenders of a newly *global* nature, not unlike the securitized indigenous forest custodians of Peru. Here, however, defending the global commons embodied in the genetic biodiversity of Mexico's native landraces of maize seems to have a greater consonance with popular struggles for social justice.

In chapter 3, Fábio de Castro takes a closer look at the relationship between environment, citizenship and social justice. He offers a hybrid perspective that integrates the top-down and bottom-up assemblages of nature and citizenship examined in the first two chapters. Focussing on Afro-Brazilian and indigenous peoples living in areas of Brazil that have been identified as megabiodiversity zones, de Castro explores the links between changing modes of subsistence, evolving identities and the multi-scalar politics of conservation, alongside struggles over the concrete parameters of citizenship within local political organizing and state-directed processes of policy development. Like the natures of REDD and Mexican maize, the nature that emerges at this crossroads of influences is both local and global. In exchange for more secure land tenure, the traditional communities examined by de Castro are enlisted as custodians of newly constituted global ecological commons that are embedded in their local landscapes. As part of their custodial duties to preserve biodiversity and carbon reserves, these communities – like their Peruvian counterparts – often face new restrictions on their own rights to local resources. De Castro observes that this manifestation of global ecological citizenship has significantly greater impacts on livelihood when compared to the duties taken on by 'green' consumer-citizens in the Global North.

In all three of these chapters, emerging assemblages of citizens and natures are intimately linked to transformations in socio-ecological knowledge regimes. Such transformations pave the way for both new kinds of knowers and new objects of knowing, enabling the calculation of carbon credits, the tracking of biological diversity levels and the increasing global monopoly over seeds for staple commodities like corn. The final chapter in this section focuses directly on the dimension of knowledge in the environment/citizenship nexus. Renzo Taddei explores the regional politics of climate in the state of Ceará, in Northeast Brazil, where state agencies preoccupied with the climatological component of rural agricultural development employ scientific and technocratic frameworks that compete with traditional ecological knowledge. In this fraught encounter we see the way that different ways of knowing and responding to changing climate are intimately intertwined with the evolution of social subjectivity and agency. When local rain prophets are pitted against meteorologists, the encounter between tradition and modernity transforms the former into folklore and defuses the insurgency of rural citizens by converting the keepers of traditional knowledge into tabloid celebrities.

Taddei's chapter also points us towards a final insight about the deeply intertwined relationships between ecology and subjectivity. Part of the local resistance to modern climatological knowledge that is explored in his chapter has to do with a popular conception of nature as an independent agent that will ultimately reject meteorological scientists' efforts at diagnosis and control. Taddei's analysis here opens a window to the way that nature conserves a degree of autonomy as it is drawn into relationships of social construction. To be more precise, the unpredictability of weather and climate underlines the way that the co-construction of nature and subjectivity occurs in hybridized socio-ecological space, rather than inhering in the discourses and practices of human actors alone.

Environmental Marginality and the Struggle for Justice

The second section of the book highlights the connections linking citizenship as a mode of inclusion/exclusion to particular discourses and practices of land distribution, resource extraction and environmental management. By 'environmental marginality' we aim to signal that social exclusion and exploitation is invariably embedded in geographically specific power relations that shape access to and control over environmental 'goods' as well as differential exposures to the 'bads' of environmental degradation and risk. At the same time, the title of this section signals the way in which marginalized populations respond to such power relations by pursuing various kinds of agency in pursuit of more just socio-ecological arrangements, engaging in what James Holston (2008) calls 'insurgent citizenship'.

In significant part, the thematic focus of this section is indebted to a now burgeoning scholarship on environmental justice. From its origins in U.S. social movements against toxic waste facilities and other forms of pollution disproportionately affecting populations of colour, the concept of environmental justice has risen in profile to become one of the central foci of the broader global justice movement. Since the field of environmental justice deals explicitly with issues of race, gender and class in relation to access to natural resources and exposure to environmental risks, the concept offers a valuable point of reference for scholarship that seeks to connect citizenship with the politics of nature. In fact, despite reservations about compatibility expressed by key figures in the respective fields of environmental justice and environmental citizenship (Dobson 2003; Agyeman and Evans 2006) others have already argued for an inherent connection between environmental justice and citizenship (Smith and Pangsapa 2008; Latta 2009). Since a recent volume (Carruthers 2008) highlights the way that the environmental justice paradigm can be specifically applied to Latin America, it is a timely moment to begin connecting that research agenda with the one embodied in this volume.

Many of the chapters in the book engage citizenship in light of different kinds of environmental marginality, along with alternate forms of countermovement, but the four assembled here foreground these issues in particularly striking ways. In chapter 7, María Teresa Grillo and Tucker Sharon offer a historical genealogy of contemporary conflicts in Peru already touched on by Baldwin and Meltzer in the first section of the book. Where that earlier chapter looks ahead to the way a global biopolitics of security informs new interpolations of natures and citizens in the Peruvian Amazon, Grillo and Sharon trace the same region's earlier incorporation into the racialized bio-geographical order of Peruvian sovereignty. As the state pursued ways of ef-fectively integrating its Amazonian territories into the economic and political body of the nation, indigenous communities were rendered invisible or suf-fered marginal inclusion in citizenship as 'native' populations. In particular, Grillo and Sharon focus on the geopolitical imagination of former President Belaúnde Terry, who imagined an Amazonian highway system that would extend its arteries and veins from the cordillera down into the rainforest, circulating citizen settlers of European origin into the country's eastern hin-terland and transporting the region's wealth back to the heart of the nation. Read together, the book's two chapters on Peru offer a fascinating account of indigenous people's shifting (but consistently marginal) incorporation into citizenship as an effect of evolving visions of Amazonian nature and the wealth located therein.

The racial dimension of historical patterns of exclusion is similarly picked up by Juanita Sundberg in chapter 6, this time in the context of new ratio-nalities and practices of conservation that emerged through the decade of the 1990s. The dynamism inherent in Holston's notion of insurgent citizenship is clearly present in Sundberg's account, where contestation and conflict over the question of 'who counts' as a political actor has been fundamental to decisions over the establishment and management of Guatemala's Maya Bio-sphere Reserve. In the context of historically embedded inequalities of race, gender and class, Sundberg explores the processes of subjugation that repro-duce inequality but also the practices of contestation that sometimes open up new spaces for citizenly agency in different sites across the socio-geographical ordering of human relations, such as homes, places of work and community organizations. In the highly fraught socio-political terrain of post-war Guate-mala, emerging practices of conservation and the arrival of new actors in the form of international environmental NGOs served to reconfigure the inclusions and exclusions of citizenship. While the imposition of conserva-tion reserves often introduced new logics to time-worn patterns of political marginalization based on race and class, Sundberg locates one surprising ex-ample where new economic opportunities linked to women's knowledge of medicinal plants created a micro-insurgence against the gendered exclusions of citizenship, increasing women's voices within local civil society.

Jumping ahead in time to the newly marketized politics of conservation that have emerged over the past decade, in chapter 9 Adam Henne and Teena Gabrielson offer an account of marginalities that have been reinscribed within transnational struggles to protect native Chilean forest through a certification and consumer labelling campaign. In an extended reprise of the theme explored in the first section of the book, Henne and Gabrielson centre their analysis on the emergence of a singular 'Chilean forest' out of complex and multiple assemblages of humans, biophysical landscapes and technologies. They turn to Damian White and Chris Wilbert (2009) to label these emergent singularities 'technonatures', underlining the way that entities such as 'the Chilean forest' come together as a result of hybridized socio-natural agency situated across a range of scales. The Chilean forest certification campaign depended upon a conception of native forest that ironically linked industry and environmentalists together in a technonatural project, where the forest became inserted into transnational logics of capital and commodity flows, animated by scientific forestry, corporate branding and 'green' consumption. As Henne and Gabrielson emphasize, this technonatural forest is far from innocent, but rather serves as a new basis for excluding indigenous Mapuche communities from debates over the use of their ancestral territories – now converted largely to tree farms – privileging instead non-Mapuche political subjectivities, ways of knowing and regimes of environmental management.

In chapter 8 Jason Tockman takes discussion of marginality and environmental justice to the epicentre of political change in Latin America, examining the interwoven struggles over citizenship and nature that have led to the dramatic transformation of the Bolivian state under Evo Morales and the Movimiento al Socialismo (MAS). The broad-based movements that surged onto the political stage in 2000 and eventually brought Morales to power in 2006 clearly sought to overturn historical patterns of racial and class hierarchy in Bolivian citizenship, but they simultaneously called for the nationalization of the country's hydrocarbon resources. Once in office, Morales almost immediately reasserted state control over the oil and gas sectors, while his government began simultaneously working towards the eventual constitutional changes that in 2009 introduced new collective and individual rights promising greater social and political inclusion for Bolivia's indigenous and *campesino* populations. Tockman convincingly argues that the pairing of citizenship and natural resource policy as key planks in the MAS's political platform is simply the latest instance in a long history linking natural resource extraction regimes to the ordering of Bolivian society and politics. From the colonial era mines of Potosí, to the tin boom of the early twentieth century, through to modern struggles over water, gas and oil, Tockman offers a sweeping historical account of the way that control and exploitation of natural resources has fundamentally shaped the Bolivian polity according to class divisions and mobilizations, generating alternate modes of inclusion/exclusion based on racial categories and regional conflicts over access to wealth and political power.

Citizens, the State and Environmental Governance

Citizenship as a substantive embodiment of both political being and territorial ordering evolves in relationship with a host of institutional norms and practices. As such, the lens of citizenship brings a new dimension to the study of environmental governance, with its preoccupation over the interactions between different institutional actors in establishing the legal, economic and administrative infrastructures that render human-nature relationships an object of management. If processes of globalization have opened up a complex and multi-scalar landscape of institutional actors (Díez and Dwivedi 2008), among them the state nevertheless retains a singular importance in environmental governance. By increasingly working in concert with other actors, the state authorizes and enables new spaces of deliberation and management along with alternative notions of territory and sovereignty, while alternately shutting out or domesticating forms of socio-ecological agency that challenge its authority. At the same time, innovation and contradiction within and between different arms of the state can sometimes open unexpected opportunities for insurgent forms of citizenship practice. The chapters in this section highlight some surprising shifts in environmental governance that force us to rethink the relationship between states and citizens.

In chapter 10, Enrique Silva describes a crisis in environmental governance that resulted when a new model of private highway concessions adopted during the 1990s by Chile's Ministry of Public Works (MOP) collided with resistance from residents of a low income Santiago neighbourhood, whose homes were threatened by a new urban highway that cut through their community. The MOP's innovative approach to infrastructure concessions involved what Silva calls 'deliberate improvisation', a kind of planning at the margins that deploys state sovereignty in new ways to insulate private investors from the political risks associated with the social and environmental impacts of highway construction. The organized resistance that rose in response to such impacts delayed the highway project for several years and provoked a prolonged public debate about the highway concession system. Silva's chapter is a study of the power of citizen insurgency, but it is also ultimately a story of the neoliberal state's ability to deflect radical criticism and conserve its institutional trajectory.

The next two chapters take us to Argentina, both with a slightly more positive outlook on the possibilities of citizen interaction with state institutions over matters of environmental governance. In chapter 11 María Gabriela Merlinsky and Alex Latta focus on the interaction between new forms of citizen mobilization and the judicial sphere, where the latter becomes an increasingly important channel by which citizens make demands on policy makers. In the case of a pulp mill conflict on the Argentina–Uruguay frontier, they highlight the dynamic relationships between grassroots organizing, transboundary harm and international judicial authority. In a second case, Argentina's constitutional guarantee of environmental rights becomes a crucial point of leverage enabling new kinds of legal claims and empowering the courts to take innovative steps to push forward dramatic changes in the institutional and legal parameters for environmental governance of an important waterway in the nation's capital. Nevertheless, this chapter also demonstrates that both popular mobilization and court actions are often beset by troubling contradictions, limiting the changes they are able to secure. Moreover, Merlinsky and Latta observe that as new citizen voices emerge into environmental policy debates, they themselves are implicated in producing new forms of socio-ecological exclusion.

Brián Ferrero's chapter takes us out of urban and industrial contexts and back into questions of rural livelihood and land use, this time in the Paraná rainforest enclave of Argentina's Misiones Province. In his examination of *colono* and indigenous participation in shaping environmental governance for the region, Ferrero argues that the global movement for forest conservation has generated fresh political space at the local level, replete with a new set of transnational actors, within which the region's inhabitants are able to pursue other long-standing socio-economic goals. Political partnerships with environmental NGOs and bilateral aid agencies have earned small farmers and the Mbya-Guaraní recognition and access to new resources from the state. As in the Mexican case examined by Richard, we see here a dialectical interplay between citizen mobilization and public institutions, where popular protest forces changes to state policies and these changes in turn reshape both citizens' socio-ecological subjectivities and their opportunities for political agency. Nevertheless, the state and citizens are not dancing alone; in many ways local peoples are part of a tug-of-war between NGOs and powerful forest companies. In concluding, Ferrero is cautious about whether or not the evolution of novel frameworks for environmental governance in Misiones will on balance support a more just and democratic basis for sustainable local livelihoods over the long term.

The final chapter addresses the question of nature's 'participation' in the contestation and evolution of the relationships linking environment to citizenship. Here, Juliet Pinto examines debates over Ecuador's 2008 constitutional reforms, which mark a watershed in the environmental dimension of constitutional law by explicitly enshrining rights for nature. Her analysis chronicles a society struggling with the implications of recognizing nature as a kind of legal subject, perhaps blazing a trail that will eventually reshape what is meant by the concept of environmental citizenship. The notion of *buen vivir*, or 'living well', is central to this struggle, part of an attempt to neutralize and displace the dominant vision of human progress through control over nature for the instrumental aims of modernization. What is revealed by Pinto's analysis of debates over the constitutional reforms in mainstream media outlets is that the joined-up human-nature worldview of *buen vivir* is far from entering into the socio-ecological consciousness of Ecuador's elites. Instead, thoroughly entrenched human/nature dualisms persist, suggesting that citizens who seek to invoke the new constitutional rights of nature to challenge resource extraction projects will face strong opposition.

Points of Departure

The themes outlined above help to highlight some of the key contributions made by the chapters in this collection, but we have necessarily left quite a number of other important threads for our readers to discover on their own. As the conceptual architects of this project, and as facilitators of the workshop discussions that comprised the intellectual encounter leading to this collection of research, we conclude this introductory chapter by identifying some of our own remaining 'loose ends'. The avenues for further exploration herein are diverse, but we nevertheless feel that several important areas of research remain un- or under-explored in the collection. We offer a summary of these avenues here as additional pieces to the emerging research agenda.

We begin where we left off, with Pinto's contribution and the possibility of somehow more fully incorporating nature into conceptions and practices of citizenship. The idea of recognizing rights for nature is complemented by the echoes of nature's autonomous agency in Taddei's discussion of climate knowledge in Brazil. Henne and Gabrielson also point towards a more active place for nature in our conceptions of citizenship, with their use of the hybridizing concept of technonature. Nevertheless, nature's specific valence in the relationships that constitute the socio-ecological substance of citizenship is an issue which lies on the fringes of this collection and of the broader literature on environment and citizenship. As we turn our attention more directly to the 'subjectivity' or 'agency' of ecological systems or non-human entities, a number of potential points of reference emerge for further inquiry. In *The Natural Contract,* Michel Serres (2003) offers us one provocative way of recognizing and constituting nature as an interlocutor in political life. Like the imaginary (but no less powerful) social contract that serves as the basis for orderly human society, a natural contract would enshrine a series of rights and responsibilities providing for peace and order in the human relationship with the planet. Perhaps Ecuador's recognition of constitutional rights for nature can be seen as the beginnings of such a contract. John Dryzek (1995) offers another widely cited model for creating a place in politics for nature's voice. Differing from Serres in that he takes a communicative rather than contractarian approach to socio-ecological relations, Dryzek argues that through a combination of scientific interpretation and an open public sphere humans can effectively allow nature's voice – most especially its calls of distress – to register in democratic deliberation. Finally, the theoretical innovations of Bruno Latour, along with the broader literature on actor-network theory (ANT) that has emerged from science and technology studies, provide a third and final site from which to think through socio-ecological hybridity. Where Dryzek and Serres see the need to 'bring nature in', theorists of ANT proclaim that it is already integral to the evolution of the dynamic assemblage that we have previously labelled *society* (Callon 1986; Latour 1993, 2000, 2005; Law and Hassard 1999; Murdoch 2001). In this assemblage, human and non-human elements alike are intermingled in the co-construction of agency, such that action at any one node of a network is a product of its relationship with other nodes. This perspective allows us to consider the material agency of nature and even conceptualize nature itself as an 'actant' or independent force within a larger encompassing socio-natural system. What citizenship might mean in the context of hybrid actor networks remains an entirely open question.

Along a second (though related) conceptual front, we assert that future work on environment and citizenship in Latin America, and other parts of the Global South, needs to increase its level of scepticism towards the concept of citizenship itself. In the post-colonial conjuncture of the contemporary world it is easy to efface alternate traditions of collective organization and assume that 'citizenship' is a universally suited analytical lens, rather than a key part of what in some cases amounts to a neo-colonial ideological apparatus. We suggest that citizenship, because it embodies the possibility of contestation, is more open-ended than other hegemonic Western concepts like modernization or markets. Nevertheless, it is important to probe the limits of citizenship and to track the ways that it can be employed as a subordinating discourse or an apology for systemic oppression and violence. Baldwin and Meltzer's chapter offers one striking example of such innovative scepticism at work, but similar caution is not widely evident in the rest of the collection. Here we think that building further links between the dimensions of justice and subjectivity, such as emerging work on 'cosmopolitics' (de la Cadena 2010) and ontological conflicts (Blaser 2010), may provide ways to think through alternatives to the Western concepts of politics and citizenship, contributing to processes of intellectual socio-ecological decolonization.

The last reorientation that we propose has to do not with conceptual but rather with empirical foci. Only two of our contributors (Silva and Merlinsky/Latta) touch on urban contexts for exploring the intersection between citizenship and environment. This is despite the fact that human population in

Latin America is overwhelmingly urban, in a landscape of cities marked by stark inequalities in both economic and ecological terms. Scholars such as José Esteban Castro (2006), John Guidry (2003) and James Holston (2008) all demonstrate that material struggles over access to land and environmental services are entangled with competition over the shape of political rights and broader battles over the control of urban space. Citizenship in the city has everything to do with the possibility for more inclusionary urban habitats. Urban political ecology provides one starting point for broadening existing inquiry along these lines (see, for example, Heynen, Kaika and Swyngedouw 2005), and recent efforts to describe the socio-ecological challenges of cities through the lens of technonature provide another (in White and Wilbert 2009, see chapters by Guy; Hinchliffe and Whatmore; and Swyngedouw). Urban intersections of environment and citizenship must be at the centre of the research agenda in years to come.

The chapters in this collection are illustrative of the wide array of fresh insights that can be obtained by approaching environmental questions in Latin America through the lens of citizenship. At the same time, they offer key rejoinders to the dominant conceptions of environmental citizenship that populate scholarship in and about the Global North. In sum, we are optimistic about the volume's potential to spark new inquiry and debate. At the same time we are also conscious of its limitations, and we invite others to join in the task of clarifying key questions, theoretical frameworks and research methodologies. It is our hope that this collection marks only the beginning of efforts to map the contours of this vibrant but difficult terrain, where the multifaceted imaginaries and practices of citizenship and environment meet in an encounter that leaves them mutually transformed.

References

Agyeman, J., and B. Evans. (2006) 'Justice, Governance, and Sustainability: Perspectives on Environmental Citizenship from North America and Europe,' in A. Dobson and D. Bell (eds), *Environmental Citizenship*. Cambridge, MA: MIT Press, pp. 185–206.

Bachmann, P. L., L. E. Delgado and V. H. Marín. (2007) 'Analysis of the Citizen's Participation Concept Used by Local Decision Makers: The Case of the Aysén Watershed in Southern Chile,' *International Journal of Sustainable Development*, Vol. 10, No. 3, pp. 251–266.

Barns, I. (1995) 'Environment, Democracy and Community,' *Environmental Politics*, Vol. 4, No. 4, pp. 101–133.

Barry, J. (1999) *Rethinking Green Politics: Nature, Virtue and Progress*. London: Sage.

Bell, D. R. (2005) 'Liberal Environmental Citizenship,' *Environmental Politics*, Vol. 14, No. 2, pp. 179–194.

Blaser, M. (2010) *Storytelling Globalization from the Chaco and Beyond*. Durham: Duke University Press.

Bryant, R. L., and S. Bailey. (1997) *Third World Political Ecology*. London: Routledge.

Callon, M. (1986) 'Some Elements of a Sociology of Translation: Domestication of the Scallops and the Fishermen of St. Brieux Bay,' in J. Law (ed.), *Power, Action and Belief: A New Sociology of Knowledge*. London: Routledge and Kegan Paul, pp. 196–229.

Carlsson, M., and B. B. Jensen. (2006) 'Encouraging Environmental Citizenship: The Roles and Challenges for Schools,' in A. Dobson and D. Bell (eds), *Environmental Citizenship*. Cambridge, MA: MIT Press, pp. 237–261.

Carruthers, D. V. (2008) *Environmental Justice in Latin America: Problems, Promise, and Practice*. Cambridge, MA: MIT Press.

Castro, J. E. (2006) *Water, Power, and Citizenship: Social Struggle in the Basin of Mexico*. New York: Palgrave Macmillan.

Chihuailaf, E. (1999) *Recado Confidencial a los Chilenos*. Santiago: LOM Ediciones.

de la Cadena, M. (2010) 'Indigenous Cosmopolitics in the Andes: Conceptual Reflections Beyond "Politics",' *Cultural Anthropology*, Vol. 25, No. 2, pp. 334–370.

Díez, J., and O. P. Dwivedi (eds). (2008) *Global Environmental Challenges: Perspectives from the South*. Peterborough: Broadview Press.

Dobson, A. (2003) *Citizenship and the Environment*. Oxford: Oxford University Press.

Dryzek, J. S. (1995) 'Political and Ecological Communication,' *Environmental Politics*, Vol. 4, No. 4, pp. 13–30.

———. (2000) *Deliberative Democracy and Beyond: Liberals, Critics, Contestations*. Oxford: Oxford University Press.

Flynn, R., R. Bellaby and M. Ricci. (2008) 'Environmental Citizenship and Public Attitudes to Hydrogen Energy Technologies,' *Environmental Politics*, Vol. 17, No. 5, 766–783.

Gabrielson, T. (2008) 'Green Citizenship: A Review and Critique,' *Citizenship Studies*, Vol. 12, No. 4, pp. 429–446.

Gilbert, L., and C. Phillips. (2003) 'Practices of Urban Environmental Citizenships: Rights to the City and Rights to Nature in Toronto,' *Citizenship Studies*, Vol. 7, No. 3, pp. 313–330.

Gudynas, E. (2009) 'Ciudadanía ambiental y meta-ciudadanías ecológicas. Revisión y alternativas en América Latina,' in J. Reyes Ruiz and E. Castro Rosales (eds), *Urgencia y Utopía Frente a la Crisis de Civilización*. Guadalajara: Universidad de Guadalajara y Ayuntamiento de Zapopan, pp. 58–101.

Guidry, J. (2003) 'Trial by Space: The Spatial Politic of Citizenship and Social Movements in Urban Brazil,' *Mobilization*, Vol. 8, No. 2, pp. 189–204.

Guy, S. (2009) 'Fluid Archetectures: Ecologies of Hybrid Urbanism,' in D. White and C. Wilbert (eds), *Technonatures: Environments, Technologies, Spaces and Places in the Twenty-First Century*. Waterloo, ON: Wilfrid Laurier University Press, pp. 215–238.

Hailwood, S. (2005) 'Environmental Citizenship as Reasonable Citizenship,' *Environmental Politics*, Vol. 14, No. 2, pp. 195–210.

Hayward, T. (2002) 'Environmental Rights as Democratic Rights,' in B. A. Minteer and B. Pepperman Taylor (eds), *Democracy and the Claims of Nature: Critical Perspectives for a New Century*. Oxford: Rowman and Littlefield, pp. 237–256.

Heynen, N., M. Kaika and E. Swyngedouw. (2005) *In the Nature of Cities: Urban Political Ecology and the Politics of Urban Metabolism*. London: Routledge.

Hinchliffe, S., and S. Whatmore. (2009) 'Living Cities: Towards a Politics of Convivality,' in D. White and C. Wilbert (eds), *Technonatures: Environments, Technologies, Spaces and Places in the Twenty-First Century*. Waterloo, ON: Wilfrid Laurier University Press, pp. 105–123.

Hochstetler, K., and Keck, M. E. (2007) *Greening Brazil: Environmental Activism in State and Society*. Durham: Duke University Press.

Holston, J. (2008) *Insurgent Citizenship: Disjunctions of Democracy and Modernity in Brazil*. Princeton: Princeton University Press.

Jagers, Sverker C. (2009) 'In Search of the Ecological Citizen,' *Environmental Politics*, Vol. 18, No. 1, pp. 18–36.

Jelin, E. (2000) 'Towards a Global Environmental Citizenship,' *Citizenship Studies,* Vol. 4, No. 1, pp. 47–62.

Latour, B. (1993) *We Have Never Been Modern.* Cambridge, MA: Harvard University Press.

———. (2000) 'When Things Strike Back: A Possible Contribution of 'Science Studies' to the Social Sciences,' *British Journal Of Sociology,* Vol. 51, No. 1, pp. 107–123.

———. (2005) *Reassembling the Social: An Introduction to Actor-Network-Theory.* Oxford and New York: Oxford University Press.

Latta, P. A. (2007a) 'Citizenship and the Politics of Nature: The Case of Chile's Alto Bío Bío,' *Citizenship Studies,* Vol. 11, No. 3, pp. 229–246.

———. (2007b) 'Locating Democratic Politics in Ecological Citizenship,' *Environmental Politics,* Vol. 16, No. 3, pp. 377–393.

———. (2009) 'The Ecological Citizen,' in E. F. Isin (ed.), *Recasting the Social in Citizenship.* Toronto: University of Toronto Press, pp. 239–260.

Latta, A., and H. Wittman. (2010) 'Environment and Citizenship in Latin America: A new paradigm for theory and practice,' *European Review of Latin American and Caribbean Studies,* Vol. 89, pp. 107-116.

Law, J., and J. Hassard. (1999) *Actor Network Theory and After.* Oxford and Malden, MA: Blackwell.

MacGregor, S. (2006a) *Beyond Mothering Earth: Ecological Citizenship and the Politics of Care.* Vancouver: University of British Columbia Press.

———. (2006b) 'No Sustainability Without Justice: A Feminist Critique of Environmental Citizenship,' in A. Dobson and D. Bell (eds), *Environmental Citizenship.* Cambridge, MA: MIT Press, pp. 101–126.

Menegat, R. (2002) 'Participatory Democracy and Sustainable Development: Integrated Urban Environmental Management in Porto Alegre, Brazil,' *Environment and Urbanization,* Vol. 14, No. 2, pp. 181-206.

Murdoch, J. (2001) 'Ecologising Sociology: Actor-Network Theory, Co-Constructionism and the Problem of Human Exceptionalism,' *Sociology,* Vol. 35, No. 1, pp. 111–133.

Newby, H. (1996) 'Citizenship in a Green World: Global Commons and Human Stewardship,' in M. Bulmer and A. M. Rees (eds), *Citizenship Today: The Contemporary Relevance of T.H. Marshall.* London: UCL Press, pp. 209–221.

Nuijten, M., and D. Lorenzo. (2009) 'Ruling by Record: The Meaning of Rights, Rules and Registration in an Andean Comunidad,' *Development and Change,* Vol. 40, No. 1, pp. 81–103.

Palerm, J., and C. Aceves. (2004) 'Environmental Impact Assessment in Mexico: An Analysis From a Consolidating Democracy,' *Impact Assessment and Project Appraisal,* Vol. 22, No. 2, pp. 99–108.

Perreault, T. (2010) *Personal Communication and Photo Record of Graffiti in Cochabamba.* 11 March, 2010.

Perreault, T., and G. Valdivia. (2010) 'Hydrocarbons, Popular Protest and National Imaginaries: Ecuador and Bolivia in Comparative Context,' *Geoforum,* Vol. 41, No. 5, pp. 689–699.

Poole, D., and B. Alonso Rascón. (2009) 'Eating to Dream: A Tortillería in Oaxaca,' *NACLA Report on the Americas,* Vol. 42, No. 3, pp. 32–33.

Postero, N. G. (2007) *Now we are Citizens: Indigenous Politics in Postmulticultural Bolivia.* Stanford: Stanford University Press.

Schlosberg, D., S. Shulman and S. Zavestoski. (2006) 'Virtual Environmental Citizenship: Web-Based Public Participation in Rule Making in the United States,' in A. Dobson and D. Bell (eds), *Environmental Citizenship.* Cambridge, MA: MIT Press, pp. 207–236.

Serres, M. (2003 [1992]) *The Natural Contract,* trans. E. MacArthur and W. Paulson. Ann Arbor: University of Michigan Press.

Smith, M. J. (1998) *Ecologism: Towards Ecological Citizenship.* Minneapolis: University of Minnesota Press.

Smith, M. J., and P. Pangsapa. (2008) *Environment and Citizenship: Integrating Justice, Responsibility and Civic Engagement.* London and New York: Zed Books.

Swyngedouw, E. (2005) 'Governance, Innovation and the Citizen: The Janus Face of Governance-Beyond-the-State,' *Urban Studies,* Vol. 42, No. 11, pp. 1991–2006.

UNEP/PNUMA. (2006) 'Definición del Concepto "Ciudadanía Ambiental Global,"' PNUMA Officina Regional Para América Latina y el Caribe.

Valencia Sáis, A. (2005) 'Globalisation, Cosmopolitanism and Ecological Citizenship,' *Environmental Politics,* Vol. 14, No. 2, pp. 163–178.

Walker, D., et al. (2007) 'When Participation Meets Empowerment: The WWF and the Politics of Invitation in the Chimalapas, Mexico,' *Annals of the Association of American Geographers,* Vol. 97, No. 2, pp. 423–444.

White, D. F., and C. Wilbert. (2009) *Technonatures: Environments, Technologies, Spaces and Places in the Twenty-First Century.* Waterloo, ON: Wilfrid Laurier University Press.

Wittman, H. (2009) 'Reframing Agrarian Citizenship: Land, Life and Power in Brazil,' *Journal of Rural Studies,* Vol. 25, No. 1, pp. 120–130.

———. (2010) 'Agrarian Reform and the Environment: Fostering Ecological Citizenship in Mato Grosso, Brazil,' *Canadian Journal of Development Studies,* Vol. 29, No. 3, pp. 281–298.

Wolf, J., K. Brown and D. Conway. (2009) 'Ecological Citizenship and Climate Change: Perceptions and Practice,' *Environmental Politics,* Vol. 18, No. 4, pp. 503–521.

Wright, A. (2008) 'Is a Better World Possible? The Experience of the Brazilian Environmental Movement and the "Construction of Citizenship",' in J. Díez and O. P. Dwivedi (eds), *Global Environmental Challenges: Perspectives From the South.* Peterborough: Broadview, pp. 275–300.

Yashar, D. J. (2005) *Contesting Citizenship in Latin America: The Rise of Indigenous Movements and the Postliberal Challenge.* New York: Cambridge University Press.

Assembling Nature's Citizens

Environmental Citizenship and Climate Security

Contextualizing Violence and Citizenship in Amazonian Peru

Andrew Baldwin and Judy Meltzer

In June 2009, thousands of indigenous peoples living in the Amazon region of Peru staged a mass protest against the Peruvian state. Led by the Inter-ethnic Association for the Development of the Peruvian Rainforest (AIDE-SEP),[1] their claim was that through a series of executive decrees, the Peruvian state was bypassing its international obligations under International Labour Organization (ILO) Convention 169 to consult indigenous peoples on issues related to development in their ancestral territories. The decrees were put in place as measures that would fast-track oil and gas extraction in Andean Peru and were coincident with the Free Trade Agreement (FTA) that Peru had entered into with the United States. The decrees were designed to assure would-be investors in Peruvian oil and gas that indigenous peoples' territorial claims would not impede investment. On 5 June 2009, Peruvian President Alan García authorized the Peruvian police to put down the protest. The result was a violent confrontation in Bagua, in which the police are said to have massacred fifty-four indigenous protesters (some estimate the number to be much higher). Twenty-three policemen were also killed and 169 indigenous and mestizo protesters injured (Bebbington 2009).

The Bagua massacre is typical of ongoing colonialism and the use of state military violence to suspend indigenous peoples' political rights, in this case in the name of trade liberalization. Peru has a long history of violent struggle over land, in which state-led violence is routinely legitimized through recourse to narratives of civilization, national security and economic development (see Lopez 1997; de la Cadena 2000; Klarén 2000). The Bagua massacre was no different. The Peruvian government framed the AIDESEP opposition to the decrees as a state security issue. It argued that economic development in the Peruvian Amazon (mainly oil, gas and logging) was threatened by the supposed lawlessness represented by indigenous peoples in their struggle for secure tenure rights. The police violence authorized by President García was meant to send a message to indigenous peoples (and others) that opposition to Peruvian state authority in this brave new world of liberalized trade with the United States would not be tolerated.

These scenes of violence construct the notion of security in a very particular way. They frame security as a set of practices carried out by the state (whether in the form of military or police violence) in order to safeguard state sovereignty against what are perceived to be illegitimate counter-claims. One might argue with whether the Peruvian state has the right to enact this violence, and in this case, we feel strongly that the Peruvian state was criminal in its use of violence against the AIDESEP opposition movement. However, for the purpose of this chapter, the scenes of violence that unfolded in Bagua in the summer of 2009 are important for the way in which they reinforce the idea that security is associated with the use of state violence, legitimate or otherwise. In this sense, the case of Bagua is important because it repeats a familiar geopolitical narrative in which it is assumed that the use or threat of physical coercion by the state is the exclusive route to national security.

This chapter presents a different interpretation of security. In particular, it argues that environmental citizenship is a productive category through which to rethink this conventional, geopolitical notion of security. This may seem like an odd proposition given that environmental citizenship carries rather innocent connotations. However, given that climate change – arguably the most important global environmental problem of the twenty-first century – is now routinely figured as an issue of national and international security by western governments, notably the U.S., U.K. and European Union,[2] we feel a more expansive understanding of security and environmental citizenship is warranted. As such, we use the notion of biopolitical security to read the discourse of environmental citizenship in the context of Peruvian forest politics. We elaborate on this below. However, for now we take biopolitical security to mean a politics that takes 'life' to be the referent object of security rather than some notion of sovereign territoriality, which is the referent object of conventional geopolitical security. Consequently, we consider forest conservation a form of biopolitical security, and we consider the environmental citizen one of its principle agents. In framing environmental citizenship this way, we depart from conventional notions of environmental citizenship, which tend to frame environmental citizenship through the canon of normative political theory (Dobson and Bell 2006), and arrive at the unsettling proposition that far from innocent, the environmental citizen arbitrates the politics of life and death.

Peru in the aftermath of the Bagua massacre is a productive site through which to interrogate the biopolitical security of environmental citizenship. Indeed, as Peru's Minister of Environment Antonio Brack stated just weeks after the Bagua massacre, 'Peru can contribute enormously to the world in preserving biodiversity, native cultures and forest management, and we're laying down a big challenge to protect those forests, create wealth from them and not destroy them' (*Latin American Herald*, 31 July 2009). At first glance,

Brack's environmental rhetoric does not make reference to the violence in Bagua; it offers the promise of life, not death. His message presents an optimistic vision for indigenous peoples in Peru, one in which a new kind of citizenship is made available to a population for whom formal citizenship has historically been denied. Against the backdrop of the Bagua massacre, this offering by the Peruvian state seems like a welcome change of heart in which an ethic of state violence is replaced by an ethic of environmental protection. For us, however, at stake in Brack's rhetoric is the need to cultivate a citizenry capable of securitizing neoliberalism through forest conservation in Andean Peru. Central to this project, alongside the FTA and oil and gas investment, is the emergent policy of reduced emissions from deforestation and degradation (REDD), a forest conservation policy that has gained in international popularity since the publication of the Stern Review in 2006. We elaborate on REDD below, but for now REDD simply refers to a policy in which the financialization of forest carbon makes intact forests economically more valuable than if converted for other land uses like agriculture.

Environmental Citizenship as Security Discourse

Environmental citizenship is routinely framed in political discourse as an innocent form of political subjectivity. It conjures up images of the passionate environmentalist minimizing her daily carbon throughput, activists demanding strong legislation to limit greenhouse gas emissions and transnational environmentalists cultivating alliances with indigenous peoples around shared visions of forest conservation that synchronize cultural and natural survival. Our contention, however, is that the notion of environmental citizenship is never quite so innocent, even in its liberal progressive form. Alternate ways of imagining and constituting environmental citizenship are proposed throughout this volume. In this chapter, we seek to challenge the innocence that attaches to the concept by arguing that environmental citizenship extends the project of U.S. national security in the era of climate change. Our claim is that environmental citizenship is implicated in an ongoing reconfiguration of threat, a reconfiguration in which the geopolitical and biopolitical are beginning to coincide in the delivery of a new form of security.[3]

What is this new form of security? Broadly, it is security deployed in response to a new risk landscape, a landscape in which emergent risk has replaced the clearly definable 'enemy' as a source of national and international insecurity. Emergent risk in this sense refers to those immanent events that strike without warning, are inherently unpredictable and are indiscriminate in their effects. Examples of emergent risk include earthquakes and extreme weather events, the 2007–2008 financial crisis and Al-Qaeda. The new mode of security to which we are referring is being deployed by Western governments as a means of responding to unpredictable events of insecurity and a future of everlasting uncertainty, or in the words of Michael Dillon and Julian Reid (2009), 'the emergency of emergence'. In this sense, the new security can take numerous forms. Borrowing from Ben Anderson's (2010) typology of the politics of the future, this mode of security can be precautionary in that it can limit certain behaviours; it can prepare for the unexpected through preparedness planning; it can be pre-emptive, as we saw in Iraq; or it can be the embodiment of resilience, as in the capacity to withstand and recover from unexpected events.

A topical illustration of this new mode of security is found in the discourse of climate security (Barnett 2001; Brown, Hammill and McLeman 2007; CNA 2007; Mabey 2007; American Security Project 2009; Detraz and Betsill 2009). *Climate security* is a tricky term, but we take it to mean a political rationality that seeks to limit insecurity induced by climate change, where the eventualities of climate change (rising sea levels and extreme climatic events) are thought to catalyse emergent forms of insecurity (scarcity, disease, mass migration, war, failed states and terrorism). Important here is that climate security discourse reframes climate change as an issue of national and international security. In the language of climate security, climate change is thus considered to be a threat or risk multiplier (Campbell et al. 2007; CNA 2007). To mitigate climate change is therefore also to ameliorate these risks. As such, the reduction of greenhouse gas emissions is no longer simply an issue of economic competitiveness. Emissions reductions are also made to carry the promise of national and international security. For instance, in a well-cited report, the CNA Corporation (2007) recommends the reduction of greenhouse gas emissions as integral to U.S. national (and global) security and stability.

This discourse captures perfectly the overlap between the geopolitical and the biopolitical. By *geopolitical* we mean the efforts of sovereign nation-states to secure state territory, enhance competitiveness or reconstitute political relations elsewhere. In this sense, climate security discourse is geopolitical to the extent national security, or more properly the nation, remains the referent object of security. It spells a new era in climate change discourse and raises important questions about what it means to be an environmental citizen when geopolitics are foregrounded in contemporary climate change discourse. As such, we argue that environmental citizenship cannot be understood outside its geopolitical context, outside the operation of sovereign power.

However, discourses of climate security are simultaneously biopolitical to the extent they promote human life, make life live in Foucault's terms (Foucault 2003; Dillon and Reid 2009), or ensure that through the living of life, we do not undermine the life-giving capacity of earth itself. In other words, this is an environmental narrative in which managing the circulation of carbon in the interest of promoting life becomes a security imperative. This is a narrative saturated by the notion that with every megatonne of carbon released into the stratosphere, the emergency of emergence draws the world ever closer to the brink. Thus, in rethinking the innocence of environmental citizenship, climate security discourse prompts us to ask several questions. What kind of citizenry is required to deliver this new mode of security? Where and how will it intervene? What specific geographic locations will it be applied to? And through what areas of policy will it intervene?

The mode of environmental citizenship we have in mind is one that guarantees or at least aims to guarantee climate security. As such, it provides a good example of Michael Dillon's (2008) notion of the biopoliticization of security. For Dillon, the biopoliticization of security means that life (species life, human life) and its mechanisms (that which sustains life, for instance, nature, economy and culture) are the referent objects of security. Biopolitical security is practiced through what he calls 'combinatorial transactional freedom', or more simply the capacity of living things to interact, or transact, in a way that enables their life to reproduce through daily life. In this sense, security is not prophylactic; it does not protect or safeguard. Rather, biopolitical security is precisely that which allows life to be governed by the emergent properties internal to life itself and the systems that enable its propagation. The carbon cycle is absolutely critical here. The carbon cycle provides one of the many biological circuits that form the basis of life (others include the hydrologic cycle and nitrogen cycles). Without the carbon cycle, photosynthesis would not exist and without photosynthesis our capacity to (re)produce food and oxygen are severely undermined. Yet through REDD policy, we have, at least in principle, a deliberate attempt to synchronize circuits of carbon with circuits of capital in the name of planetary survivability and life. Or more baldly, through REDD, forest carbon and capital become synonymous. REDD financializes forest carbon. It enables the export of forest carbon to the global carbon market where it is purchased by all manner of market actors from banks to insurance companies to manufacturers to offset their carbon risk. At the same time, forests are said to be life-giving through the provision of ecosystem services like clean drinking water and biodiversity. Thus, through their sequestration and storage of carbon, forests are also said to forestall climate change. They enable life and limit apocalypse and death.

For us, all of this means that environmental citizenship cannot be understood as something whose meaning is derived straight from the canon of political theory. Instead, it suggests that the meaning of environmental citizenship ought to be understood as something shaped by context, in this case, geopolitical and biopolitical context. In so far as Peru lies squarely within the United States' sphere of influence, and to the extent that the political context of the Bagua Massacre and REDD in Peru were shaped by the FTA, we argue that U.S. political culture is important for helping us understand the links between environmental citizenship and security. Important in this regard is that early in his first term in office, and in a decisive shift away from Bush-era environmental foreign policy, U.S. President Barack Obama is hailing a new green America and with it a new environmental citizenry. Through Obama's rhetoric, such as the New Energy Plan for America, the realization of a low-carbon economy extends the project of American security by ensuring its consistency with United States' national energy security.

Environmental Citizenship and Biopolitical Security in Peru

The case of Peru provides an empirical base for our theoretical claims. The Bagua massacre exemplifies the conventional geopolitical narrative in which the state, through its monopoly on the use of violence, is said to be the ulti-mate guarantor of national security (in this case, national security defined as neoliberal economic development). We contrast this with a different con-figuration of security, one in which the geopolitical security of the neoliberal state intersects with the biopolitical security of 'life', guaranteed, for example, through the circulation of carbon as a way to mitigate the contingent threat of climate change. In particular, we look at how this narrative operates through the practice of forest conservation, specifically the REDD program in Peru's Amazon region, focusing on the role of the environmental citizen in this context. As previously mentioned, we argue that the environmental citizen is neither an innocent nor obvious subjectivity, but is implicated as an impor-tant agent in this reconfiguration of security. Moreover, to the extent that this form of citizenship is encouraged to be simultaneously environmental and entrepreneurial, we regard this subject as an 'enviropreneurial' citizen.

The narrative of citizenship and security underpinning the violence in Ba-gua provides a useful counterpoint to the alternate conceptions of security, risk and citizenship that are at the centre of this chapter. The Bagua mas-sacre was part of a longer history of struggles over land framed in terms of a national security that excluded indigenous peoples, particularly in the Ama-zonian region. In Peru, the biopolitical impulse to produce and secure the 'Peruvian population' post-Independence and through the twentieth century involved a sharp demarcation between indigenous populations in the Andean highlands, who were recast as peasant farmers, and indigenous peoples of the Amazon, who were not considered fit to 'count' as part of the national body. Indeed, in Peru's first national census in 1940 they were literally not counted. As the lead census official put it, 'It is common knowledge that the Peruvian jungle ... is unlike the rest of the country in every respect, physical, and human. ... The jungle aboriginal still keeps his freedom; he likes to move from place to place; he accepts no other rule than that of his own community. It would be useless to try and count him' (Parro 1942, 8). This sentiment also informed development policy, where even in the 1960s and 70s the indigenous peoples of the Amazon lowlands were conceived merely as 'native communities', with limited potential for citizenship (see de la Cadena 2000; García 2005). Grillo and Sharon (this volume) provide a detailed account of the shifting discursive constructions of the Peruvian Amazon and the Amazonian native during this period, illustrating the way that the distinction between citizen and native was integral to the construction of the Amazon as an empty space to be incorporated (and civilized) through the settlement of non-indigenous Peruvians and the exploitation of the region's resources to generate wealth for the national economy. In the face of this national project, Amazon populations, as well as the emptiness and unproductivity of the region itself, have been historically constituted as a risk to the Peruvian nation and national development (Larson 2004; Yashar 2005).

Security in this narrative is contingent on the economic development of the Amazon region through the extraction of oil and gas as well as logging. It is reliant on insecure tenure rights for indigenous populations in order to maximize access for private capital, and was the basis for the Peruvian government's recent violent crackdown against indigenous protesters in the Bagua region. Leading up to this massacre were months of escalating protest against ninety-nine presidential decrees enacted by President García in 2007–2008, under special powers granted by Congress to implement the FTA signed with the United States in 2007 (and with Canada in 2008). Collectively, these decrees repealed or modified existing laws protecting indigenous land rights, making it easier for communally held lands to be acquired by private investors, enabling the government to take control of indigenous land deemed to be 'unproductive' or 'idle', and eliminating the informed consent requirement for extractive industries to operate in indigenous territory – violating Peru's international commitment under ILO Convention 169 (Barrera-Hernández 2009). The measures were designed to open the region to expanded biofuel, oil and mineral development, as envisaged by the FTA.

The characterization of security and citizenship underpinning the decrees and the ensuing massacre was explicit in an article written by President García and published in a national newspaper in 2007. Entitled 'The Syndrome of the Dog in the Manger', the article made the claim that Peru's central problem was that its natural resources were 'unproductive' – neither drawing investment nor generating employment – because they were not legally titled. García emphasized that the key obstacle to realizing Peru's resource potential were 'lazy' indigenous populations whose resistance he equated with that of 'the dog in a manger' in reference to Aesop's fable of the mean-spirited dog who slept in a manger only to prevent others from doing so (García 2007). Shortly before the Bagua massacre, García made a public statement against the protests, reiterating the native/citizen distinction: 'Enough is enough. These people ... are not first-class citizens. ... Who are 400,000 natives to tell 28 million Peruvians that you have no right to come here? This is a grave error, and whoever thinks this way wants to lead us to irrationality and a retrograde primitivism' (cited in Bebbington 2009, 13). In fact, oil development in the Amazon region has been expanding rapidly, while community land titling that the government claims to have carried out (Forest Carbon Partnership Facility 2008) has had dubious results in actually protecting indigenous territories from encroachment (Bebbington 2009). Matt Finer and Martí Orta-Martinez (2010) recently estimated that nearly 50 per cent of the Peruvian Amazon is now covered by oil and gas concessions, up from only 7.1 per cent in 2003, and as much as 72 per cent of the region is zoned for hydrocarbon activities (4–5). The annual rate of deforestation is officially estimated to be over 150,000 hectares per year (Povéda and Sanchez-Triana 2005, 463), and is likely much greater. The active oil concessions overlap with over half of all titled indigenous lands and about 17 per cent of protected areas (Finer and Orta-Martinez 2010, 4).

A New Risk Landscape: Climate Insecurity and REDD

In the context of García's disqualification of indigenous citizens in favour of rapid expansion of oil and gas exploitation in the Amazon, Environment Minister Antonio Brack's claim just weeks after the Bagua massacre – that forest conservation and indigenous communities play a pivotal role in creating national wealth – seems to reflect a paradoxical ethic of environmentalism and indigenous citizenship. We suggest, however, that this is in fact part of an alternate characterization linking Amazonian subjects to the problem of security, centred on ensuring the circulation of carbon and capital according to the biopolitical and geopolitical imperatives of climate security.

Environmental concerns have not been framed as an important problem of government in Peru until fairly recently. Policies and institutions have been limited and weak, and governments at all levels have remained apparently unconcerned with environmental issues, including protecting designated 'protected areas'. It was the U.S. FTA that required that a Ministry of the Environment be established in Peru. However, in the past several years, climate change has been increasingly identified as an important threat facing Peru. The National Commission on the Environment (CONAM) stated that Peru was one of the countries at greatest risk to climate change, in particular due to loss of glaciers. Climate change is identified as a 'menace' to development, and in an interview with the BBC, Brack stated that he was seeking international funds for a 'new 3,000-strong environmental police force to try to stop deforestation in remote regions' (Painter 2008). The financialization of forest carbon in Peru's Amazon region is increasingly portrayed as a crucial new asset to mitigate the risks presented by this emergent threat – a way to secure life (i.e. biopolitical security) through the carbon cycle as a supplement to geopolitical imperatives of national development and economic competitiveness. This alternate security problematic can be traced through nascent REDD programs underway in Peru.

REDD programs are promoted as a form of 'carbon offsetting,' offering another way of converting carbon reductions into an abstracted, tradable commodity purchased by polluters as a cost-effective way to reduce emissions. REDD programs commodify forests in a novel way by calculating quantities of carbon stored and converting this into tradable credits. This operates through an assemblage of new experts and institutions set up to calculate, track and certify carbon credits, linking carbon to biological and capital circuits, fostering life and facilitating the circulation of capital. In creating new incentives to limit deforestation, REDD is frequently portrayed as a 'win-win' solution and has garnered support from key environmental organizations. As Randall Hayes, founder of the Rainforest Action Network put it 'done properly, this is our number one hope' (cited in Cohen 2009).

In Peru, REDD programs are part of voluntary carbon offset agreements and a national REDD system is also being developed for recognition under the UN-REDD program. There are presently at least four privately funded REDD programs at various stages of development in Peru's Amazon region. Briefly, these include a two million dollar investment by the Walt Disney Company in a REDD program in Peru's Alto Mayo Protected Forest, in the regions of San Martin and Amazonas. The project consists of reforestation and 'avoided deforestation' initiatives, and is undertaken in partnership with two NGOs as well as the Ministry of the Environment and National Service for Natural Protected Areas (SERNANP). Two timber companies (Maderacre and Maderyja) have partnered with local and international NGOs (Greenoxx and Asociación para la Investigación y Desarrollo Integral; or AIDER, the World Wildlife Foundation and Pronaturaleza) to implement a REDD forest conservation project of 100,000 hectares in the Madre de Dios (Amazonian) region in Peru (Cenamo et al. 2009). To develop its national REDD program, Peru is seeking funding from the World Bank Carbon Finance Unit's Carbon Partnership Facility (FCPF), which helps countries 'build capacities' and ensures that they can demonstrate 'REDD readiness' as a precondition for presenting a REDD plan and eventually receiving funding for implementation (Forest Carbon Partnership Facility 2009). Such readiness depends on the development of a new set of expert knowledge and administrative practice to manage the securing of life, including the elaboration of monitoring apparatuses to generate data on indigenous populations and rates of deforestation, as well as legal frameworks to govern the interface between cycles of carbon and capital.

In contrast to the Bagua massacre, in which indigenous peoples were constituted as a barrier to national security and development, REDD is contingent on a different subjectivity: the environmental – or more properly, the enviropreneurial – citizen. Through REDD, indigenous peoples (and the region itself) no longer embody a threat to the nation, but are reconfigured as environmental citizens, responsible for managing new risks against the threat of climate change through forest conservation and the circulation of carbon.

Constituting the Environmental Citizen

To say that REDD programs help produce a particular kind of environmental citizen is not to presume their effects, but rather to raise questions as to how citizenship is defined and circumscribed in this context. As Barbara Cruikshank (1999) has made clear, programs to 'empower' citizens are also projects of reform, and they reflect the varying ways in which security, integration and progress are imagined over time.

The environmental citizen in this context is constituted through new responsibilities related to the management of forest carbon as a way to allay uncertain risks of climate change and ensure the circulation of capital, and with it national economic development – including oil and gas development within the region. This is embedded in a neoliberal logic that aligns the responsible, moral citizen with an economic-rational individual (*homo economicus*) with the capacity to manage individualized risk (Lemke 2001).[4] Environmental citizenship is practised through maintaining and monitoring tracts of preserved forest, to be supported, in principle, by a more robust system of land tenure: the FCPF Manual for the REDD program (2009) states that 'land rights of forest communities urgently need to be re-examined, and restored or confirmed by countries seeking to participate in REDD' (5). This makes a similar link between security and productivity (and competitiveness) that was used to justify the state violence perpetrated in Bagua, but through a different form of capital investment. Conversion into capital in this context does not involve deforestation for resource extraction, but requires legal titling of the forest as an economic asset that can be converted into capital, accumulated and traded – a process which well-known conservative Peruvian economist Hernando de Soto (1989, 2000) has argued is the principle path to development.

While the indigenous environmental citizen has a responsibility (and assumed immanent capacity) for oversight of the forest (specifically its carbon content), new skills and attitudes must be cultivated for this to be realized. Some of these new skills and attitudes are set out in Peru's REDD Readiness Plan Idea Note (RPIN) submitted to the World Bank's Carbon Finance Unit's Carbon Partnership Facility, which suggests training will be required to build the capacity of indigenous populations to conserve forest carbon stocks (Forest Carbon Partnership Facility 2008). REDD training manuals also offer insight into how these capacities are to be instilled. Source books, such as the *Global Observation of Forest and Land Cover Dynamics* (2009) or the *Field Guide for Assessing and Monitoring REDD* (Verplanke and Zahabu 2009) and the Intergovernmental Panel on Climate Change's (IPCC) *Good Practices Guidance* (Penman et al. 2003) detail standard operating procedures for monitoring and reporting forest carbon, including how communities should be adapted and trained to self-monitor carbon. For carbon to be credited and registered, communities must first conduct mapping (using GPS technology) to assess the carbon stock. Participating communities are trained to measure the forest in terms of different amounts of carbon stored, undertake surveys to calculate variance and identify and measure sample plots (Verplanke and Zahabu 2009, 23–46). Framed as a new form of Community Forest Management, these activities also require extensive expert oversight for independent verification involving complex calculations of carbon 'stocks' and associated uncertainties, to quantify risk and exposure to contingency.

The monitoring and oversight required of the environmental citizen under REDD is critical to the larger network of surveillance required to secure carbon and commodify it through the calculation of 'additional' reductions. This is done using various projection models that try to incorporate historical land-use patterns using satellite images, as well as projections of future deforestation in the area (see GOFLCD Sourcebook 2009 for a detailed account). Vigilance through surveillance and local monitoring by environmental citizens is a constant requisite of pre-emption against a perpetual risk of 'leakage'. Anticipating this risk, REDD programs also require physical buffer zones to be set up around each of the protected areas, as well as virtual credit buffers that set aside credits to compensate for future risks of leakage.[5] Such strategies of pre-emption thus operate at several levels against emergent threats from climate change and carbon containment, and reflect the contingency which Dillon (2008: 314) refers to as 'the epistemic object for biopolitics of security in the 21st century'. Environmental citizens play a constitutive role in the operation of these new metrological regimes and forms of surveillance, helping make visible 'a forest … composed of pools of carbon' (GOFLCD Sourcebook 2009, 43). They are thus essential to coordinating circuits of carbon and capital in which neoliberal norms of efficiency and 'value-for-money' articulate with biopolitical and geopolitical concerns related to climate security.

At the same time, securing against risks from climate change through carbon offsetting has not disrupted the expansion of oil and gas exploration and extraction in the region. In May 2010, Perupetro announced that it intended to auction off twenty-five additional lots for oil and gas exploration in Peru's Amazon region, totalling an additional area of approximately ten million hectares, resulting in 75 per cent of the region now being open to oil and gas exploration and drilling (Perupetro 2010).

There are obvious contradictions between the impetus to develop oil as a means of national development, and preserving carbon to mitigate the risks of climate change. Oil and gas development, and the deforestation it entails (directly and indirectly through road building and the repercussions of opening up the region to other forms of encroachment) are directly at odds with the REDD mandate of preserving forests, reflecting the new sites of emergent contradiction created by climate change (see Urry 2010). Official discourse attempts to neutralize this in part by attributing deforestation to unsustainable land use by local populations rather than private industry. This was manifest in Peru's REDD RPIN submitted to the World Bank's Carbon Finance Unit's Carbon Partnership Facility, which stated that 'dwellers in the Amazon region ... tend to disregard the importance of forested land. This trend can be changed by education and training, dissemination of successful forest management practices and adequate incentives' (2008, 5).

These dual narratives of security and development present ambivalent, contradictory roles for indigenous peoples as both obstacle and instrument – required on the one hand to step aside and allow forest destruction for fossil fuel extraction, they are exhorted on the other hand to become custodians of those same forests in order to preserve and accumulate valuable carbon stocks. While official discourse on indigenous rights is being harnessed to carbon offsetting and other 'conservation' projects, forest conservation (for example through the creation of national parks and protected areas) has historically been at odds with the recognition of indigenous access, usage and territorial rights. Increasing the value of forests through carbon commodification presents new risks of appropriation. It is therefore not surprising that there is growing opposition to REDD programs – as Article 6 in the Anchorage Declaration from the Indigenous Peoples' Global Summit on Climate Change (2009) attests: 'We challenge States to abandon false solutions to climate change that negatively impact Indigenous Peoples' rights, lands, air, oceans, forests, territories and waters. These include nuclear energy, large-scale dams, geo-engineering techniques, "clean coal", agro-fuels, plantations, and market based mechanisms such as carbon trading, the Clean Development Mechanism, and forest offsets.'

Conclusion

Drawing upon Dillon's (2008) idea of a biopolitics of security, we have sought to show how a new mode of security and risk, operating through uncertainty (specifically the emergent risks associated with climate change) and environmental citizenship, extends the project of national security in the United States and other industrialized countries.

In contrast with the conventional geopolitical narratives in which state coercion is the exclusive route to national security, this chapter presented a different interpretation of security, in which the geopolitical security of the neoliberal state intersects with the biopolitical security of 'life'. In particular, it argues that environmental citizenship is a productive category through which to rethink this conventional, geopolitical notion of security. As such, we have sought to challenge assumptions about environmental citizenship as being inherently progressive or fixed and to understand how environmental citizenship is implicated in this new mode of security, in this case in REDD programs that seek to manage carbon to ensure life. The context for this is a contingent biosphere in which unpredictable risks must be pre-empted.

REDD programming also shows how the responsibilities of the environmental citizen – a subjectivity that is pivotal to the carbon-capital circuit – is conceived and instilled. Good citizenship in this context is performed through risk management, and is not limited to REDD. Recently, Peru's Ministry of the Environment defined '*ciudadanía ambiental*' as 'the exercise of environmental rights and duties by citizens … manifest through their active and responsible participation in decision-making in environmental management' (Ministerio del Ambiente, 2008). The environmental citizen thus represents a new mode of citizenship in a region where racial, class-based and gendered hierarchies have historically constituted the boundaries of citizenship and social order (see Larson 2004; Wilson 2003). It also carries assumptions about the immanent capacity and moral authority of 'the Indian' to conserve nature (defined in terms of carbon), but nonetheless requires new attributes and capacities to be instilled in order for this capacity to be realized. This echoes longstanding colonial projects of improvement and reform, reconfigured according to a neoliberal/market logic under which the rational-economic citizen operates as 'an entrepreneur of himself' (Foucault 2008, 226).

While it is still too early to assess its (intended and unintended) effects, REDD's emphasis on land titling opens the possibility that historically excluded indigenous populations may lay claim to certain previously unrecognized rights (although as a way to secure carbon rather than in recognition of the 'right to have rights'). This is, of course, an enticing proposition, explored elsewhere in this volume in somewhat similar contexts in Brazil and Argentina (see de Castro's and Ferrero's chapters). We wish to end, however, with a caution. While this new citizenship might be said to enable life – it ensures the life-giving capacity of the earth system, it attracts capital, it contributes to various forms of national and international security and thus enables life citizens – opposition to it can easily be construed as an apologetics for death. This is important to bear in mind given that while some indigenous peoples may well embrace REDD, others may not. It seems that Peruvian politics after Bagua may well continue to turn on matters of life and death.

Notes

1. AIDESEP is an umbrella organization representing six indigenous regional organizations and sixty-five federations – over 350,000 indigenous people in the Peruvian Amazonian region (Hughes 2010).
2. For instance, the U.S. Quadrennial Defense Review 2010 contains the first clear statement by the U.S. military on its strategic approach to climate change. So, too, the 2008 U.K. National Security Strategy positions climate change as one of the drivers of global insecurity.
3. Underpinning this is an understanding of citizenship and 'the citizen' not just as a particular form of membership or legal status, but as a subjectivity and strategy of government (see Cruikshank 1999; Procacci 2001).
4. Neoliberal or marketized citizenship was entrenched in Peru through the 1980s and 1990s in international structural adjustment programs and reforms implemented under Fujimori. It has persisted in subsequent governments, which not only imposed orthodox economic models but reoriented government according to a market logic (see Panfichi 2007). Neoliberal environmental governance in the region tends to be understood in terms of a reinstitutionalization of economic management, manifest in resource privatization and commercialization, enclosure of environmental commons, new markets for environmental goods and services and new forms of capital accumulation (see Perreault and Martin 2005; Liverman and Vilas 2006).
5. For example, in Peru, the REDD project in San Martin, Ucayali, Huanuco and Loreto (which covers an area of about 1.3 million hectares) has a so-called 'leakage belt' around it of over 2.3 million hectares as well as a separate credit buffer of 15 to 20 per cent of credits to underwrite risk of leakage (Cenamo et al. 2009, 55).

References

American Security Project. (2009) *Climate Security Index*. Washington, D.C.: American Security Project.

Anchorage Declaration. (2009) Article 6, Anchorage Declaration, Indigenous People's Global Summit on Climate Change. 24 April 2009, online report, http://www.unutki.org/down loads/File/Events/2009-04_Climate_Change_Summit/Anchorage_Declaration.pdf.

Anderson, B. (2010) 'Preemption, precaution, preparedness: anticipatory action and future geographies,' *Progress in Human Geography*, Vol. 34, No. 6, pp. 777–798.

Barnett, J. (2001) 'Security and Climate Change: Tyndell Centre for Climate Change Research Working Paper Seven,' Tyndell Centre for Climate Change Research, October 2001.

Barrera-Hernández, L. (2009) 'Peruvian Indigenous Land Conflict Explained,' *Americas Quarterly*, 12 June 2009, online report, www.americasquarterly.org/peruvian-protests-explained.

Bebbington, A. (2009) 'The New Extraction: Rewriting the Political Ecology of the Andes?' *NACLA,* Vol. 42, No. 5, pp. 12–40.

Brown, O., A. Hammill and R. McLeman. (2007) 'Climate Change as the "New" Security Threat: Implications for Africa,' *International Affairs,* Vol. 83, No. 6, pp. 1141–1154.

Campbell, K. M., et al. (2007) 'The Age of Consequences: The Foreign Policy and National Security Implications of Global Climate Change.' Washington, D.C.: Center for Strategic and International Studies and Center for a New American Security.

Cenamo, M., et al. (2009) *Casebook of REDD Projects in Latin America.* Brazil: Idesam.

CNA. (2007) 'National Security and the Threat of Climate Change.' Alexandria: CNA Corporation.

Cohen, T. (2009) 'Climate change proposal would revolutionize value of forests,' *CNN,* 22 September 2009, online report, www.cnn.com/2009/TECH/science/09/22/climate .forests/index.html.

Cruikshank, B. (1999) *The Will to Empower: Democratic Citizens and Other Subjects.* Ithaca: Cornell University Press.

de la Cadena, M. (2000) *Indigenous Mestizos: The Politics of Race and Culture in Cuzco Peru, 1919–1991.* Durham: Duke University Press.

de Soto, Hernando. (1989) *The Other Path: The Invisible Revolution in the Third World.* New York: Harper & Row.

———. (2000) *The Mystery of Capital: Why Capitalism Triumphs in the West and Fails Everywhere Else.* New York: Basic Books.

Detraz, N., and M. Betsill. (2009) 'Climate Change and Environmental Security: For Whom the Discourse Shifts,' *International Studies Perspectives,* Vol. 10, No. 3, pp. 303–320.

Dillon, M. (2008) 'Underwriting Security,' *Security Dialogue,* Vol. 39, No. 2–3, pp. 309–332.

Dillon, M., and J. Reid. (2009) *The Liberal Way of War: Killing to Make Life Live.* London: Routledge.

Dobson, A., and D. Bell (eds). (2006) *Environmental Citizenship.* Cambridge, MA: MIT Press.

Finer, M., and M. Orta-Martinez. (2010) 'A Second Hydrocarbon Boom Threatens the Peruvian Amazon: Trends, Projections, and Policy Implications,' *Environmental Research Letters,* Vol. 5, pp. 1–10.

Forest Carbon Partnership Facility. (2008) 'Peru Readiness Plan Idea Note' (RPIN), online report, www.forestcarbonpartnership.org/fcp/sites/forestcarbonpartnership.org/files/Doc uments/PDF/Peru_R-PIN_07-31-08.pdf.

———. (2009) 'Capacity Building Program for Forest-Dependent People on REDD+,' online report, www.forestcarbonpartnership.org/fcp/sites/forestcarbonpartnership.org/files/ Documents/PDF/Nov2009/Program_Description_English_11-15-09_updated.pdf.

Foucault, M. (2003) *'Society Must be Defended': Lectures at the College de France.* New York: Picador.

———. (2008) *The Birth of Biopolitics.* Translated by Graham Burchell. Houndmills: Palgrave Macmillan.

García, A. P. (2007) 'El Síndrome del Perro del Hortelano,' *El Comercio,* Lima: 28 October.

García, M. E. (2005) *Making Indigenous Citizens: Identity, Development and Multicultural Activism in Peru.* Stanford: Stanford University Press.

Global Observation of Forest and Land Cover Dynamics (GOFLCD). (2009) *Sourcebook,* online report, www.gofc-gold.uni-jena.de/redd/sourcebook/Sourcebook_Version_Nov_2009 _cop15-1.pdf.

Hughes, N. (2010) 'Indigenous Protest in Peru: The 'Orchard Dog' Bites Back,' *Social Movement Studies,* Vol. 9, No. 1, pp. 85–90.

Klarén, P. (2000) *Peru: Society and Nationhood in the Andes.* Oxford: Oxford University Press.

Larson, B. (2004) *Trials of Nation Making: Liberalism, Race, and Ethnicity in the Andes, 1810–1910.* Cambridge: Cambridge University Press.

Latin American Herald Tribune. (2009) 'Peru to Pay Indians for Conservation of Amazon Jungle,' *Latin American Herald Tribune*, 31 July 2009, online report, http://laht.com/article.asp?CategoryId=14095&ArticleId=340515.

Lemke, T. (2001) '"The Birth of Bio-Politics": Michel Foucault's Lecture at the College de France on Neo-Liberal Governmentality,' *Economy and Society*, Vol. 30, No. 2, pp. 190–207.

Liverman, D. M., and S. Vilas. (2006) 'Neoliberalism and the Environment in Latin America,' *Annual Review of Environmental Resources*, Vol. 31, No. 1, pp. 327–363.

Lopez, S. J. (1997) *Ciudadanos Reales e Imaginarios: Concepciones, Desarrollo y Mapas de la Ciudadanía en el Perú*. Lima: Instituto de Diálogo y Propuestas.

Mabey, N. (2007) 'Summary,' *Whitehall Papers*, Vol. 69, No. 1, pp. 1–7.

Ministerio del Ambiente. (2008) *Documento de Trabajo: Programa Ciudadanía Ambiental Conceptos*, online report, www.minam.gob.pe.

Painter, J. (2008) 'Peru Aims for Zero Deforestation,' *BBC News*, 12 July, online report, http://news.bbc.co.uk/go/pr/fr/-/2/hi/americas/7768226.stm.

Panfichi, A. (2007) 'Democracia y Participación: El Fujimorismo y los Gobiernos de Transición,' in A. Panfichi (ed.), *Participación Ciudadana en el Perú: Disputas, Confluencias y Tensiones*. Lima: Fondo Editorial de la Pontificia Universidad Católica del Perú, pp. 1–23.

Parro, A. (1942) 'Census of Peru, 1940,' *Geographical Review*, Vol. 32, No. 1, pp. 1–20.

Penman, J., et al. (eds). (2003) 'Good Practice Guidance for Land Use, Land Use Change and Forestry,' paper prepared for the IPCC National Greenhouse Gas Inventories Programme, online report, http://www.ipcc-nggip.iges.or.jp/public/gpglulucf/gpglulucf_contents.html.

Perreault, T., and P. Martin. (2005) 'Geographies of Neoliberalism in Latin America,' *Environment and Planning*, Vol. 37, pp. 191–201.

Perupetro. (2010) 'Bidding Call for the Bidding Round 2010,' *News Source: Perupetro*, 28 June.

Povéda, R., and E. Sanchez-Triana. (2005) 'Setting Environmental Priorities in Peru,' in M. Guigale, V. Fretes-Cibils and J. Newman (eds), *An Opportunity for a Different Peru: Prosperous, Equitable, and Governable*. Washington, D.C.: The World Bank.

Procacci, G. (2001) 'Governmentality and Citizenship,' *The Blackwell Companion to Political Sociology*, K. Nash and A. Scott (eds). Oxford: Blackwell Publishing.

UN Collaborative Programme on Reducing Emissions from Deforestation and Forest Degradation in Developing Countries (UN-REDD). (2008) *Framework Document*, June, online report, www.undp.org/mdtf/un-redd/docs/Annex-A-Framework-Document.pdf.

Urry, J. (2010) 'Consuming the Planet to Excess,' *Theory, Culture & Society*, Vol. 27, No. 2/3, pp. 191–212.

Verplanke, J. J., and E. Zahabu (eds). (2009) *A Field Guide for Assessing and Monitoring Reduced Forest Degradation and Carbon Sequestration by Local Communities*. Kyoto: Think Global, Act Local Project, online report, http://www.communitycarbonforestry.org/Online%20Fieldguide%20full%20123.pdf.

Wilson, F. (2003) 'Reconfiguring the Indian: Land Labour Relations in the Postcolonial Andes,' *Journal of Latin American Studies*, Vol. 35, pp. 221–247.

Yashar, D. (2005) *Contesting Citizenship in Latin America: The Rise of Indigenous Movements and the Postliberal Challenge*. Cambridge: Cambridge University Press.

3

Multi-Scale Environmental Citizenship

Traditional Populations and Protected Areas in Brazil

Fábio de Castro

Since the late 1980s, Brazil has been in a process of democratization where minority groups have actively demanded their rights and, in some cases, fostered institutional change to address their claims (Kingstone and Power 2000). Environmental movements and policy have been particularly relevant in this process, as rural populations have framed their discourses on environmental concerns as a matter of social justice (Hochstetler and Keck 2007). Among other initiatives, local management systems have been proposed by different groups in order to combine sustainable use of natural resources with rights to land, food security and rural development (Brown and Rosendo 2000; Cunha and Almeida 2000; Diegues and Vianna 2000).

The links between democratization, social justice and the environment can be usefully drawn out by deploying the lens of environmental citizenship. In the Global North this concept is frequently associated with the notion of citizens' responsibility to engage in voluntary behavioural change to reduce the ecological impact of their lifestyles (for example, see Dobson 2003; Dobson and Valencia Saíz 2005; Horton 2006; Jagers 2010). As argued in chapter 1 of this volume, the focus on a politics of sustainable consumption says little about socio-ecological realities in other parts of the world. A number of scholars have argued that a closer look at other dimensions of citizenship can help us understand and problematize issues of equity, participation, identity formation and justice in environmental politics (MacGregor 2006; Latta 2007; Gabrielson 2008). These approaches are suggestive of the way that the concept of environmental citizenship can be deployed to describe the engagement of local populations in evolving discourses and practices of environmental governance to secure livelihoods and increase protection of environmental space at various scales in the Global South (Gudynas 2009; Wittman 2010).

Environmental governance in the South has been characterized by reconfigurations in scalar relationships among social actors engaged in environmental politics (Swyngedouw 1997). Cross-scale interactions are the outcome of struggles around access to and control of natural resources by different social and political actors (Adger, Brown and Tompkins 2006). In many cases, emerging environmental citizens have strategically 'jumped scales' and engaged in transnational networks (Keck and Sikkink 1998). In some cases, states have also been repositioned within a 'glocalization' process as major partners in participatory initiatives at the local level. A focus on the reconfiguration of cross-scale interactions can unpack the emergence of new local-national-global connections, along with their implications for environmental citizenship. The environmental justice approach offers a key complementary avenue for such analysis. Although scholarship on environmental justice has also primarily emerged from studies in urbanized, industrial contexts (Mohai, Pellow and Roberts 2009), its focus on distributional issues, social heterogeneity and collective action make it well-suited to approaching a broader array of socio-ecological realities. Indeed, the concept has already found fertile ground in the developing world context of Latin America (see, for example, Carruthers 2008), where struggles for access to land, natural resources and safe environments by rural families and communities are combined with struggles for livelihood, cultural recognition and access to social benefits (Gudynas 2009). Across the diverse societies of Latin America, access to and management of nature play different and often conflicting roles in social, cultural and political life. Moreover, citizenship in the region is mediated by complex local, national and international politics, as it becomes stretched between local demands, measures to propel national economic growth and increasing efforts to sustain global commons.

In particular, the actions and livelihood strategies of peoples located in mega-diversity biomes have received increased attention as potential targets for conservation practices, due to the increased salience of the ecological services of tropical forests at an international scale. Ecosystem degradation and global climate change have become emergent issues alongside persistent concerns for social justice, poverty alleviation and economic growth. This confluence of issues has shaped a political agenda embraced by many left and centre-left national governments in Latin America (Barrett, Chaves and Rodriguez-Garavito 2008), where a range of hybrid policies have sought to combine social, ecological and economic goals (Lemos and Agrawal 2006). These policies have a major influence on the way citizens claim their rights towards nature at various scales. As mobilizations for environmental justice have increasingly attracted national attention, new political spaces for the expression of conservationist discourses by local populations have also emerged.

Using the combined normative frames of historical justice and environmental conservation, local populations, including various kinds of traditional groups, have partnered with national government institutions to embark on the design of new models for protected areas that combine territorial rights, conservation and sustainable production (hereafter territorial-environmental governance). This chapter examines the way local populations in the Brazilian

Amazon frame their discourses and practices in order to seek active involvement in the creation of protected areas for biological and cultural diversity. I analyse the processes through which local populations living in mega-biodiversity areas claim rights to land, consider the role of the state in mediating institutional innovations required for legal recognition of such rights and discuss the implications of these processes for local and traditional populations – especially in light of the fact that new rights become interwoven with new responsibilities. By exploring the case of territorial-environmental governance in Brazil and unpacking the politics of nature that shape claims to rights, impositions of duties and the formation of new institutions, I hope to demonstrate the way that national policies mediate environmental citizenship among local populations. Combining environmental citizenship with environmental justice perspectives not only helps to better understand the relationship between citizenship and nature across a range of socio-environmental contexts, but also promises to reveal the contradictions between rights and duties at local and global scales as individuals and collectivities become the targets of new modes of environmental governance.[1]

The chapter is divided into four sections. In the first section, I present the socio-environmental context of territorial-environmental governance in Brazil, based on official documents and academic literature. In the second section, based on empirical data from twenty years of longitudinal research in the region of Santarém in the Lower Amazon, I analyse how a local fishing management system has been transformed into a core element of the design and implementation process for a patchwork of Agro-Extractive Settlement (AES) in the region – a new territorial model for sustainable production within local communities. In the third section I discuss how indigenous populations and other traditional groups are being enlisted as local and global environmental citizens, through a combination of rights and duties influenced by national policies. In the last section I highlight the contradictions between the land rights granted in response to social justice claims and newly emergent duties meant to safeguard the global commons as part of a national strategy to mitigate climate change.

Territorial-Environmental Governance in Brazil

Brazil's environmental challenges are directly linked to the country's vibrant economic growth, which relies on primary and secondary industries with significant and increasing energy demands. Brazil occupies the uncomfortable position of being one of the world's top greenhouse gas emitters, with 80 per cent of carbon emissions coming from deforestation (Fearnside 2008). At the same time, Brazil is host to approximately 65 per cent of a mega-biodiversity biome, the Amazon basin, which also serves as an important carbon sink. Together, these facts make land cover changes in Brazil a key environmental concern at the global level. Meanwhile, in domestic environmental politics, conflicts over unequal access to natural resources, social exclusion and increased ecological risks are pressing issues (Carneiro-Filho and Braga de Souza 2009). In order to sustain steady economic growth, the Brazilian government has developed the Growth Acceleration Program, which foresees the expansion of agricultural land, energy production and infrastructure supported by a 'green' energy grid based on hydroelectric power and agro-fuel, intensive agro-pastoral activities and a broad conservation program of protected areas (República Federativa do Brasil 2010). In this complex socio-environmental context, territorial-environmental governance in Brazil has gone through major institutional changes since the early 1990s, from a centralized, national structure to a 'participatory' approach in which local populations have increasingly been engaged in the design and implementation of land tenure and land-use models in protected areas. A brief historical account of territorial-environmental governance in rural Brazil is helpful to understanding how this process came about.

Until the 1980s, territorial-environmental governance was controlled by national agencies and organized into three pillars: indigenous territories, agrarian reform settlements and conservation units. The three territorial models developed separately during the military government, served different purposes and did little to advance land rights for rural populations. Plans to establish indigenous territories were overshadowed by ongoing efforts to integrate indigenous populations into the national society (Souza 1995). Likewise, agrarian reform settlements were mainly driven by military colonization projects and land conflict resolution, leading to the establishment of small farms in marginal lands with little additional technical or financial support (Alston, Libecap and Mueller 1999). Meanwhile, the preservationist model of conservation units restricted local populations living in the area from using natural resources that had long been part of their livelihood traditions (Diegues 1994). While local communities struggled for access to land and natural resources, rural development policies related to agribusiness, infrastructure expansion and extractive activities drove environmental degradation and social conflicts (Zhouri and Laschefski 2010). Along the new agro-pastoral frontiers, mostly in the savannah and Amazonian biomes, the rural elite gradually appropriated new agricultural lands and pushed rural populations into more isolated areas with limited access to markets, infrastructure and information (Wolford 2008).

The democratization process that followed the end of the military government in the 1980's opened new political spaces for the exercise of citizenship among local actors, who organized themselves into a broad range of social movements (Acselrad 2008). This period was marked by the incorporation of a green discourse into social justice agendas and the development of alliances between local populations and transnational organizations as communities sought to strengthen their political power in the struggle for territorial rights (Hochstetler and Keck 2007). In particular, communities in the Amazonian basin have emphasized the value of their local management systems, based on low-impact practices, as a strategy for conservation of mega-biodiversity regions (Redford and Padoch 1992). By linking the local identities of indigenous communities and other traditional groups to sustainable production and natural resource extraction, and connecting cultural with biological diversity, these rural populations have been able to increase their political visibility at national and international levels. In doing so, they have become inserted into national and international networks of NGOs and researchers.

The bottom-up mobilization of these populations has found political support in the strong discourse of social inclusion, participation and empowerment deployed by the national government over the last decade. As part of a strategy to reposition themselves in the centre of the territorial-environmental governance agenda, national agencies responded to claims from social movements by promoting institutional innovation for conservation and development in rural areas. Social movement networks and local peoples in turn influenced the design of new legislation for protected areas and new categories of agrarian reform settlements, leading to a policy framework that seeks to conserve both cultural and biological diversity.

Together with indigenous populations, *quilombolas* (Afro-Brazilian rural communities) were the first to be formally recognized and granted special territorial rights by the 1988 Constitution. A decade later, other social groups such as rubber tapper, riparian and coastal communities were granted rights to live in agrarian reform settlements and conservation units. The agrarian reform agency recognized collective land tenure and local management systems in special agrarian settlement categories in the early 1990s, while the National System for Conservation Units (SNUC), approved in 2000, included several categories of conservation units, with local residents under the definitional umbrella of 'traditional populations', legally defined as 'groups who self-recognize as culturally differentiated and hold their own social organization, territorial and natural resource use as a way to reproduce their cultural, social, religious, ancestral, and economic conditions, using knowledge, innovation, and practices generated and transmitted through traditional means' (Brazil 2007).

Since 1988, numerous co-management initiatives have been developed in the country under a range of land-use designation categories, including indigenous lands (Lisansky 2005), extractive reserves (Rosendo 2007) and *quilombo* settlements (French 2009). With oversight from different governmental agencies, these designations combine conservation, social inclusion and rural development goals in their management plans (Paz, Freitas and Souza 2006), while granting local residents exclusive, collective, land-use rights. Though based on the overarching supposition of shared interests, the different goals and motivations driving participation in such partnerships have created a complex and not always harmonious set of relationships. Indeed, it would be fair to say that territorial-environmental governance in Brazil has been shaped by both collaboration and conflict between local and national actors. It is this tension which has come to define the emergence of environmental citizenship in mega-biodiversity areas.

The institutional framework for this emerging governance/citizenship milieu is multifaceted. Although numerous state and non-state agencies collaborate in this process, five national agencies play a major role in the governance of protected areas[2]: the National Agency for Agrarian Reform (INCRA), the National Foundation for Indigenous Populations (FUNAI), the Palmares Cultural Foundation (FCP), the Chico Mendes Institute of Conservation and Biodiversity (ICMBio) and the Institute of Environment and Renewable Natural Resources (IBAMA). Protected areas in state and municipal territories are governed by corresponding agencies at the state and municipal levels, which can create more complexity and conflicts with federal environmental governance. Each agency is located in a different Ministry and they differ in their historical backgrounds, political motivations and principle goals. INCRA was created during the military government in 1970 to carry out agrarian reform, monitor rural property titles and administer public lands. Until recently, its policy blueprint focused narrowly on the provision of individual land titles, infrastructure and credit lines, with little consideration for environmental issues or social diversity. FUNAI, created in the same period, is in charge of the identification, regulation and protection of indigenous land. However, only after the Constitution of 1988 was passed were concrete steps towards the protection of indigenous territories undertaken (Lisansky 2005). The FCP, created in 1988 as part of a new constitutionally mandated social inclusion program for Afro-Brazilian society, has the mission of formulating programs and projects to support the inclusion of Afro-Brazilians, which includes the creation and implementation of *quilombolas* (rural Afro-Brazilian territories). The ICMBio, recently created in 2007, oversees the creation and governance of national conservation units. It maintains a preservationist model of protected areas without human presence that was inherited from its predecessor agency and which has begun to change only recently (Rylands and Brandon 2005). Finally, IBAMA is the agency in charge of the evaluation, approval and monitoring of management plans for national protected areas, except in cases where a state-level environmental agency is institutionally capable of performing this role. In cases of protected areas with local residents, management plans are formulated in collaboration with traditional populations, and the approval of each plan depends on its compliance with national environmental legislation.

Since the mid 1990s, the spatial configuration of protected areas in Brazil has evolved to become a mosaic covering approximately 25 per cent of the national territory. There are 1.1 million square kilometres in conservation units (Rylands and Brandon 2005), from which approximately one-fifth is devoted to sustainable-use categories – extractive reserves and sustainable development reserves – that include traditional populations (CNUC/MMA 2011). Another 1.1 million square kilometres are devoted to indigenous territories (Carneiro-Filho and Braga de Souza 2009). The percentage of land in protected areas is raised to nearly half within the Amazonian territory (Rolla and Ricardo 2009), where most of the ethnic territories have been created. Table 3.1 shows the current picture of the most relevant national protected areas that involve traditional populations in Brazil. Indigenous lands alone occupy 13 per cent of the national territory (ISA N.d.), as part of the accomplishment of the Indigenous Lands Demarcation Project (PPTAL) initiated in the mid 1990s (Lisansky 2005; ISA N.d.). Between 1995 and 2011, 1,188 *quilombola* territories have been identified and are under different stages of land-regulation process: 120 territories have been granted land titles covering nearly 10,000 square kilometres, 135 demarcated territories are awaiting legal confirmation covering over 15,000 square kilometres and 933 are ter-

Table 3.1 Agencies, Protected Areas and Traditional Populations in Brazil.

Ministry	Agency	Main Mission	Settlement Category	Number of Settlements	Total Area (km²)
Ministry of Justice	FUNAI	Human rights	Indigenous reserves	674	1,115,236
Ministry of Education and Culture	FCP	Cultural diversity	*Quilombolas*	1188	25,366
Ministry of Environment	ICMBio IBAMA	Environmental conservation	Extractive and sustainable development reserves	93	242,611
Ministry of Agriculture and Rural Development	INCRA	Rural development	Agro-extractive settlements	246	21,574

Sources: CNUC/MMA 2011; INCRA/DFQ 2011; ISA N.d.; INCRA personal communication, 2011.

ritories currently under evaluation (INCRA/DFQ 2011). In addition, 93 conservation units associated with traditional communities have been created in both inland and coastal areas (CNUC/MMA 2011), while INCRA has initiated a program in 2006 to expand agro-extractive settlements on the Amazonian floodplain to include more than 240 new areas.[3]

Social justice, rural development and environmental conservation are elements of all four territorial models. However, the ethos of each agency varies according to the goals and political motivations of the ministries responsible. INCRA's focus on rural development is usually motivated by land conflicts, demands from social movements such as the Landless Workers Movement (MST) and election campaigns. Due to a history of ethnic annihilation, FUNAI is located in the Ministry of Justice and is driven by a human rights orientation, while FCP is influenced by the culturally oriented mission of the Ministry of Education and Culture. Despite the new emphasis on social justice, ICMBio and IBAMA, both part of the Ministry of the Environment, focus on stringent environmental protection, which often involves local residents limiting their livelihood to subsistence agriculture and low-impact extractive activities.

As a result of these differences, the formal rights and duties of human populations within protected areas vary widely across the different models and are not always in consonance with past traditions of livelihood. The tension among the three main goals – land rights, conservation and local development – is especially evident in the agrarian reform settlements implemented by INCRA. Among all agencies, INCRA is the one with the longest history of territorial governance based on private land rights for landless peasants. For this reason, it is also the agency that has most struggled to leave behind its top-down policy blueprint and adapt to the new impetus for the creation of collective settlements based on participatory management plans. The challenge of developing land-use models that explicitly provide space for the exercise of citizenship rights related to the environment is illustrated in the next section through an examination of INCRA's implementation of agro-extractive settlements in the floodplain.

Agro-Extractive Settlements in the Lower Amazon

The Amazonian floodplain comprises four interconnected ecological zones: river channels crossing high natural levees and natural grasslands that are seasonally flooded, creating a system of interconnected lakes which changes in area, depth and connectivity throughout the year. In general, river channels are considered to be open access commons, high natural levees are held privately, while lakes and grasslands, which are seasonally overlapping, are held collectively. Informal environmental management in this ecosystem dates back to pre-Colombian times (Castro 2002). However, intentional territorial-environmental governance at the local level emerged in many floodplain communities in the 1980s as a response to the intensification of commercial fishing in the region (McGrath et al. 1993). 'Fishing accords' constitute an informal local governance model developed for the floodplain, which was the outcome of collective action by local users with the support of Catholic Church organizations in the region.

A fishing accord is a document usually prepared by community residents, where rules of access, use and monitoring are recorded and approved by a voting system (Castro 1999). These accords define an explicit resource tenure system based on the local perception of the floodplain as an integrated ecosystem. However, until the 1990s, fishing accords were mostly fragmented, created by single communities and focused primarily on fishing resources (Castro and McGrath 2003). As ranching on the floodplain grasslands and the 'invasion' of lakes by urban commercial fishers escalated in the region, floodplain residents organized politically in their communities and in the region to claim their formal exclusive-use rights of their territories and natural resources. The informal management model of fishing accords found supporters in governmental and non-governmental organizations in the region, while innovations in environmental governance at the national level during the 1990s provided a legal framework by which the accords were gradually formalized as co-management systems in collaboration with the IBAMA and other agencies. These co-management systems were based on three main pillars: the formalization of the fishing accords and elaboration of local monitoring systems; the formulation of agreements between local residents and cattle ranchers regarding land-use activities; and the creation of regional councils, comprised by different stakeholders, for broader discussions over sustainable production in the floodplain (McGrath et al. 2008).

Despite these advances, co-management efforts were limited to conservation goals and did not address the economic and land-tenure issues necessary to support local participation and accountability (McGrath et al. 1993). After several discussions among representatives of government agencies, NGOs, grassroots organizations and floodplain dwellers, the agro-extractive settlement (AES) model of INCRA was chosen as the most suitable category for further institutionalizing environmental governance in floodplain communities. Created in 1986 by INCRA to regulate rubber tapper communities in the western Amazon region, the AES is the territorial model available that can best provide legal tools to incorporate informal fishing accords into integrated territorial governance for the floodplain. Specifically, via the AES, exclusive collective land-use rights can be granted to local residents by means of a renewable concession contract of ten years, negotiated between the local association and INCRA. Moreover, INCRA provides financial benefits for improvement in local infrastructure and production systems.

The floodplain AES was therefore the outcome of a gradual process of incorporation of informal local management into an integrated territorial governance model. As a result, the community-based, fishing-oriented management systems that emerged in the 1980s became part of a regional, floodplain-oriented conservation and development program, which included new goals such as regulation of land tenure, sustainable production and rural development. As part of this formal incorporation into the INCRA model, the implementation of the AES has included technical assistance and financial support to each eligible resident for basic housing, production and community infrastructure, as well as lines of credit for farmers.

The most important additional aspect provided by the AES designation has been the institutionalization of local tenure and management rules into a formal legal infrastructure. As a territorial-environmental entity, the AES is defined through cultural, ecological and socio-economic criteria. In the floodplain, an AES is usually comprised by a lake system and its surrounding lowland, where communities and farms are located. In the whole Lower Amazon, more than forty AESs were created, covering nine different municipalities along the river. In five municipalities where more detailed fieldwork has been carried out since 2008 (Santarém, Óbidos, Alenquer, Curuá and Prainha), fifteen AESs were created between July and December 2006, covering an area of approximately 2,300 km², including about one hundred communities and more than four thousand dwellers. All community residents with traditional ties to the area are eligible to live in an AES. The management plan for an AES includes rules of use, a system of monitoring and sanctions and a local council that includes representatives of all communities within an AES. Compliance with the management plan must be monitored by the local council in collaboration with supporting governmental agencies.

The creation of an AES is initiated through a formal request from the local population to INCRA, followed by a socio-environmental assessment carried out by INCRA and the elaboration of a management plan with participation of local residents. Upon the approval of the management plan by the State Environmental Agency (SEMA), technical and financial assistance is released to the community, completing the implementation cycle. Ongoing monitoring is led by the local council, which carries out regular evaluation and contemplates both adjustments to the plan and the levelling of sanctions against non-compliant members of the community. Residents who do not comply with the rules face eventual expulsion from the area.

Despite the innovative elements of the AES, key problems emerged during the creation of a number of AESs in the Lower Amazon floodplain. First, formal requests to create more than forty AESs were issued by different Fishers'

Unions in the region instead of community associations. As the formal representative organizations of the floodplain communities, the Fishers' Union of each municipality is entitled to issue such requests on behalf of the communities, but it is expected that they do so in consultation with local residents. In many cases such consultation had not occurred: during the six month period in 2006 in which the fifteen AESs were demarcated by means of preliminary socio-environmental assessment, there was little public participation. Part of the problem seems to be the organizational culture of INCRA, which has employed a universal AES model across the region, with no attention to specific social and historical context. Nevertheless, some of the communities themselves also appear to have lacked capacity for effective engagement with this kind of planning process. Despite the number of fishing accords in the region, most of the communities have diffuse leadership and local organizational structures. As such, even when some consultation has occurred, promises of new infrastructure, access to small grants and lines of credit have secured local approval without any significant degree of deliberation. In other words, the long-term democratic and participatory process of almost fifteen years to agree on a territorial model for the floodplain culminated in the top-down imposition of rules based on the rushed technocratic implementation of an inappropriate blueprint. Not surprisingly, the lack of transparency, which fed existing mistrust of governmental agencies, ultimately triggered opposition from floodplain dwellers.

In addition to problems with the design of the AESs, new issues arose during the implementation process. Entitled to develop their own management plans, local populations were eager to add rules to restrict the activities of cattle ranchers and urban fishers in the area. However, they were unaware that stringent environmental laws would now also restrict local practices such as hunting, farming and collection of non-timber products. As the designation of an AES suggests, the production system in this territorial model is focused on agro-extractive activities. In the floodplain, artisanal fishing, agroforestry and small-scale farming are the main activities foreseen. However, many traditional practices such as slash-and-burn agriculture, hunting and collection of turtle eggs are restricted by national environmental legislation. In addition, the growing engagement of local residents in cattle ranching, fomented in part by the new availability of lines of credit, may conflict with restrictions formulated in the management plans.

In another dimension, the limited organizational capacity of some communities, combined with the technocratic procedures of INCRA, has not only hampered the participation of local residents in some places, but also enhanced internal disagreements within and between communities, leaving the management plans to be formulated and implemented mostly by small numbers of community members and local NGOs. Interestingly enough, communities with strong political organizations were the most resistant to the AES designation. Some continued to seek a different territorial model over which they could have more control. For example, a few floodplain communities sought their territorial rights by claiming *quilombola* identity.

In sum, though the decision to make the AES the territorial model for the floodplain was the outcome of a gradual process incorporating informal local practices into an integrated floodplain tenure framework, the approach taken by INCRA has jeopardized the participatory approach that had developed in the region over the last decades.

From Rights to Duties

Rural populations in Brazil have a history of struggle for social justice based on the defence of traditional livelihood strategies. Long regarded by the national state as inefficient producers and as a threat to nature preservation, some members of this group have found new opportunities for political agency with the global turn toward local populations as important allies in biodiversity conservation. By linking local identities with 'sustainable' production, different rural groups have been able to enshrine their territorial rights in the 1988 Constitution and new conservation legislation passed in 2000. Of particular note, such identity claims have been made not only by indigenous and Afro-Brazilian peoples but also by other social groups such as rubber tappers, riparian and coastal communities.

In a context where the worldwide implementation of protected areas has had major impacts on local populations (Adams and Hutton 2010), territorial rights allotted to traditional populations by the Brazilian state must be recognized as a positive step towards greater social justice in environmental governance. As Ferrero observes (this volume) local peoples have been able to tap into concern over the sustainable use of natural resources in order to secure new recognition and resources from state actors. Nevertheless, despite the institutional innovations in Brazilian territorial-environmental governance, including the expansive definition of 'traditional populations', the implementation of protected areas has had other, less positive, implications that deserve close attention.

One major implication of the new social category of 'traditional populations' is the fragmentation of the rural population, which shares similar social demands but is now split into several different identity groups pursuing various institutional paths in order to claim their rights to land (Castro et al. 2006). Indigenous groups seek rights to indigenous territories through FUNAI, Afro-Brazilian groups claim rights as *quilombola* communities through FCP and other traditional groups pursue rights through special categories of conservation units or agrarian settlements through ICMBio and INCRA, respectively. In many cases, the pursuit of such rights has involved active identity reconstruction (French 2009), while others engaged in forum shopping between identities – such as the case of certain floodplain communities described earlier, who claimed their *quilombola* identity over their riparian identity as a way of securing a more favourable mode of local environmental governance. Such strategic use of identity to secure political power and legal rights has meant that these various rural groups have distanced themselves from each other in their struggles to access land and natural resources.

In addition to this problem of new and newly entrenched identities, the category of 'traditional populations' implies the simultaneous existence of 'non-traditional peasants', who lack similar avenues for claiming rights to land, a fact that not only impinges on their own well-being but also has led to conflictive interactions with other rural groups (Carneiro-Filho and Braga de Souza 2009). In response to their lack of ethnic status, landless peasants have pursued a different political strategy, organizing themselves into one of the largest social movements in Latin America, the Landless Workers Movement (MST). In their demand for agrarian reform and land redistribution, the MST emphasizes social justice, citizenship, food security and health (MST 2009), converting territorial rights into a social issue. On this basis, the MST calls for rural development through provision of basic infrastructure, technical assistance, market access and credit in order to halt rural-to-urban migration, generate employment and promote food security along with sustainable land-use practices (Wright and Wolford 2003). The MST discourse shares something of the 'green' dimension associated with traditional populations. Designing sustainable land-use practices such as agro-forestry, promoting environmental education and condemning high-input, large-scale mono-crop agriculture are examples of practices of environmental citizenship by individuals and groups affiliated with the MST as a way to combine ecological and social concerns (Wittman 2010).

In contrast to the non-traditional populations, ethnic groups gain political capital by emphasizing their low-tech, subsistence-based, land-use practices, which ironically limit their future development options and reinforce their impoverished conditions. As a result, these populations are increasingly not treated as peasants by governmental agencies, which prescribe non-consumptive economic activities as an alternative source of income, such as the program of community-based ecotourism launched in 2008 by the Ministry of Tourism to support local initiatives to develop the economy in extractive reserves (MTUR 2008). Despite the positive outcomes of ecotourism in certain contexts (Alencar and Peralta 2008), some authors call attention to the danger of promoting the impoverished lifestyles of rural communities as an idealized existence to be appreciated by outsiders (Penna-Firme and Brondizio 2007). In addition, as Sundberg observes in the case of the Maya Biosphere reserve (this volume), a focus on traditional identity often accentuates the discriminatory perceptions of professionals working for state agencies or conservation organizations, who often view local groups as incapable of making informed decisions about local environmental management.

Finally, another implication of the reliance on traditional identities to make claims to land rights has to do with the distribution of the burden of nature protection. The cost of managing protected areas is often born by local populations, who are left to defend their territories from development pressures with limited outside support (Brondizio, Ostrom and Young 2009). Indeed, the presence of populations in protected areas acts as a cost-cutting measure for underfunded government agencies, since it minimizes the resources required for monitoring. Meanwhile, as traditional populations are charged with preserving global commons such as biodiversity and carbon storage, socio-economic actors in other parts of the landscape can often see a relaxation in environmental regulation. Policy innovation for conservation in Brazil has to be understood as fundamentally linked to development policy, where the preservation of some landscapes means the allocation of others to the ongoing expansion of economic activities with significant ecological impacts. This trend can be observed when national government measures to protect the Amazonian biome are contrasted with large-scale development projects recently implemented in the region. A plan to include almost half of the Amazon in protected areas (MMA 2009), to implement a moratorium on soy cultivation in Amazonian soils and an ecological-economic zoning for the Amazon (MMA 2010) are some of the measures in progress to protect Amazonian ecosystems. On the other hand, construction of gas pipelines through protected areas, along with the projected doubling of biofuel production and export by 2017 (MME 2009), raises concerns about ecological and social impacts in and around protected areas. Finally, the plan to expand agricultural land for agribusiness by 170 million hectares, although mostly outside the Amazon region, is expected to have indirect impacts on protected areas in the region (Carneiro-Filho and de Souza 2009).

Even though traditional populations are key to the success of conservation strategies in protected areas, they frequently have little say in their design and implementation. Despite the fact that participation is promoted through the establishment of co-management systems, the everyday politics of decision making tends to exclude local groups. Since leadership and social networks vary across communities, territorial-environmental governance in Brazil has led to a range of outcomes. In the case of the AESs in the Lower Amazon, some communities have been equal partners in the initiatives, others have tried to withdraw from the process and still others have accepted the new governance regime with limited participation. The result is a paradoxical combination of more secure land rights along with reduced rights to carry out traditional production activities. Meanwhile, these communities are expected to take on new duties in monitoring and enforcement of protected areas. In sum, the glocalization of conservation governance in Brazil, significantly mediated by the efforts of various state agencies to reposition themselves relative to demands for local land rights, has produced a new scalar configuration of responsibility, with local populations enlisted as guardians of global commons.

Linking Local and Global Environmental Citizenship

The contradictions between the local rights and global duties of traditional populations emerging from territorial-environmental governance in Brazil have major implications for the environmental citizenship debate. Environmental citizenship has been a contentious concept in the analysis of emerging questions about the link between political agency, rights, obligations and the cultivation of sustainable societies. Emphasis on the consumptive behaviour of citizens in industrialized countries promotes a globalized notion of environmental responsibility that is often disconnected from local socio-ecological contexts. Turning our attention to the way that traditional populations become integrated into the territorial-environmental governance of mega-biodiversity regions offers an important remedy to this shortcoming, demonstrating the way that citizenship becomes entangled with the environmental policies carried out by the state.

The environmental citizenship promised to traditional peoples in Brazil is meant to be bi-directional, in which their rights to land, livelihood and political participation are granted along with responsibilities to conserve local environments. In contrast to the diffuse global responsibility taken on by the ecologically enlightened northern consumer, environmental citizenship for Brazil's traditional populations entails a form of stewardship that is embedded in local ecological contexts. At the same time, since the ecosystems they are meant to protect have a broad value to humanity as a shared world heritage and as a carbon sink, their duties as environmental citizens also have an important global dimension. While somewhat comparable to the duty-oriented global environmental citizenship of the northern consumer, globalized duty for the Amazonian citizen-steward has key differences in terms of motivations and outcomes. Where the northern consumer voluntarily foregoes a degree of material luxury in order to reduce an excessive ecological footprint, her Amazonian counterpart is compelled to take on responsibilities in exchange for rights, often implying behavioural changes that have direct livelihood impacts. Finally, the responsibilities taken on by Amazonian communities involve not only changes in their members' conduct but also the expectation that they will play a role in monitoring the conduct of others who might threaten the protected areas that they inhabit.

The way this scalar reconfiguration has been influenced by the national state is of particular relevance to environmental citizenship research in Latin America. The decentralization measures implemented during the neoliberal period have redefined the role of the nation-state as a facilitator of market relations between local producers and global market. Recently, some Latin American countries have undergone political changes and are now represented by post-neoliberal, non-elite parties. As a result, attempts of the state to regain control of environmental governance have been accompanied with discourses of social inclusion, rural development and poverty alleviation (Baud, Castro and Hogenboom 2011). Scalar reconfigurations emerging from this trend have fostered new opportunities for environmental citizenship such as cases in Bolivia and Argentina (see both Tockman and Merlinsky and Latta, this volume). However, as the case examined here suggests, the outcomes of such scalar reconfigurations are multifaceted and often ambiguous (see also Perreault 2005).

From an environmental justice perspective, converting marginalized traditional populations into the 'guardians' of collectively valued resources in exchange for moderate improvements to their social and political rights entails a rather problematic basis for citizenship. Depending on traditional populations to protect Amazonian ecosystems reduces costs for government agencies, hence lowering the price tag of conservation for society at large. At the same time, it plays into a politics of conservation that legitimizes the escalation of unsustainable practices by other actors elsewhere on the landscape, many of whom stand to accrue significant profits as a result. The stringent limitations on resource use in protected areas contrasts with the limited monitoring of land-use activities on private properties. Therefore, although new policies of territorial-environmental governance have reduced inequality in terms of land rights, not all kinds of land rights are created equal in terms of the distributions of welfare and responsibilities that they entail.

Traditional populations' evolving socio-political agency is intertwined with new approaches to environmental governance, a relationship which has meant their emergence as environmental citizens in both local and global dimensions. Their environmental citizenship is distinct from that of the green citizen-consumers of the Global North, and the peculiar distribution of rights and duties it entails raises the spectre of new forms of environmental injustice. This citizenship arises from the interplay among individuals, collectivities, state agencies and international actors, requiring a multi-dimensional and multi-scale analytical approach. Probing the way that scalar configurations are 'produced, undone, and reproduced through political struggle' (Brown and Purcell 2005, 607) can help us understand how environmental governance and citizenship are connected. Global climate change and biodiversity agendas become refracted through government agencies with broader institutional agendas, while local actors respond in different ways to policy innovations, especially taking advantage of the points of contact between social, cultural and environmental policy. How we see this interplay of actors, interests and agendas depends on the perspective from which we view them. Where environmental NGOs and some government agencies see nature conservation, other government agencies see social or cultural policy. Local people may in turn see land rights and new economic development possibilities, or may instead perceive new efforts by the state to constrain traditional means of livelihood. Ultimately, it is fundamental to ask how these different perceptions of environmental governance connect to form the spaces of environmental citizenship that the peoples of Amazonian traditional communities inhabit.

Notes

1. This research was funded by WWF-Brazil, the Centre for Latin American Research and Documentation (CEDLA), and the European Commission (FP7-SSH-2010-3, Grant Agreement no. 266710). I am thankful to IPAM staff in Santarém for their logistical support during my visits to the field, and to Alex Latta and Hannah Wittman for their thoughtful comments on earlier drafts of this chapter. This version remains my own responsibility.
2. Protected areas are usually defined as territories set aside for environmental conservation. In this text I use this term to also include ethnic territories such as indigenous and rural Afro-Brazilian communities, which are primarily set aside for cultural diversity.
3. Agro-extractive settlements emerged as an institutional design for several rubber tapper communities in the late 1980s. According to an INCRA agent, only a few settlements were developed before 2006. Data on the program since 2006 have been provided to the author by INCRA on 21 June 2011.

References

Acselrad, H. (2008) 'Grassroots Reframing of Environmental Struggles in Brazil,' in D. V. Carruthers (ed.), *Environmental Justice in Latin America: Problems, Promises, and Practice.* Cambridge, MA: MIT Press, pp. 75–97.

Adams, W. M., and J. Hutton. (2010) 'People, Parks, and Poverty: Political Ecology and Biodiversity Conservation,' *Conservation and Society,* Vol. 5, No. 2, pp. 147–183.

Adger, W. N., K. Brown and E. L. Tompkins. (2006) 'The Political Economy of Cross-Scale Networks in Resource Co-Management', *Ecology and Society,* Vol. 10, No. 2, paper 9.

Alencar, E. F., and N. Peralta. (2008) 'Ecoturismo e Mudança Social na Amazônia Rural: Efeitos Sobre o Papel da Mulher e as Relações de Gênero,' *Campos,* Vol. 9, No. 1, pp. 109–129.

Alston, L. J., G. D. Libecap and B. Mueller. (1999) *Titles, Conflict, and Land Use: The Development of Property Rights and Land Reform on the Brazilian Amazon Frontier,* Economics, Cognition, and Society Series. Ann Arbor: The University of Michigan Press.

Barrett, P., D. Chaves and C. Rodriguez-Garavito (eds). (2008) *The New Latin American Left: Utopia Reborn.* London: Pluto Press.

Baud, M., F. Castro and B. Hogenboom. (2011) 'Environmental Governance in Latin America: Towards an Integrative Research Agenda,' *European Review of Latin American and Caribbean Studies,* Vol. 90, pp. 79–88.

Brazil. (2007) 'Investimentos em Infraestrutura para o Desenvolvimento Econômico e Social,' República Federativa do Brasil, online report, http://www.brasil.gov.br/pac/o-pac/investi mentos-em-infraestrutura-para-o-desenvolvimento-economico-e-social.

Brondizio, E., E. Ostrom and O. R. Young. (2009) 'Connectivity and the Governance of Multi-level Social-Ecological Systems: The Role of Social Capital,' *Annual Review of Environment and Resources,* Vol. 34, No. 1, pp. 254–278.

Brown, J. C., and M. Purcell. (2005) 'There's Nothing Inherent About Scale: Political Ecology, the Local Trap, and the Politics of Development in the Brazilian Amazon,' *Geoforum,* Vol. 36, pp. 607–624.

Brown, K., and S. Rosendo. (2000) 'Environmentalists, Rubber Tappers and Empowerment: The Politics and Economics of Extractive Reserves,' *Development and Change,* Vol. 31, No. 1, pp. 201–228.

Cadastro Nacional de Unidades de Conservação / Ministerio do Meio Ambiente [CNUC/ MMA]. (2011) Tabela Consolidada das Unidades de Conservação. Governo Federal do Bra-sil. Table updated 6 June 2011. http://www.mma.gov.br/sitio/index.php?ido=conteudo .monta&idEstrutura=119&idConteudo=11227&idMenu=12153 (accessed 13 July 2011).

Carruthers, D. V., ed. (2008) *Environmental Justice in Latin America: Problems, Promises, and Practice.* Cambridge, MA: MIT Press.

Castro, F. (1999) 'Fishing Accords: The Political Ecology of Fishing Intensification in the Ama-zon,' *CIPEC Dissertation Series,* No 4. Bloomington: Indiana University.

———. (2002) 'From Myths to Rules: The Evolution of the Local Management in the Lower Amazonian Floodplain,' *Environment and History,* Vol. 8, No. 2, pp. 197–216.

Castro, F., and D. McGrath. (2003) 'Community-Based Management of Lakes and Sustain-ability of Floodplain Resources in the Lower Amazon,' *Human Organization, Vol. 62,* No. 2, pp. 123–133.

Castro, F., et al. (2006) 'Use and Misuse of Concepts of Tradition and Property Rights in the Conservation of Natural Resources in the Atlantic Forest (Brazil),' *Ambiente e Sociedade,* Vol. 9, No. 1, pp. 23–39.

Carneiro-Filho, A., and O. Braga de Souza. (2009) 'Atlas of Pressures and Threats to Indig-enous Lands in the Brazilian Amazon.' São Paulo, Brazil: Instituto Socioambiental.

Cunha, M. C., and M. W. B. Almeida. (2000) 'Indigenous People, Traditional People, and Conservation in the Amazon,' *Daedalus,* Vol. 129, No. 2, pp. 315–338.

Diegues, A. C. S. (1994) *O Mito da Natureza Intocada.* São Paulo, Brazil: NUPAUB.

Diegues, A. C. S., and V. M. Vianna, orgs. (2000) *Comunidades Tradicionais e Manejo dos Re-cursos Naturais da Mata Atlântica.* São Paulo, Brazil: NUPAUB.

Dobson, A. (2003) *Citizenship and the Environment.* New York: Oxford University Press.

Dobson, A., and A. Valencia Saíz (2005) 'Introduction,' *Environmental Politics,* Vol. 14, No. 2, pp. 157–162.

Fearnside, P. M. (2008) 'Deforestation in Brazilian Amazonia and Global Warming,' *Annals of Arid Zone,* Vol. 47, No. 3–4, pp. 1–20.

French, J. H. (2009) *Legalizing Identities: Becoming Black or Indian in Brazil's Northeast.* Chapel Hill: University of North Carolina Press.

Gabrielson, T. (2008) 'Green Citizenship: A Review and Critique,' *Citizenship Studies,* Vol. 12, No. 4, pp. 429–446.

Gudynas, E. (2009) 'Ciudadanía Ambiental y Meta-Ciudadanías Ecológicas: Revisión y Alterna-tivas en América Latina,' *Desenvolvimento e Meio Ambiente,* Vol. 19, pp. 53–72.

Hochstetler, K., and M. E. Keck. (2007) *Greening Brazil: Environmental Activism in State and Society*. Durham: Duke University Press.

Horton, D. (2006) 'Demonstrating Environmental Citizenship? A Study of Everyday Life Among Green Activists,' in A. Dobson and D. Bell (eds), *Environmental Citizenship*. Cambridge, MA: MIT Press, pp. 127–150.

Instituto Nacional de Colonização e Reforma Agrária / Coordenação Geral de Regularização de Territórios Quilombolas [INCRA/DFQ]. (2011) Quadro Atual da Política de Regularização de Terrirórios Quilombolas no Incra. Table updated 29 June 2011. http://www.incra .gov.br/index.php/estrutura-fundiaria/quilombolas/file/109-quadro-atual-da-politica-de-regularizacao-de-territorios-quilombolas-no-incra (accessed 13 July 2011).

Instituto Socio-Ambiental [ISA]. (N.d.) *Povos Indígenas do Brasil: Localização e Extensão das TI's*, http://pib.socioambiental.org/pt/c/terras-indigenas/demarcacoes/localizacao-e-extensao-das-tis, (accessed 13 July 2011).

Jagers, S. C. (2010) 'In Search of the Ecological Citizen,' *Environmental Politics*, Vol. 8, No. 1, pp. 18–36.

Keck, K. E., and K. Sikkink. (1998) *Activists Beyond Borders: Advocacy Networks in International Politics*. Ithaca: Cornell University Press.

Kingstone, P. R., and Y. J. Power (eds). (2000) *Democratic Brazil: Actors, Institutions and Processes*. Pittsburgh: University of Pittsburgh Press.

Latta, P. A. (2007) 'Locating Democratic Politics in Ecological Citizenship,' *Environmental Politics*, Vol. 16, No. 3, pp. 377–393.

Lemos, M. C., and A. Agrawal. (2006) 'Environmental Governance,' *Annual Review of Environment and Resources*, Vol. 31, pp. 297–325.

Lisansky, J. (2005) 'Fostering Change for Brazil's Indigenous People: The Role of the Pilot Programme,' in A. Hall (ed.), *Global Impact, Local Action: New Environmental Policy in Latin America*. London: Brookings Institution Press, pp. 170–186.

McGrath, D., et al. (1993) 'Fisheries and the Evolution of Resource Management on the Lower Amazon Basin,' *Human Ecology*, Vol. 21, No. 2, pp. 167–195.

McGrath, D., et al. (2008) 'Constructing a Policy and Institutional Framework for an Ecosystem-Based Approach to Managing the Lower Amazon Floodplain,' *Environment, Development and Sustainability*, Vol. 10, pp. 677–695.

MacGregor, S. (2006) 'No Sustainability Without Justice: A Feminist Critique of Environmental Citizenship,' in A. Dobson and D. Bell (eds), *Environmental Citizenship*. Cambridge, MA: MIT Press, pp. 101–126.

Ministério do Meio Ambiente [MMA]. (2009) 'Programa Areas Protegidas da Amazonia – ARPA – Fase II,' Ministério do Meio Ambiente, Secretaria de Biodiversidade e Floresta. Brasília.

———. (2010) 'Estratégias de Transição para a Sustentabilidade,' Proposta Preliminar para Consulta Pública. Brasília, online report, http://www.mma.gov.br/estruturas/225/_arquivos/ macrozee___proposta_preliminar_para_consulta_26_jan_225.pdf

Ministério de Minas e Energia (MME). (2009) Plano Decenal de Expansão de Energia 2008-2017. Vol. 1 and 2, online report, http://www.mme.gov.br/mme/galerias/arquivos/publi cacoes/pde_2008_2017/PDE2008-2017_VOL2_CompletoM.pdf.

Ministério de Turismo [MTUR]. (2008) 'Seleção de Propostas de Projetos para Apoio às Iniciativas de Turismo de Base Comunitária,' Edital de Chamada pública de Projetos, MTur/Nº 001/2008, online report, http://www.turismo.gov.br/export/sites/default/turismo/con venios_contratos/selecao_projetos/Edital_Chamada_Pxblica_de_Projetos_0012008.pdf

Mohai. P., D. Pellow and J. T. Roberts. (2009) 'Environmental Justice,' *Annual Review of Environment and Resources*, Vol. 34, pp. 405–430.

Movimento dos Trabalhadores Rurais Sem Terra [MST]. (2009) 'Nossas Bandeiras,' online report, http://www.mst.org.br/taxonomy/term/329

Paz, R. J., G. L. Freitas and E. A. Souza. (2006) *Unidades de Conservação no Brasil: História e Legislação*. João Pessoa, Brasil: Ed. Universitária/UFPB.

Penna-Firme, R., and E. Brondizio. (2007) 'The Risks of Commodifying Poverty: Rural Communities, *Quilombola* Identity, and Nature Conservation in Brazil,' *Habitus,* Vol. 5, No. 2, pp. 355–373.

Perreault, T. (2005) 'State Restructuring and the Scale Politics of Rural Water Governance in Bolivia,' *Environment and Planning A*, Vol. 37, pp. 263–284.

Redford, K. H., and C. Padoch (eds). (1992) *Conservation of Neotropical Forests: Working from Traditional Resource Use*. New York: Columbia University Press.

República Federativa do Brasil. (2010) 'Programa de Aceleração do Crescimento,' online report, http://www.brasil.gov.br/pac/.

Rolla, A., and F. Ricardo (eds). (2009) 'Amazonia Brasileira 2009.' São Paulo, Brasil: Instituto Socioambiental.

Rosendo, S. (2007) 'Partnerships Across Scales: Lessons from Extractive Reserves in Brazilian Amazonia,' in M. A. F. Ros-Tonen (ed.), *Partnerships in Sustainable Forest Resource Management: Learning from Latin America*, Latin America Studies 94, CEDLA. Leiden, The Netherlands: Brill, pp. 229–254.

Rylands, A. B., and K. Brandon. (2005) 'Brazilian Protected Areas,' *Conservation Biology*, Vol. 19, No. 3, pp. 612–618.

Souza, C. F. M. (1995) 'On Brazil and its Indians,' in D. L van Cott (ed.), *Indigenous Peoples and Democracy in Latin America*. New York: St. Martin's Press, pp. 213–234.

Swyngedouw, E. (1997) 'Neither Global nor Local: 'Glocalization' and the Politics of Scale,' in K. R. Cox (ed.), *Spaces of Globalization: Reasserting the Power of the Local*. New York: Gilford Press, pp. 137–166.

Wittman, H. (2010) 'Agrarian Reform and the Environment: Fostering Ecological Citizenship in Mato Grosso, Brazil,' *Canadian Journal of Development Studies*, Vol. 29, No. 3–4, pp. 281–298.

Wolford, W. (2008) 'Environmental Justice and Agricultural Development in the Brazilian Cerrado,' in D. V. Carruthers (ed.), *Environmental Justice in Latin America: Problems, Promises, and Practice*. Cambridge, MA: MIT Press, pp. 213–238.

Wright, A. L., and W. Wolford. (2003) *To Inherit the Earth: The Landless Movement and the Struggle for a New Brazil*. Oakland: Food First Books.

Zhouri, A., and K. Laschefski (eds). (2010) *Desenvolvimento e Conflitos Ambientais*. Belo Horizonte: Editora UFMG.

'Sin Maíz No Hay País'

Citizenship and Environment in Mexico's
Food Sovereignty Movement

Analiese Richard

The struggle for food sovereignty has become one of the most important social movements in recent Mexican history, incorporating a broad range of actors including campesinos, environmentalists, human rights activists, academics and urban consumers. Beyond food security, defined as access to adequate quantities of food,[1] proponents of food sovereignty advocate the reconfiguration of global systems of food production, distribution and consumption to enable local control over basic food supplies. Leading international advocates like La Vía Campesina and Food First assert that traditional food systems are better adapted to local environments and hence more ecologically sustainable than large-scale industrial agriculture. Food sovereignty activists in Mexico have built upon the momentum of fifteen years of anti-NAFTA protests, referencing older nationalist discourses which portray Mexico as a 'maize civilization' characterized by a deep history of symbiosis between land and society mediated by a staple food crop. Mexico's 'Tortilla Crisis', one of many popular uprisings that punctuated the 2006–2008 global food crisis, catalysed renewed debate over the future of native maize and small-scale agriculture. The movement enjoins citizens and authorities alike to defend native maize as national patrimony, but also engages notions of the global commons to represent Mexican farmers as stewards of genetic biodiversity. This chapter analyses the political discourse of the Mexican food sovereignty movement as a response to environmental degradation, global economic integration and changing political frameworks.[2] Embedded in this discourse is a nascent notion of environmental citizenship, which helps to illuminate how the politics of the commons informs environmental struggles in Latin America.

The concept of citizenship provides important tools for theorizing political mobilization around the management of public goods such as traditional food systems. Environmental researchers have employed the idea of the commons to conceptualize contemporary struggles over nature, critiquing neoliberal policies as a new form of enclosure (Nonnini 2006; Scharper and Cunningham 2006). Meanwhile, agrarian scholars have examined the role of agriculture in mediating metabolic relationships between society and nature, highlighting the increasing politicization of crop germplasm (Kloppenberg

1988; Phillips 2005; Wittman 2009). These developments point towards mounting theoretical interest in the rights and responsibilities implied by the construction of nature as a public good. Viewed through this lens, maize is more than an agricultural commodity; it is also a genetic repository of collective knowledge and labour, a symbol of national heritage and a mediator of relationships between humans and ecosystems. The food sovereignty movement's identification of Mexicans as '*gente de maíz*' (people of maize) conjures an implicit model of environmental citizenship, in which citizens exercise rights to an autonomous food system while incurring responsibility for stewardship of the ecological and social relations that undergird it. The movement's rights-based rhetoric indexes national debates over democratic participation and accountability which are echoed within the scholarly literature on citizenship and the environment.

Food Sovereignty and Environmental Citizenship

From the 1970s onwards, the formulation of 'nature as part of the entitlements of humanity' enabled the creation of strategic coalitions between environmentalists and human rights advocates (Jelin 2000, 50). The Mexican food sovereignty movement links concerns regarding the relationship of the global food regime to local food systems with human rights and global environmental issues. It is led by a coalition of national-level agricultural producer networks, regional campesino and indigenous organizations, human rights and civil society associations, environmental organizations and groups of concerned academics. Two major networks lead the movement. Sin Maíz No Hay País (Without Maize There is No Country, SMNHP) incorporates many agrarian organizations from the earlier Movimiento El Campo No Aguanta Más (The Countryside Can Endure No Longer, MCNAM), along with environmental and academic NGOs. Red en Defensa del Maíz Nativo (Maize Defense Network, RDMN) is composed of smaller regional campesino and indigenous organizations. Over six hundred organizations have participated in the national campaigns described here. The movement's campaign for nutritional rights further enables it to appeal to everyday consumers, while articulating the importance of native maize in the environmentalist idiom of biodiversity gives the movement global reach.

The planetary scale of environmental crises and the activist networks confronting them coexist with renewed emphasis on local identities and symbolic points of reference (Jelin 2000, 48). Environmental politics necessarily involve cultural processes aimed at conceptualizing the relationships between specific societies and environments. The discourse of the Mexican food sovereignty movement centres on the notion of 'sustainable agrobiodiversity', conceived as an enduring web of reciprocal relationships among humans, ecosystems and food crops, namely maize. This relationship figures as a collectively produced public good which forms the basis of national identity and social order.[3] For example, the properties of the plant are said to influence the structure of the civilization; the nutritional efficiency, versatility and ease of preparation of the grain itself and the low-capital intensity and high biodiversity of the intercropped *milpa* system of production imply a degree of productive self-sufficiency (Warman 2003, 20). This autonomy, however, is tempered by the necessity of reciprocity. Since domesticated maize cannot self-propagate, reproduction depends upon its relationship with those who cultivate and consume it. Maize is a 'promiscuous' plant, an open pollinator highly vulnerable to hybridization. Cross-pollination, selection and sharing of seeds among farmers across millennia have produced 250 native landraces adapted to specific ecological zones and uses (Warman 2003, 15). The food sovereignty movement contends that Mexicans are duty bound to defend these relationships upon which their civilization is said to be founded. It alleges that failure to protect native maize and traditional agriculture endangers the body politic and undermines the legitimacy of the state (see, for example, Red en Defensa del Maíz et al. 2009).

The concept of citizenship – the rights and responsibilities of members of a political community, especially with regard to the management of public goods – provides a useful framework for theorizing environmental struggles. Whereas Northern theorists have proposed environmental citizenship as a means of fostering individual responsibility towards nature (Dobson 2003; Dobson and Bell 2006), debates in the Global South tend to focus on conflicts over ecological commons and the collective rights to livelihoods dependent upon these commons (see de Castro, this volume). These commons are conceived neither as pristine wilderness nor as mere resources, but rather as complex (often anthropogenic) ecosystems which provide basic means of biological and social reproduction. Some differences between the two perspectives may be attributed to the relative political and economic concerns of Northern and Southern countries within the international system, as reflected in ongoing struggles over the Doha Development Round of the WTO. Others are related to the practical challenges of institutionalizing environmental rights and responsibilities in specific contexts.

All humans may be imagined to be 'citizens of the planet', but rights and responsibilities associated with the global ecological commons must be claimed and enacted in relation to specific political communities. The constitution of these communities is widely debated among theorists. Andrew Dobson (2003) proposes 'ecological citizenship' as a new form of citizenship practice based upon the material relations embodied in the ecological footprint concept. In a situation of ecological scarcity, he argues, unequal use of ecological space generates a political obligation on the part of beneficiaries towards the victims of ecological deprivation. Eschewing traditional models of citizenship based on a bounded polity, Dobson suggests this new form of citizenship may be enacted in the course of 'everyday living' via horizontal relations of global civil society (2003, 138). He rejects a focus on rights to the commons, instead arguing that the virtue of justice is capable of producing obligations of ecological citizenship.

Though virtue is crucial to encouraging individuals to pursue the common good, on its own it provides insufficient grounds for citizenship. Alongside the present case study, other contributors to this volume demonstrate the failure of Dobson's normative approach to account for the concrete geopolitical and biopolitical contexts through which environmental citizenship regimes are currently enacted. Baldwin and Meltzer highlight the stark inequalities enshrined both in emergent methodologies for assessing and managing global ecological commons, as well as in the differential responsibilities these assign to Northern and Southern 'ecological citizens'. Likewise, de Castro notes that the 'downloading' of responsibility for protecting the commons onto disadvantaged populations in specific locations (such as areas of mega-biodiversity) enables the de facto legitimization of unsustainable practices (like overconsumption) by actors elsewhere in the global system. Finally, as Taddei and Henne and Gabrielson show, any model of environmental citizenship which fails to substantively address the role of transnational capital in shaping both the geopolitical and biopolitical contexts in which struggles over ecological commons take place is misguided.

Dobson's model is thus ill-suited to elucidate the citizenship practices or institutional frameworks advocated by Mexican food sovereignty activists. This movement attempts to adapt existing structures and practices (drawn both from nationalist traditions and more recent struggles for indigenous autonomy and human rights) to address the democratic management of an ecological commons – the landraces of native maize and the social and ecological systems which perpetuate them. These efforts are informed by existing constitutional principles regarding the management of public goods such as land, water and energy, categorized as sovereign possessions of the Mexican nation to be managed by the state in accordance with the public interest.[4] As Tim Hayward notes, Dobson's 'ecological citizenship' fails to establish a concrete polity to which both the victims and beneficiaries of unequal use of ecological space are bound, leaving aside consideration of the 'procedural standards of political legitimacy' (2006, 440). Without a framework of rights, victims of environmental injustice are excluded from agency as 'ecological citizens'. This is especially problematic in Mexico, where the most vulnerable and disenfranchised actors are left to defend a very valuable commons. In fact, the issue of legitimate use of sovereign power is crucial to the way the Mexican food sovereignty movement links food systems, biodiversity and democracy. In Mexico as elsewhere, social movements' attempts to amplify social, ecological and cultural rights face strong resistance from transnational corporations. Successful movements may gain enough popular support to force the government to negotiate, but converting conciliatory rhetoric into reality often proves more difficult.[5] Trade agreements and structural adjustment packages limit the Mexican state's ability to radically alter macroeconomic policy, and the desire to attract foreign investment (and close connections between the political class and corporations) strongly influences policy and budget decisions. Food sovereignty campaigns in Mexico have routinely linked the struggle for sustainable agro-biodiversity directly to ongoing national debates around the meaning of the country's democratic transition, explicitly condemning measures like the 2004 Law on Biosafety as corporate giveaways that violate national sovereignty.

The global food sovereignty movement demands recognition of the right to local control over the systems of food production, consumption and distribution (Forum for Food Sovereignty 2007). However, attempts to institutionalize such rights have necessarily involved appeals to specific states to regulate markets in land, labour, goods and natural resources (including genetic resources and biodiversity). For instance, the Mexican food sovereignty movement has advocated for limiting the importation of foreign maize, seen as a threat to the biological integrity of Mexican landraces, by renegotiating the North American Free Trade Agreement (NAFTA) and increasing federal reinvestment in small-scale agriculture. It opposes patents on living organisms, and has called for a moratorium on both importation and open-field testing of genetically modified maize (UNORCA 2007; Sin Maíz No Hay País 2008). Finally, the movement has lobbied the legislature to pass new laws requiring the labelling of foods containing GMO ingredients and the strengthening of enforcement capacity among consumer protection agencies. The movement not only advocates domestic policies to enable food sovereignty for Mexicans, it also enjoins the Mexican state to assert its sovereignty internationally by rejecting treaties and trade agreements which endanger the cultural and nutritional rights of its citizens. Conflicts over agro-biodiversity in the world's 'cradle of corn' have planetary implications, but the movement also acknowledges that international dynamics shape the conditions under which democracy is practiced in Mexico.

Environmental citizenship, simultaneously a status and a practice, derives from membership in a political community. Such polities need not be coterminous with nation-states, but must be sovereign in the sense of a 'body politic ... vested with power and authority by the people', capable of accommodating difference and mediating disagreements via processes which are accepted by all as legitimate (Hayward 2006, 437). Because environmental rights and obligations stem from social relations, they are subject to constant renegotiation. Alex Latta notes that theories of environmental citizenship tend to overlook 'both the degree of exclusion in existing polities and the role of subaltern actors in politicizing the injustices of existing socio-ecological orders' (2007, 378). In Mexico, indigenous peoples and rural denizens have long been excluded from full participation in the public sphere. Recent movements for indigenous territorial autonomy and cultural rights have not only fostered coalitions between environmental, human rights and civil society groups but have also enabled food sovereignty campaigns to politicize food systems by demonstrating the links between sustenance and self-determination. In this way, the lens of environmental citizenship yields insight into broader debates in Mexico over the nature of democracy and rule of law, particularly the ongoing struggle to institutionalize citizen participation in policy making beyond the ballot box and mass protests. The rhetorical strategies employed by the food sovereignty movement also make evident the challenges of reconciling individualist citizenship frameworks with calls for collective rights and common responsibilities.

'Maize and Liberty': Food Policy and Food Sovereignty in Mexico

Historically, food policy has been an important tool for mediating relationships between the state and civil society in Mexico. The consolidation of the post-Revolutionary state was accomplished in part via the creation of the official Partido Revolucionario Institucional (Institutional Revolutionary Party, PRI), which staked its legitimacy upon claims to 'institutionalize' the ideals of the Revolution. It established a corporatist model of government, incorporating peasants, workers and other social sectors into a unified national development plan. Food self-sufficiency was deemed crucial to industrialization and food subsidies (particularly subsidized tortillas) became part of the social pact with expanding ranks of urban workers (Fox 1992). In rural areas, the PRI co-opted the revolutionary legacy of Emiliano Zapata, who fought under the slogan '*Tierra y Libertad*' (Land and Liberty). There, the corporatist pact was embodied in a land-reform scheme based upon collective land holdings combined with agricultural extension and credit programs, distribution infrastructure and price supports. Campesinos developed both a nationalist consciousness and a sense of themselves as historical protagonists via struggles to claim these new rights (Boyer 2003). Citizen participation was mediated almost exclusively through the organs of the official party, leaving clientelism and mass protests as the major modes of political engagement. However, the debt crisis of the 1980s initiated three decades of divestment from the countryside, and eventually the state abandoned even rhetorical ties to redistribution programs in favour of free trade and export oriented agro-industry. In the 1990s, agrarian issues re-emerged as major points of contention in Mexico's 'democratic transition' (Richard 2008). As Gillian Hart (2002) points out, in the Global South agrarian questions are not limited to land or agricultural policy. They also conjure debates over disappearing social rights and redistributive justice, which tend to be sidelined as official democratization projects become wedded to economic liberalization schemes.

Hubert de Grammont and Horacio Mackinlay (2009) document the struggles of campesino and indigenous organizations to negotiate new relationships to government agencies and political parties during Mexico's long transition to democracy. Independent peasant organizations began to emerge in the late 1970s and early 1980s as the pace of land reform slowed, rural populations grew and small-scale agriculture became less profitable. Increased competition for land and water, combined with erosion, deforestation and agrochemical pollution associated with the Green Revolution led to the foundation of grassroots environmental organizations, like the Grupo de Estudios Ambientales (Environmental Studies Group, GEA). They focused on soil and water conservation, helping campesinos in central and southern Mexico develop and disseminate sustainable agricultural techniques. As these regions contain the highest concentration of small maize farmers, GEA's emphasis on caring for scarce common resources was an important innovation during a period in which land redistribution diminished. Official responses to the political unrest and land invasions occasioned by deepening rural poverty included strategic investment in development programs targeted to highly marginalized regions and the organization of small producer cooperatives to generate rural entrepreneurialism (de Grammont and Mackinlay 2009, 25).

The Unión Nacional de Organizaciones Regionales Campesinas Autónomas (National Union of Autonomous Regional Peasant Organizations, UNORCA), founded in 1985, was among the earliest campesino groups to seek greater autonomy from the political organs of the official party. De Grammont and Mackinlay (2009) argue that UNORCA exemplified the 'political-social' approach employed by many campesino and indigenous organizations during this period, in that 'participation and representation are in the hands of the social organization, while political negotiation with the state is shared with political parties' (2009, 22). In the 1980s UNORCA formed alliances both with the official organs of the PRI and with independent campesino groups, mobilizing campesinos in favour of land reform and price supports for basic crops (UNORCA 1989; de Grammont and Mackinlay 2009, 26). These early experiences left their mark on the food sovereignty movement that UNORCA would later help to build, by emphasizing the development of social solidarity among autonomous organizations and leveraging existing state institutions to press for policy reform.

In the 1990s, the Mexican government deprioritized rural development in favour of export-oriented manufacturing and agribusiness, and independent peasant associations and allied organizations like GEA struggled to find new ways to put the fate of small farmers back onto the national agenda. The 'Reform of the Agrarian Reform', initiated under Carlos Salinas (1988–1994), entailed a massive public divestment from rural development at the same time as it privatized collective landholdings, ended price supports and opened Mexican markets to highly subsidized agricultural imports from the United States. The Salinas administration relied on neocorporatist social programs to reconsolidate control in rural areas, but under Salinas's successor, Ernesto Zedillo (1994–2000), independent peasant organizations were largely excluded from such programs. Commercial tortilla processors and meat producers increasingly substituted Mexican-grown maize with U.S. imports that were lower in cost as a result of the subsidies enjoyed by U.S. farmers (de la Tejera et al. 2007, 18–19). In the decade following NAFTA's implementation, maize prices fell 70 per cent, plunging rural Mexico into a deep economic and social crisis (de la Tejera et al. 2007, 3). In response, UNORCA sought out links with transnational agrarian movements like La Vía Campesina, which it joined in 1996 (Borras, Edelman and Kay 2008). La Vía Campesina helped UNORCA to integrate debates around GMO crops and peasant stewardship of agro-biodiversity into its official platform (Poitras 2008, 274).

The process of drafting national biosecurity laws and devising federal institutions to implement the 2000 Cartagena Protocol created new opportunities for the food sovereignty movement to broaden its appeal and gain greater political traction. In 1999, Greenpeace México alerted the Mexican government to the illegal presence of genetically modified maize in commodity imports arriving from the U.S. Mexico's new biosecurity commission (CIBIOGEM) called upon the agricultural ministry to detain maize imports from the U.S., but it refused. The Mexican government later moved to block the publication of scientific research which demonstrated that native maize crops in Southern Mexico had already been contaminated with GMO strains (Poitras 2008, 269–272). Later, the movement succeeded in depicting the Fox administration's 2004 Law on Biosafety and Genetically Engineered Organisms as an imposition supported by large U.S.-based corporations, which would damage Mexico's ability to feed itself. While the law was ostensibly aimed at regulating the evaluation of risks and prevention of harm to human and environmental health, campesino groups complained that the consultation process was rushed and that the resulting legislation failed to address their economic, ecological and cultural concerns or those of consumers (for examples of these allegations, see Red en Defensa del Maíz 2008). Instead, the main provisions of the 'Monsanto Law' facilitated the importation, cultivation and commercialization of GMO crops by providing legal and institutional frameworks for granting permissions for open-field experiments and collecting information on the results. Greenpeace México and the international Action Group on Erosion, Technology and Concentration (ETC) used the legislative process and ensuing legal appeals to call attention to the lack of citizen participation in the decision-making process and government agencies' lack of accountability to scientific standards. To counter government claims that the movement had taken an unnecessarily alarmist stance, GEA and Greenpeace México trained campesinos to collect maize samples for monitoring, and conducted independent studies of genetic contamination in native landraces. The movement enlisted experts from Mexican and foreign universities, who undertook research and held conferences to analyze the rural crisis and propose solutions (Esteva and Marielle 2003). In fact, there has been a notable insistence upon broadening the range of experts contributing to policy formulation beyond official ministerial and corporate representatives to include independent natural and social scientists as well as local knowledge producers.

As more established groups such as UNORCA sought out links to global environmental and agrarian movements, a new wave of independent organizations began forming in the countryside. In the 1990s El Barzón, a rural debtors' movement, sought to leverage some aspects of Mexico's transition to multiparty democracy by promoting national legislation to provide debt relief for small farmers and by launching legal challenges to bank privatization schemes (Williams 2001). Other newly formed producer networks like the Asociación Nacional de Empresas Comercializadoras de Productos del Campo (National Association of Campesino Commercial Enterprises, ANEC) used public demonstrations and national media campaigns to criticize neoliberal reforms while lobbying legislators to support alternative rural development plans (de Grammont and Mackinlay 2009, 30). In late 2002, mere months before the final elimination of tariffs on key agricultural products under NAFTA, a coalition of twelve producer organizations (including UNORCA and ANEC) joined with El Barzón to form the Movimiento El Campo No Aguanta Más, which mobilized small farmers across the country and focused national attention on the crisis in the countryside. They demanded the government renegotiate the agricultural chapters of NAFTA and enforce tariffs and quotas on maize imports that had largely been ignored since 1994. They also demanded a ban on the importation and experimental cultivation of GMO crops, arguing that transgenic maize represented the expropriation of collective intellectual property and threatened farmers' productive autonomy (El Campo No Aguanta Más 2002).

On 1 January 2003, movement protestors occupied ports of entry for U.S. agricultural products in Ciudad Juárez, a historical site where campesino armies won a significant victory against the dictatorship of Porfirio Díaz in 1911. Five days later over 100,000 protestors marched to the Zócalo, Mexico City's main square, demanding a renegotiation of NAFTA and an end to illegal dumping of subsidized agricultural commodities from the United States. Members of the movement carried out a series of direct-action protests that successfully captured media attention by creatively incorporating strong symbolic elements. Farmers marched naked through the streets, formed 'tractorcades' to the capital and staged mass giveaways of produce they claimed had been rendered worthless by NAFTA. Representatives of El Barzón rode into sessions of Congress on horseback and spilled barrels of milk onto the front steps of the National Archive. Protestors unfurled enormous signs in front of the Presidential Palace accusing the government of committing 'agricide'. The movement's slogan, 'Save the Countryside to Save Mexico', proclaimed the importance of traditional agriculture to national identity.

In press releases and protest speeches, movement leaders critiqued the irrational logic of policies which led Mexico to export farm labour whilst importing basic foods like maize. MCNAM organizers represented the dumping of U.S. maize not only as a threat to public health and economic development, but also as an affront to Mexican democracy. Activists argued that NAFTA had been negotiated and implemented without citizen input, against popular disapproval, during a period in which the PRI still maintained tight control over the political arena. They demanded that NAFTA be renegotiated on the grounds that it unfairly disadvantaged Mexican farmers and violated national sovereignty. Blanca Rubio (2004) argues that the campaign's massive demonstrations at border crossings, major ports and in the capital rendered food sovereignty visible for the first time as an aspiration which concerned both rural and urban populations.

Though these efforts garnered media attention and widespread popular support, they did not result in profound policy changes. Instead, the new Fox administration sought to deflect political pressure by launching a series of National Dialogues that culminated with the signing of a National Accord for the Countryside in April 2003. It outlined the government's commitment to re-evaluate NAFTA's impact on the agricultural sector, develop a plan for food security, revise existing government programs to make them more accessible to the poorest campesinos and increase the overall budget for agricultural development. The government also promised to revise land-tenure laws, tend to unresolved land disputes and invest more in rural social programs (de Grammont and Mackinlay 2009, 35). The consultation process between movement activists and representatives of key government ministries bore a strong resemblance to the co-optation strategies and strategic delays pursued by earlier PRI administrations. A divide emerged between organizations like El Barzón, who eventually signed the Accord and others, like UNORCA, who refused. The main disagreements were over whether the Accord represented an initial step towards the recognition of campesino rights, or whether the government had succeeded in sidelining major issues over the course of the negotiations. In the end, very few of the measures proposed in the Accord were implemented, and almost no additional resources were allocated to rural programs (Rubio 2004). By 2004, MCNAM had effectively disbanded.

Nonetheless, the struggle for food sovereignty continued, shifting focus slightly to highlight the rights and responsibilities of both producers and consumers. In 2000, ANEC teamed up with Greenpeace México to create a campaign called 'Tortillas de las buenas, tortillas de maíz mexicano, libres de transgénicos' (Good tortillas from Mexican corn, GMO free). It was aimed at raising awareness among Mexican consumers of the potential health risks of consuming U.S.-grown GMO corn and the importance of supporting Mexican campesinos (Seymour and Gzesh 2000). Then, in late 2006, President Felipe Calderón faced a major crisis as angry crowds throughout Mexico protested the skyrocketing price of tortillas. Widespread speculation on ethanol production had rapidly inflated the price of maize on the global market, dramatically underlining the dangers of food dependency. Suddenly, many of the people whose ancestors had originally domesticated maize could no longer afford their daily tortillas. A fresh grassroots alliance in defence of native maize quickly assembled, incorporating many of the same groups that had participated in the MCNAM mobilizations along with collaborators from academia, civil society and human rights and environmental organizations.

Calderón reacted to public outrage over soaring tortilla prices not by renegotiating trade agreements or augmenting the agricultural development budget, but by increasing imports of U.S. maize by nearly 32 per cent over the previous year's volume (USDA 2008). The primary objective was to control tortilla prices, thereby curbing urban protests and preventing inflation. A pact was negotiated with large industrial farmers, grain marketers and the flour and tortilla industries to temporarily fix the price of tortillas. These measures did not represent a change in the direction of agricultural policy; the Ministry of Agriculture's strategy for correcting this trade imbalance centred on increasing domestic production of yellow corn via biotechnology and expansion of large-scale industrial farming in northern states traditionally dedicated to wheat and cattle.

In the wake of the 'Tortilla Crisis', the Mexican food sovereignty movement turned its attention to the question of democratizing the food system, reworking the old Zapatista banner to reflect a new struggle: 'Maíz y Libertad.' In addition to opposition marches and direct action protests, organizations linked to the movement have developed alternative policy proposals and launched procedural challenges to the administration's current course of action. These organizations began to lobby the legislature to create and enforce national regulations that would secure the autonomy of small-scale maize producers and enable consumers to choose freely whether or not to consume GMO maize. In fact, a central focus of the movement's most recent strategy has been to open up the national policy-making process to enable broader and more meaningful participation by independent scientists and everyday citizens. Recently, Greenpeace México, ANEC and Litigio Estratégico de Derechos Humanos (Strategic Human Rights Litigation Organization, Litiga OLE) brought a lawsuit against the federal government on behalf of Mexican NGOs and citizens in connection with Calderón's decision to allow Mexican and North American corporations to resume cultivation of experimental GMO crops inside Mexican territory. The suit alleged that the Ministry of Agriculture and the Ministry of the Environment, charged with assessing risks associated with these test fields, violated their own legal charters because they did not follow standard scientific procedures, and moreover failed to take into account the concerns expressed by civil society organizations (whose right to participate in the process is guaranteed by federal law). The suit requested that the court clarify precise mechanisms by which citizen input is to be taken into account in such policy decisions, as well as how government agencies, staffed largely by appointed technocrats, are to be made accountable for protecting the rights and security of citizens.[6] These developments reflect ongoing debates in Mexican society over the need to deepen democratic citizenship, moving beyond electoral politics to develop new institutional mechanisms that both enable citizens to participate in important policy processes and hold politicians and bureaucrats accountable for their management of public goods.

Valuing the Commons: Agro-Biodiversity as National Patrimony and Global Heritage

The post-Revolutionary state grounded nationalist origin myths in pre-Columbian empires, projecting the idea of a cohesive Mexican national identity backwards across centuries. This was accomplished in part by popularizing the idea of Mexico as a 'maize civilization', a culturally diverse entity unified via the collective enterprise of domestication and diversification of a single crop (Bartra 2002). Maize figured simultaneously as national patrimony and as the nation's gift to the rest of the world. The 'cultural revolution' that accompanied the consolidation of the modern Mexican state provided a political grammar through which rural people could make claims on the government (Knight 1994). Even as Mexico urbanized, campesinos remained potent symbols of the country's roots and stewards of its patrimony. Collaboration with transnational groups like Greenpeace and La Vía Campesina has helped the food sovereignty movement's leaders to reframe their platform in terms of a defence of global genetic commons against a new corporate enclosure movement. Nonetheless, many of the idioms and images they have deployed draw upon this nationalist, historically rooted, repertoire.

This symbolic association between nation and crop was encapsulated in the name of the national campaign that organized many of the demonstrations captured by the global news media, 'Sin Maíz No Hay País.' One of the campaign's most creative and highly publicized events involved the creation of an enormous map in the Zócalo of Mexico City, in which the country's territory was overlaid with thousands of grains of native maize. The installation, constructed during a 2009 meeting of signatories to the Cartagena Protocol, was intended to represent the threatened diversity of Mexican maize as well as the sovereignty of its centre of origin. The importation of foreign maize and the cultivation of GMO varieties within national territory were framed as a calculated attempt on the part of transnational corporations to profit by imposing new forms of dependency on Mexicans. The RDMN, in a 2008 missive, accused the Mexican government of collaborating with Monsanto and other TNCs in an 'attack against our identity, autonomy, economy and health; destroying Mother Earth, life itself, and contaminating nature' (Red en Defensa del Maíz 2008). In spring 2009, when a presidential decree lifted the moratorium on cultivation of GMO maize, the RDMN issued the following declaration:

> The native peoples of Mexico created maize and they have been the guardians and creators of the diversity of varieties currently in existence. Food sovereignty and the preservation of this diversity depend on the integrity of their rights. Because of that, transgenic contamination is an assault on the identity of Mesoamerican peoples and is an act of aggression against ten thousand years of agriculture. The planting of transgenic maize is a frontal attack against native and peasant peoples and a violation of their rights. For the peoples that constitute Mexico, maize is not merchandise, but the origin of a civilization and the foundation of peasant lives and economies. We will not let our seeds be lost or contaminated by transgenes owned by transnational companies. We will not comply with unfair laws that criminalize seeds and peasant life ways. We will continue protecting maize and the life of our peoples (Red en Defensa del Maíz 2009).

The historical role of campesinos and indigenous peoples in domesticating and diversifying the native landraces of maize is highlighted by referring to them as 'stewards' and 'defenders' of the crop. This designation indexes their role in creating entire civilizations, including cuisines, cultural expressions and a highly adaptable suite of sustainable agricultural techniques embodied by the traditional *milpa* system.

The Green Revolution entailed the introduction of hybrid seed, heavy machinery, irrigation and the use of herbicides, pesticides and chemical fertilizers, posing a challenge to the *milpa* system and devaluing the knowledge of campesinos. In many areas, however, especially where maize continues to be grown primarily for local use, *milpa* techniques have persisted in some form. In this context, transgenic varieties and imported maize represent a threat to the past as well as the future of the nation, with the potential not only to enclose common goods, but to destroy or irrevocably alter the means of biological and social reproduction. High levels of out-migration from rural areas and the declining profitability of small-scale agriculture fuel fears that these techniques will be lost to future generations, while increased consumption of imported foods has been criticized as contributing to the abandonment of traditional food ways.

The food sovereignty movement aims to preserve and promote traditional agriculture and cuisines on a national level. In fact, many of the events organized by SMNHP in its initial campaign were explicitly aimed at encouraging collaboration between rural producers and urban consumers by educating consumers about the plight of campesinos and the dangers of GMO maize to public health and biodiversity. The network pressured government and industry leaders to label foods containing GMO ingredients, and Greenpeace México conducted its own research to publish a consumer guide to GMO-free foods. SMNHP circulated petitions in urban areas and online proposing the inclusion of native maize on UNESCO's World Heritage List. Concerts and other artistic events were held in the capital to raise awareness of these issues, and urban residents were encouraged to sow native maize in their neighbourhoods and in public places to signify their solidarity with campesino and indigenous 'guardians of maize'. Appreciation of native maize and of the social and ecological relationships through which it is cultivated and consumed was thus elevated to the level of civic virtue.

Campesino and indigenous communities have also sought new forms of political recognition in connection with their role as guardians of the commons. Specifically, they demand acknowledgement of the necessity of local control over food systems and ecological commons for fulfilment of their constitutional right to self-determination. Moreover, they have struggled to promote recognition of the role of campesinos as defenders of the environment and as sustainable agriculture experts. On Earth Day 2009, the Consejo Nacional de Organizaciones Campesinos (National Council of Campesino Organizations, CONOC) published a declaration denouncing the government's failure to create a comprehensive national environmental policy that could guide public and private efforts to deal with the combined effects of deforestation, desertification, water and soil contamination, climate change and the introduction of GMOs. The organization called upon the federal government to employ the expertise of local communities in creating such a policy, thus acknowledging their important role in providing ecosystems services (Consejo Nacional de Organizaciones Campesinos 2009). Importantly, CONOC's campaign and those of allied organizations bring to light the limits of the emergent model of environmental citizenship described here; in the absence of government recognition of collective and individual environmental rights, including self-determination and participation in policy processes, the capacity of campesinos, indigenous peoples and ordinary citizens to serve as defenders of the commons is compromised.

'Put Mexico in Your Mouth': Environmental Citizenship and Democratic Participation

Environmental citizenship problematizes the very foundations of traditional citizenship in that 'the status of nature' is considered alongside 'the relationship between the individual and the community in human society' (Jelin 2000, 60). In the rhetoric of the Mexican food sovereignty movement, the relationship between humans and nature is mediated through the notion of agro-biodiversity, embodied in the *milpa* system and coded as a public good. Democratic deliberation over the status of this form of 'second nature', and the future of the social and ecological systems which sustain it, is central to the implicit model of environmental citizenship espoused by the movement. SMNHP enjoins citizens to 'put Mexico in your mouth' (*pon a México en tu boca*) both by consuming native maize as a part of traditional cuisines and by participating in public debates and policy-making processes (Sin Maíz No Hay País 2009). Consequently, it could be said that the food sovereignty movement asks ordinary Mexicans to become environmental citizens who uphold the value of the commons and those who (re)produce it, who defend it from corruption and contamination and who insist that the legitimacy of their government rests upon a commitment to sustain it.

David Graeber (2001) maintains that establishing the social value of a particular object or entity is a political project which hinges on the importance given to and energy invested in creative acts. The revalorisation of native maize and of the role played by its campesino and indigenous 'stewards' is a good example of this process. In contrast to traditional Northern conservationist movements, the Mexican food sovereignty movement emphasizes the redress of social inequalities as one of its central aims. Mexican activists have attempted to expand and rework existing political and judicial institutions to create a new model of environmental citizenship which deepens public participation in policy making, democratizes expertise as a basis for public decision making and locates the fulfilment and expansion of human rights at the centre of environmental struggles. Their strategy combines older forms of government regulation, such as trade restrictions and the institutionalization of collective environmental and nutritional rights, with newer more individualized forms like independent certification of GMO-free foods and 'conscious consumerism'. This model is informed by Mexican nationalism and struggles against rural and indigenous exclusion, but also by growing consciousness of a threatened global commons. At its heart, it addresses questions fundamental to all contemporary environmental struggles, especially the urgency of developing modes of governing ecological commons in ways that enable both local autonomy and institutional accountability.

Notes

1. For a discussion of the evolution of this official definition since 1975, see Patel (2009).
2. The arguments presented here are based on textual analysis of an archive of documentary sources related to the Mexican food sovereignty movement, compiled by the author with generous support from the Pacific Fund at the University of the Pacific. The ethnographic fieldwork which informs it was carried out in Hidalgo, Mexico, and Mexico City between 2002 and 2007, with support from the John L. Simpson Memorial Research Fellowship in International and Comparative Studies and the Chancellor's Predoctoral Fellowship from the University of California, Berkeley.
3. For examples of how this is commonly articulated, see Sin Maíz No Hay País (2009) and Red en Defensa del Maíz (2003).
4. Articles I, II, IV, XXV and XXVII of the Mexican Constitution are often cited as grounds for these principles.
5. For a discussion of how these dynamics unfolded in the negotiations between Mexican federal authorities and sovereignty activists affiliated with the El Campo No Aguanta Más movement, see Rubio (2004).
6. As of 30 March 2011, the Sixth District Federal Court referred the case back to the state court of Tamaulipas, where it currently awaits the assignment of a trial date.

References

Bartra, R. (2002) *Blood, Ink and Culture: Miseries and Splendors of the Post-Mexican Condition*. Durham: Duke University Press.

Borras, S., M. Edelman and C. Kay. (2008) 'Transnational Agrarian Movements: Origins and Politics, Campaign and Impact,' *Journal of Agrarian Change*, Vol. 8, No. 2/3, pp. 169–204.

Boyer, C. (2003) *Becoming Campesinos: Politics, Identity, and Agrarian Struggle in Postrevolutionary Michoacán, 1920–1935*. Palo Alto: Stanford University Press.

Consejo Nacional de Organizaciones Campesinos. (2009) *Hacia Una Nueva Política Medioambiental*, online report, http://www.anec.org.mx/comunicados-conoc/desplegados-conoc-2009/Propuesta_de_Desplegado_Medio_Ambiente_050609.pdf.

de Grammont, H., and H. Mackinlay (2009) 'Campesino and Indigenous Social Organizations Facing Democratic Transition in Mexico, 1938–2006,' *Latin American Perspectives*, Vol. 36, No. 4, pp. 21–40.

de la Tejera, B., et al. (2007) *Maíz en México: de una política pública de dependencia y vulnerabilidad hacia una política de soberanía alimentaria con la sociedad*, paper presented at XXVII Congress of the Latin American Studies Association. Montreal, Canada.

Dobson, A. (2003) *Citizenship and the Environment*. Oxford: Oxford University Press.

Dobson, A., and D. Bell. (2006) *Environmental Citizenship*. Cambridge, MA: MIT Press.

El Campo No Aguanta Más. (2002) *Seis propuestas para la salvación y revalorización del campo mexicano*, online report, www.laneta.apc.org/anec.

Esteva, G., and C. Marielle (eds). (2003) *Sin Maíz No Hay País*. México: Consejo Nacional para la Cultura y las Artes.

Forum for Food Sovereignty. (2007) *Declaration of Nyeleni*, online report, www.worldgovernance.org.

Fox, J. (1992) *The Politics of Food in Mexico: State Power and Social Mobilization*. Ithaca: Cornell University Press.

Graeber, D. (2001) *Toward an Anthropological Theory of Value*. New York: Palgrave.

Hart, G. (2002) *Disabling Globalization: Places of Power in Post-Apartheid South Africa*. Berkeley: University of California Press.

Hayward, T. (2006) 'Ecological Citizenship: Justice, Rights, and the Virtue of Resourcefulness,' *Environmental Politics*, Vol. 15, No. 15, pp. 435–466.

Jelin, E. (2000) 'Towards a Global Environmental Citizenship?' *Citizenship Studies*, Vol. 4, No. 1, pp. 47–63.

Kloppenburg, J., ed. (1988). *Seeds and Sovereignty: The Use and Control of Plant Genetic Resources*. Chapel Hill: Duke University Press.

Knight, A. (1994) 'Weapons and Arches in the Mexican Revolutionary Landscape,' in G. Joseph and D. Nugent (eds), *Everyday Forms of State Formation: Revolution and the Negotiation of Rule in Modern Mexico*. Durham: Duke University Press, pp. 24–68.

Latta, A. (2007) 'Locating Democratic Politics in Ecological Citizenship,' *Environmental Politics*, Vol. 16, No. 3, pp. 377–393.

Nonnini, D. (2006) 'The Global Idea of "the Commons",' *Social Analysis*, Vol. 50, No. 3, pp. 164–177.

Patel, R. (2009) 'What does food sovereignty look like?' *The Journal of Peasant Studies*, Vol. 36, No. 3, pp. 663–673.

Phillips, C. (2005) 'Cultivating Practices: Saving Seed as Green Citizenship?' *Environments*, Vol. 33, No. 3, pp. 37–49.

Poitras, M. (2008) 'Social Movements and Techno-Democracy: Reclaiming the Genetic Commons,' in G. Otero (ed.), *Food for the Few: Neoliberal Globalism and Biotechnology in Latin America*. Austin: University of Texas Press, pp. 267–287.

Red en Defensa del Maíz. (2003) *La contaminación transgénica del maíz campesino en México*, online report, http://www.endefensadelmaiz.org/La-contaminacion-transgenica-del.html.

———. (2008) *Pronunciamiento de la red en defensa del maíz nativo*, online report, http://www.endefensadelmaiz.org/Pronunciamiento-de-la-red-en.html.

———. (2009) *¡No al maíz transgénico!*, online report, http://endefensadelmaiz.org/No-al-maiz-transgenico.html.

Red en Defensa del Maíz, Sin Maíz No Hay País and Red Todos los Derechos Para Todos. (2009) *Condena unánime a la siembra de maíz transgénico*, online report, http://www.anec.org.mx/campana/comunicados-campana-201csin-maiz-no-hay-pais201d-2009/09130 condena unanime a maiz ogm.pdf.

Richard, A. (2008) 'Withered Milpas: Governmental Disaster and the Mexican Countryside,' *Journal of Latin American and Caribbean Anthropology*, Vol. 13, No. 2, pp. 387–413.

Rubio, B. (2004) 'El Campo No Aguanta Más: A Un Año de Distancia,' *El Cotidiano,* Vol. 19, No. 124, pp. 33–40.

Scharper, S., and H. Cunningham. (2006) 'The Genetic Commons: Resisting the Neo-liberal Enclosure of Life,' *Social Analysis,* Vol. 50, No. 3, pp. 195–202.

Seymour, A., and S. Gzesh. (2000) 'Greenpeace and Mexico-based ANEC Launch New Project to End the Importation of US Genetically Engineered Corn,' *Mexico-US Advocates Network News,* Vol. 2, No. 8, online report, http://www.biotech-info.net/ANEC.html.

Sin Maíz No Hay País. (2008) *Declaración Final de la Asamblea Nacional por la Soberanía Alimentaria,* online report, www.ciepac.org/documento.php?id=192.

———. (2009) *Rechazamos la siembra experimental de maíz transgénico de las empresas trasnacionales en México,* online report, http://www.anec.org.mx/campana/comunicados-campana-201csin-maiz-no-hay-pais201d-2009/Postura%20campana%20transgenicos.pdf

United States Department of Agriculture [USDA]. (2008) *NAFTA's Effect on the Corn Trade Between the United States and Mexico,* Grain Inspection, Packers, & Stockyards Administration, online report, http://archive.gipsa.usda.gov/rdd/NAFTA_corn_trade.pdf.

UNORCA. (1989) 'Costa, Nuria and Union Nacional de Organizaciones Regionales Campesinas Autónomas,' *UNORCA: Documentos para la Historia.* Mexico City: Costa-Amic Editores.

———. (2007) *Chilpancingo Declaration for Food Sovereignty in Mexico,* online report, https://www.foodfirst.org/en/node/1650.

Warman, A. (2003) *Corn and Capitalism: How a Botanical Bastard Grew to Global Dominance.* Chapel Hill: University of North Carolina Press.

Williams, H. (2001) 'Of free trade and debt bondage: Fighting banks and the State in Mexico,' *Latin American Perspectives,* Vol. 28, No. 44, pp. 30–51.

Wittman, H. (2009) 'Reworking the metabolic rift: La Vía Campesina, agrarian citizenship, and food sovereignty,' *The Journal of Peasant Studies,* Vol. 36, No. 4, pp. 805–826.

5 Social Participation and the Politics of Climate in Northeast Brazil

Renzo Taddei

How does one recognize citizenship, and environmental citizenship for that matter, as it exists in Latin America? As expressed by a number of the other contributions to this volume, the idea of citizenship becomes meaningful only when analysed against specific historical and institutional backgrounds. The region has experienced a wide variety of political contexts for citizenship over the past century, ranging from centralized dictatorships to relatively decentralized liberal regimes, each context making way for different kinds of political subjectivity.

It is a given that hegemonic political agents will attempt to exert influence over the symbolic terrain upon which subject formation occurs; at the same time, this control is never absolutely effective and subjects invariably find ways of contesting the hegemonic symbolic order (Scott 1985, 1990; Bourdieu 1991). The discursive framing of ideas, problems and identities is a particularly potent element of such symbolic politics, restricting the limits of what is thinkable and legitimate in regards to different kinds of political action.

With respect to environmental politics, especially in rapidly modernizing countries such as Brazil, a particular framing of science and technology has been crucial to hegemonic discourses, but knowledge and technique have also constituted important sites of symbolic resistance. In the analysis of how different forms of environmental citizenship exist in Latin America, it is key to pay attention to subaltern actors' attempts to politicize the injustices of socio-ecological orders (Latta 2007; see also Latta and Wittman, this volume). At the same time, there is always an epistemological dimension in ecological struggles, and resistance often involves attempts to bring to debate hidden aspects of the politics of different knowledge systems in environmental governance.

The question is whether, in different Latin American realities, this type of symbolic resistance has managed to congeal into a basis for substantive challenges to existing configurations of power. In other words, has this resistance become the basis for alternate or 'insurgent' forms of environmental citizenship? On balance, in Brazil at least, it would seem that dominant discourses around science and technology (as constitutive elements of 'modernity') have successfully prevented some new forms of political-environmental consciousness from developing and transforming into radical political platforms. It is the aim of this chapter to delve into the dynamics by which emergent forms of symbolic resistance become neutralized or co-opted by hegemonic discourses of scientific knowledge and technocratic management. In a word, it focuses on what happens immediately before the moment in which resistance becomes effective, transforming frameworks of rights and making polities more inclusive (Richard, this volume). That moment, nevertheless, may never arrive; there is always the risk that some form of counter-reaction may abort the process of political transformation. And, as I intend to demonstrate, in terms of the epistemological dimension of the struggle, the most effective forms of counter-resistance are those that disarticulate subaltern discourses not through direct confrontation and physical violence, but through the reorganization of the symbolic environment in which the acts of resistance will be interpreted and understood (Taddei and Gamboggi 2009).

This chapter founds its argument in ethnographic data gathered in the state of Ceará, in the semi-arid Northeast region of Brazil, between 2003 and 2006. The field research focused on the use of scientific climate forecasts in public policy, local rural communities' reactions against such forecasting and the resulting competition between scientific and local traditional knowledge about the environment that lay at the heart of conflicts between communities and policy makers. Emerging from these conflicts, local 'rain prophets' have become regional celebrities. Nevertheless, while media attention has brought significant attention to local forms of traditional environmental knowledge during these conflicts, no organized political movement has sprung from this terrain of symbolic struggle. Instead, as holders of traditional climate knowledge have become inserted into the field of power constituted by discourses of modernization, their power to make meaning has been deflected and usurped by the media and other actors. As tradition is transmuted into folklore, the socio-ecological subjectivity of the rain prophets has become a spectral vestige of its original manifestation.

Technocratic Modernization and the Political Value of Knowledge

As debates on global warming make evident, there has been a rapid increase in scientific understanding of the global climate during the past three decades. One outcome of this knowledge is that economic development programs sponsored by agencies like the World Bank have begun to include the production of scientific climate knowledge as part of their packages of economic development. Poverty and hunger are now to be tackled not only through improved physical infrastructure, market mechanisms and re-engineered local governments, but also through the scientific capacity to forecast the climate, allowing governments and agricultural producers to adopt strategies to mitigate the impacts of extreme events and to make long-term adaptations. In the backdrop of these development-oriented practices lies the growing perception that climate is a key element in present and future international security scenarios (see Baldwin and Meltzer, this volume).

What appears to be novel in this panorama is the increasing relevance of climate knowledge for policy development. And yet, in places like rural Northeast Brazil, climate has been deeply linked to politics throughout history, even if the connections between climate events, climate knowledge and political relations have often been concealed by religious discourses around climate-related misfortunes. Such connections can be seen in innumerous examples in popular culture, such as almanacs, booklets (*cordéis*), poetry, songs and other literary genres. Moreover, at the level of more explicit relations of power and citizenship, the submission of peasants to landlords who control land, water and local politics has often been presented as 'protection' against the inclemency of climate, instead of as exploitation.

More recently, science has replaced religion as the predominant discourse of depoliticization, especially with the increasing penetration of modern media into rural settings. Scientific knowledge is a perplexing genre of discourse: it systematically decontextualizes what it talks about. Interestingly, rural populations in Brazil have resisted the decontextualizing and depoliticizing influences of science perhaps more than their urban counterparts. There are three related ways to explain this resistance. First, as other authors have demonstrated (DaMatta 1997a, 1997b; Martins 1999), Brazilian society is strongly organized around vertical hierarchies – especially in rural areas – and individuals develop their sense of identity from their positions inside the many hierarchical structures in which they are immersed. In this sense, the value and importance of everybody and everything is deeply contextual. For that reason, Roberto DaMatta called Brazil a 'relational society' (1997a, 1997b). Second, as I explore further below, science-based policies have had tangible and often negative impacts on rural livelihoods and everyday experience. Finally, most rural populations have not been fully indoctrinated into scientific discourse because they often lack long-term exposure to formal schooling.

Scientifically inspired policies appeal to an authoritative frame for political action that lies outside traditional hierarchy; they inform local populations that actions taken by the government are based on, and justified by, a non-personal form of authority – scientific authority. Not surprisingly, this new kind of authority has less purchase in marginal rural areas, where most individuals are familiar with the experience of having to accept policies because of the social position of their proponents. Policies justified through scientific discourse, however, seek legitimacy not based on the place that their purveyors occupy in the social hierarchy, but instead on the supposedly independent ontological authority that derives from the scientific method. There are actually two potent political messages in this new claim to authority. The first is that social hierarchies are no longer relevant. The second is that knowledge does not inhere in experience, but rather belongs to the realm of technique.

It is not surprising that local leaders gravitate to the first of these political messages but reject the second. They are glad to hear that the authority of knowledge is no longer based on social status (even if they might be skeptical about such claims), but they refuse to accept the pre-eminence that science allots itself when it comes to describing reality. This disjuncture creates the potential for new forms of environmental citizenship of an epistemological sort: when policies are explicitly based on scientific knowledge (rather than traditional forms of authority), local communities may feel compelled to contest the status of that external knowledge next to the veracity of their own experience. In this way, an emergent politics of knowledge offers a new space for citizen agency.

Yet, if the context of technocratic modernization in itself carries the potential for the development of new forms of environmental political consciousness and citizenship, this possibility is often neutralized by other forms of epistemological colonialism. Of these, the most prominent is the transformation of traditional knowledge into folklore, in which it is appropriated for external consumption in museums and festivals, and hence emptied of its political significance. The case of the annual meeting of the rain prophets of the state of Ceará, to which I turn further below, is an example of both popular agency in the symbolic construction of knowledge claims and the kind of epistemological colonization that neutralizes such agency. Before addressing that case, however, it is important to situate the contemporary politics of weather in Ceará within the historical practices around climate forecasting and control.

A Local History of Climate Forecasting: From Cloud Seeding to Rain Prophets

Despite having become one of the preferred tourist destinations in Brazil in the last decade, Ceará is still one of the poorest states in the country. In rural areas, over 70 per cent of the population lived below the poverty line in 2008 (IPECE 2008). Incrusted in a semi-arid region, Ceará has historically suffered droughts. In the Jaguaribe Valley, where this research was carried out, around one million people live in rural areas and depend on rain to sustain their agricultural fields of beans and corn. Restricted access to water for irrigation and the extreme concentration of land are factors that increase vulnerability to climate variations among the poorest segments of the rural population. Severe drought years have taken place on an average rate of two per decade throughout the twentieth century.

During the military regime of the 1970s there were official efforts to bring some degree of infrastructural modernization and economic development to the interior of Brazil. In 1972, the government of Ceará created the Fundação Cearense de Meteorologia (the Ceará Meteorological Foundation, FUNCEME) with the goal of increasing rain in the state through cloud-seeding activities (Orlove and Tosteson 1999, 12). Cloud-seeding technologies attempt to 'produce' rain by sprinkling silver salt over clouds with the use of airplanes. This method has been used in many parts of the world, including the United States, during the 1970s and 1980s, and it is still used in places like Spain and Israel. Since it does not produce rains, but only accelerates the physical processes inside the clouds that result in rain, cloud seeding has always been a controversial technology. The total precipitation often remains the same, and the cost of seeding clouds is high. FUNCEME eventually abandoned cloud seeding in Brazil during the late 1980s, and instead started to further develop their technological capacity for weather and climate forecasting.

Cloud-seeding activities represented a historical period of tension in the relationship between government, the population and the state's environment. The rural population was accustomed to seeing local elites and government authorities construct dams for accumulating water during the region's short rainy season. But with airplanes flying through the skies and official propaganda about the 'miracle' made possible by means of science – the production of rain – the government was seen to be using science to change nature in a radically new way. Popular reactions towards cloud seeding were strongly negative. One of the most important popular poets of Ceará, Patativa do Assaré, composed a piece of verse that criticized cloud seeding, portraying it as arrogance, imprudence and stupidity. In parts of the poem, titled 'Ao dotô do avião' (To the doctor of the airplane, in Assaré 1997), we read:

No Nordeste do país,	In the Northeast of the country
O dotô propaga e diz	The doctor[1] says and announces
Que o avião faz chuvê. (...)	That the airplane makes rain. (...)
Com a chuva de artifício,	With artificial rains,
Pru que não fez benefício	Why didn't (you) assist
Do povo do Ceará? (...)	The people of Ceará? (...)
Se Jesus não protegesse,	If Jesus didn't protect (us),
E o povo daqui vivesse	And our people lived
Esperando a solução	Waiting for the solution

Eu sei que tudo morria,	We would all die,
Sem vê um pé de feijão. (...)	Without seeing a bean sprout. (...)
Seu dotô, tome um conseio,	Dear doctor, hear my counsel,
E aquete seu parêio,	And leave your equipment to rest,
Não pode inverno mandá.	It can't send us rain.
Empregue em outro trabalho,	Use it for another task,
Arranje outro quebra-gáio,	Find yourself another occupation,
Que desse jeito não dá.	Cause it's no good as it is.
Chuve quero pruque quero,	'Rain because I want it to'
É coisa que eu não tolero,	Is something I can't tolerate,
E é fato que eu nunca vi.	It is a reality I have never seen.
Vivo muito encabulado,	I live very embarrassed,
Pru que no ano passado,	Because last year,
A minha roça eu perdi.	I lost my fields.
Seu avião, seu besouro,	Your airplane, your bug,
Ta fazendo um grande agouro	Is bringing a lot of foreboding,
Contra as coisas naturá.	Against natural things.
Respeite o Deus verdadeiro,	Respect the true God,
Não mexa no nevoeiro, seu dotô	Don't mess with the fog, doctor,
Vá se aquetá.	Quiet down.

The last six lines of the poem question the real possibility of using technology for changing rains, not because the technology available was capable of doing so or not, but because it involved acting upon things existing beyond the human domain, and instead in the realm of the divine. Cloud seeding was therefore understood as a dangerous form of arrogance against God, which could bring bad luck or some form of divine punishment, such as drought (Taddei 2005, 2009b).

Another local common attitude towards cloud seeding questioned the political use of such a technological marvel, without challenging the efficacy of the method. If science can produce rains, why do people still suffer through droughts? A general interpretation was that the elites in power profited from keeping resources – the most valuable of which being water – concentrated in the hands of a few, maintaining the population dependent and miserable and reproducing local clientelistic relations. According to this interpretation, cloud seeding was strategically carried out over the lands of the powerful, in order to fill their reservoirs (Lemos et al. 2002, 488). It was therefore seen as a form of usurping rain, one of the few common (even if uncertain) resources.

What the cloud seeding project seems to have done, in fact, was to create a discursive context in which different interpretations of nature (in its relation to politics and to transcendental spheres[2]) clashed publicly, with the rural population on one side and the government's experts on the other. In doing so, it gave shape to a political field in which new forms of environmental citizenship could emerge in the future.

In the early 1990s, FUNCEME changed its mission from climate control to climate forecasting, and soon became one of the most technically sophisticated regional climate agencies in Brazil. The 1990s were also when the climate sciences leaped forward dramatically in their understanding of the global climate, especially after the El Niño phenomenon was finally modelled, and later predicted. In Ceará, in the first free democratic elections (1986) after Brazil's period of military rule (1964–1985), a new group of young businessmen came into power and huge investments were made to improve the infrastructure of the state. In this context, the government brought FUNCEME into greater proximity with many state secretariats – especially agriculture, water management and civil defence – and scientific knowledge started being used integrally in a range of public policies.

One policy, called *Hora de Plantar* ('Planting Time'), is exemplary of the rising status of science in policy, and the problems it has generated (Finan and Nelson 2001; Lemos et al. 2002; Lemos 2003; Taddei 2005, 2009a; Pennesi 2007). In the mid 1990s, the state government decided to buy drought-resistant seeds from national agricultural research companies, and to distribute them to small producers in the state's rural areas. Yet because these seeds were expensive, the government decided to distribute them only after meteorology signalled that the rainy season had finally started and the soil had reached the required levels of humidity for optimal planting. The government feared that the farmers would use the seeds at the wrong time and lose their crops as a result. The plan required farmers to wait for a 'green light' provided by the climate scientists.

The attitude of the government infuriated local agricultural leaders. According to local planting practices, farmers plant on each and every rain occurrence that humidifies the soil to the depth of one palm. The rationale for this is that seeds can be bought on the market, but rains cannot. In general, the first rains of the season do not last long, and the sprouts soon die. But during some years, the first rains are intense and last long enough to sustain the crops, and during such years farmers enjoy two harvests of green beans and corn, greatly improving their annual income. Farmers know they will lose some seeds in the process, but expect that the total gain during good years will compensate for the seeds lost during others. Meteorology can predict, with high rates of success, the total amount of rain to be expected during a rainy season, but cannot predict when the first rains of the season will fall, or if dry periods will occur during the middle of the rainy season. As a result, seeds distributed by the government very often reached the communities too late, when farmers had already used regular seeds.

For many years a large number of local leaders complained, during meetings with agricultural extension officers and in the media, about this misplaced use of the meteorological forecasts. Meteorologists also complained about the program, although less vocally, particularly once they perceived it as seriously damaging the public image of meteorology. In the early 2000s, the government finally decided to abandon the program and to transfer the decision of when to distribute the seeds to local leaders and local managers of agricultural extension services.

Apart from local economic reasoning about the different values attributed to rain and seeds, the government's attitude was taken as a tacit and offensive lack of recognition for local climate knowledge. One can see this reflected in many of Patativa do Assaré's poems. It is also visible in jokes widely told in the rural areas, which make fun of meteorologists by playing up the science–tradition schism. There are also cases in which meteorologists suffer verbal attacks. In interviews, local meteorologists have affirmed that sometimes they limit their visits to public places like supermarkets because they feel there is a general perception that their forecasts have failed, and they are fearful of being verbally attacked or ridiculed. One meteorologist who travels frequently to the state's interior in order to fix broken pluviometers said that he prefers to travel in a car without the FUNCEME logo, in order to avoid facing the negative attitudes held towards FUNCEME that he constantly encounters in the rural areas. As I discuss elsewhere, this kind of experience is not restricted to the meteorologists of Ceará, but is also found in many other parts of the globe (Taddei 2009b).

Perhaps the most visible and relevant form of local climate knowledge in competition with the expertise of the meteorologists is the elaboration of forecasts for the rainy season through the use of traditional forecasting methods (for details, see Pennesi 2007; Taddei 2005). The rain prophets of the Sertão are individuals who read the signs of nature in order to produce and disseminate seasonal forecasts. The practice of reading nature's signs, especially in regard to the approaching rains, is common in the rural areas of the Brazilian Northeast. Gilton de Araújo is one widely recognized rain prophet. At the end of 2003, Gilton observed that the red ants he usually finds on his lands close to a riverbed were abandoning their nests on low-lying ground, and migrating to higher ground. According to Gilton, this was a sign that rain was on the approach, because when it rains, the river stream flow increases, and washes away any nests located in the riverbed. In this same year, he also observed that some of these ants were migrating to the top of local palm trees. However, he did not give this too much thought until the rains arrived, as he had predicted, in mid January. There had never been, in recorded history, a January with such intense rains. In Ceará alone, forty-three municipalities declared a state of emergency; over sixty thousand people had to leave their flooded homes and at least fifteen people died due to the heavy rains. Gilton retrospectively interprets the abnormal behaviour of the ants as a sign that the approaching rains were to be considerably above their usual level.

The existence of such traditional forecasts was not taken seriously by the urban population and politicians until, in 1997, local shop owners in the municipality of Quixadá started organizing an annual meeting of the rain prophets. The meeting was created by Helder Cortez, an engineer working for the water agency of the town of Quixadá, and a member of the local chapter of the Rotary Club. In an interview (Taddei 2005), Helder declared that the meeting was organized with three different goals: first, to provide local shop owners, most of whom were Rotarians, with forecasts that would enable them to better anticipate the demand that typically revolves around the rhythms of agricultural production; second, to create an institutional context in which the ability to forecast the climate could be preserved and transmitted to younger community members; and third, to raise the profile of local climate knowledge among government decision makers and the broader public.

The annual meeting of the rain prophets is carefully choreographed. First, attendees recite the Lord's Prayer. Then local politicians speak, followed by academics and meteorologists, if present. After that, each prophet comes to the microphone and announces his or her forecast (as seen in photo 5.1), usually followed by questions from Helder on the methods they use. In total

Illustration 5.1. Antonio Lima announces his forecast during the rain prophet meeting of 2004. Photo by the author.

there are usually around twenty prophets, and they are allocated no more than five minutes each. Before and after the meeting, the many media crews that attend the event interview the rain prophets. The media coverage is key to Helder's third goal, of raising the public profile of local climate knowledge. The local, state and national media quickly realized the potential of the meeting for 'making news', and eventually an article on the rain prophets and their meeting was published on the front page of *The Wall Street Journal* (see Moffett 2006). From the outset, the media framed the event as a battle between 'science' and 'tradition', and this is how the meeting has been presented ever since.

In sum, through exploring alternative 'scale frames' (Kurtz 2003, 892; see also Henne and Gabrielson, this volume), rural populations in Ceará have achieved an important level of agency vis-à-vis climate-related politics over the past decade. First, they managed to convince the government not to use meteorological information as the basis for timing the distribution of drought-resistant seeds, but instead to transfer this responsibility to local leaders. Second, through humour and verbal hostility, rural individuals and communities have delimited the spaces that science and its representatives can occupy, both in the local imaginaries and in geographical space. Finally, in founding the annual meeting of the rain prophets they have managed to draw a significant amount of media attention, to the point that most newspaper articles covering rainy season forecasts in local and state-wide media present rain prophets' knowledge as a complement or alternative to official meteorological information. Nonetheless, despite this resistance to the state's claims to authority via the epistemological credentials of climate science, a more fulsome and enduring local environmental citizenship – in terms of meaningful agency to shape agricultural policy – has failed to emerge.

What Kind of Voice Creates Citizenship?

One could interpret the clashes over climate-related policies and climate knowledge in Ceará as an example in which 'disobedient knowledge' (Igoe, Sullivan and Brockington 2010), or 'insurgent knowledge' (Holston 2008; Latta and Wittman, this volume) constitutes alternative forms of citizenly agency. Yet, none of the achievements mentioned above represent a permanent or stable political transformation. This raises the question of what turns resistance into citizenship.

One possible way to conceptualize citizenship is to understand it as a form of insertion inside a political field, where actors recognize each other as effective players, as subjectivities that 'count', to use Sundberg's formulation (this volume). For instance, since its foundation in 1984 the activities of the Landless Rural Workers Movement (MST) – to cite the example of 'insurgent citizenship' used by James Holston (2008) – have been a thorn in the side of successive Brazilian governments. None of them have been able to ignore its existence, given the effectiveness of its political strategies and the broadly recognized legitimacy of its cause. Political elites have systematically attempted to criminalize the actions of MST and many of its leaders have been incarcerated; this, nevertheless, has not erased the general perception that land distribution in Brazil is one of the country's most acute social problems.

When we return to the case of traditional knowledge about climate and its political relevance, however, we are faced with a different situation. Here there is a disconnection between localized modes of resistance, such as the ones described above, and the larger narratives that frame the way these local actions are perceived by the broader Brazilian polity. It is important, therefore, to understand how local actions gain new meaning when taken up into larger political arenas. It could be argued that new forms of citizenship are only established when they become capable of interacting with the discourses and narratives that organize the larger political field, while still retaining their own unique coherence (Taddei and Gamboggi 2009).

The most prominent discourse concerning knowledge and science that organizes political interactions between governments and local communities in Brazil is that of modernization. Modernity has been a classic fixation of the Brazilian national project (as for several other national projects in Latin America) since the late nineteenth century, and is now a pervasive feature of the country's urban imaginaries. The military regime that ruled the country from 1964 to 1985 invested in a wide array of programs of technocratic modernization. After the 1985 return to democracy, the national political landscape was flooded with the discourse of democratic order and national economic reconstruction, also encapsulated within the rubric of modernization.

In terms of the organization of meaning, modernization discourses reify and oppose backwardness and underdevelopment on one side, with modernity and progress on the other. These terms are fuzzy in meaning, but powerful in the feelings they invoke, and are thus valuable resources for political manipulation (Taddei 2011). As with any discourse that becomes dominant and pervasive, the modernization discourse in Brazil imposes a specific symbolic reorganization upon the social and cultural processes with which it establishes relations. Modernization puts social relations in a particular temporal frame, presenting certain elements of social life as representing the past, being therefore of little value, while other elements are presented as representing the future, and hence progress. This temporal ordering has a corollary in spatial relations, where the urban is progressive and the rural regressive (Lipton 1977; Tacoli 1998). Because modernity constitutes such a pervasive set of assumptions, it is often linguistically unmarked, made evident simply by its juxtaposition with the negatively marked categories of 'traditional', 'rural' and 'underdeveloped'.

In the case of Ceará, political voices and actions that were effective in the local sphere became subject to symbolic reorganization along these dualistic lines when they moved into visibility at regional and national scales. This has occurred both because of the way that local knowledge is performed during the rain prophets meetings, and due to the framing in media coverage. Clearly, in the relationship between action and meaning that constitutes citizenship as a social practice, citizen agency is mediated by both institutional configurations and communicational processes.

The annual meeting of rain prophets is an example of institutional mediation that can dramatically transform the nature of local knowledge. The structure of the meeting makes for a radical decontextualization of the prophets' activities as they are normally carried out in their respective communities. Ethnographic evidence demonstrates that most of these individuals do not understand their forecasts as strictly related to climate or having solely economic purposes (Taddei 2005). In general, the rain prophets are elders of rural villages, who besides predicting rain also produce herbal medicine, perform healing rituals (*benzeção*), mediate local conflicts, provide astrological analyses and carry out other types of predictions. João Ferreira de Lima, for instance, besides concocting medicine from local roots (*garrafadas*) and forecasting rains, forecasted the days in which one should avoid leaving home or travelling in order not to meet with enemies or wrongdoers. As local leaders of diverse communities, these elders may have very little in common. The meeting, by gathering many of them in one place and giving them only a few minutes to talk about their climate forecasts, erases most of the diverse and unique contextual elements that give social significance to their forecasting activities for the communities in which they dwell (see Pennesi 2007; Taddei 2005, 2009a, 2009c).

The media coverage has a similar but more pronounced perverse effect. Since all newspapers and TV channels come from the capital city of Fortaleza or other urban centres like São Paulo and Rio de Janeiro, where the urban middle class is the main audience, the theme is generally approached through a heavily orientalizing perspective (Souza-Fuertes 2007). Most urban individuals do not have any personal experience of rural life, and are therefore incapable of understanding the phenomenological relations coded into the forecasts. More often than not, there is a tendency to associate the rain prophets' phenomenon with another class of discourse, where rural life is understood as quaint or backward, and yet simultaneously iconic of a past that is supposedly more authentic than the contemporary urban experience. Local individuals, both rain prophets and farmers, are referred to as 'simple' people, with a 'direct' connection to nature, having learnt their methods from oral traditions. The message is organized according to a polarization between rural and urban, simple and complex, immediate and technologically mediated perception, oral traditions and textual learning, past and future. One of the largest Brazilian newspapers, *Folha de São Paulo,* for instance, referred to the 2004 annual meeting of rain prophets as something that was *'quase inverossímil'* (almost implausible).

This romanticized view of the rural world is what sustains the rural tourism industry, which extends from the nation-wide celebrations of the *Festas Juninas* (June Festivals) – where urban individuals dress and dance like 'country bumpkins' – to the multiplication of 'regional' restaurants in cities like Fortaleza, Recife, São Paulo and Rio de Janeiro, with adobe walls and waiters dressed as peasants, producing what Irene Portis-Winner (2002) has called 'fakelore'. The annual meeting of rain prophets is therefore transformed into a rural life spectacle for urban audiences, and the rain prophets are converted into icons of a folkloric rural world, subjected to a process of museumification by urban societies that are unable to identify any other legitimate socio-cultural lens for understanding this kind of practice. Misrecognition is a crucial element in exclusion. The end result is that, for larger audiences and in key decision arenas in Ceará, the perception that rural knowledge is devoid of all political significance is further strengthened.

Beyond the conversion of knowledge to folklore, the media coverage also creates realignment both in the social identities of the rain prophets and in the mechanisms through which their authority is constructed. While most individuals in the *Sertão* know how to practice the methods used for forecasting, very few would feel comfortable sharing their forecasts in front of TV cameras. Indeed, the whole idea of the meeting as a media event scared away most of the rain prophets of the Quixadá region. So the event in itself became a mechanism of distinction. A true rain prophet is increasingly seen as a person who can forecast the climate *and* perform it in front of the cameras. Since the size of state newspapers' and TV news programs' audiences is much larger than the social networks of each rain prophet, the aggregate result is that their authority now comes in proportion with their appearance in the media. The pragmatic effects of the meeting recast the socio-political identities of the rain prophets, in ways that were outside their control. For most of the state's population, rain prophets have become folkloric media celebrities rather than local leaders. And, it must be said, very few of the prophets who participate in the meeting express discomfort with their celebrity. In 2006, when Antonio Lima found out that he had his face stamped on the front page of *The Wall Street Journal* (see illustration 5.2 below), he became visibly happy. He has brought copies of the newspaper article to every meeting since its publication.

Illustration 5.2. Antonio Lima in *The Wall Street Journal*. Photo by the author.

Citizenship as Spectrality

It could be said that the epistemological citizenship embodied in local re-sistance to climate science in Ceará has taken on a kind of spectrality (Der-rida 1994), making its presence felt but never materializing into concrete political space for marginal groups. If the construction of citizen-subjects is related to the mobilization and contestation of knowledge, then we must be cognizant of the way knowledge is performed at different scales and within different fields of power. Treating citizenship as dependent on control over contested forms of knowledge that are themselves inserted into a field of power helps us understand that performance. The metaphor of 'field' gives centrality to the idea of strategic political action and to the need to deal with larger discursive configurations and meaning-making practices. In the case of climate forecasting in Ceará, individuals have been able to strategically act upon their immediate material and environmental contexts, negotiating with the government over specific agricultural policies, shooing away un-desired meteorologists and even organizing a widely publicized meeting of rain prophets. Yet in the higher-level field of discursive configurations and meaning-making practices of citizenship, such local performances have been unable to escape the neutralizing impacts of their insertion into the meta-discourse of modernization. De Castro's discussion (this volume) of how some traditional communities in Brazil increase their political capital through presenting themselves as low-tech and 'environment friendly' (and therefore as good candidates for participating in REDD programs, for instance) could be seen as a case that is almost structurally inverted, when compared to the rain prophets: communities focus on their low technological capacity (rather than trying to compete with central powers in regard to knowledge and technical capacity), and through that explore new options for political insertion. In a similar vein, Baldwin and Meltzer (this volume) present evidence from Peru showing that in order to participate in REDD programs, traditional communities have to adopt techno-scientific forms of understanding the natural environment that may be in direct contradiction with their identities as traditional forest dwellers, and that made them good candidates for participating in REDD programs in the first place. Instead of opening spaces for further agency, practices of local knowledge have become subject to folkloric frames that hollow-out their political content.

The case of Ceará also calls attention to normative questions of reciprocity and accountability as fundamental elements of political relations, and therefore of citizenship practice. Science in general, and meteorology in particular, operate according to the premise that they are not responsible or accountable for the social implications or impacts of what they produce. But for the general population – especially in rural areas – no one occupies a place of non-accountability. A more balanced relationship between local communities, central political powers and meteorology requires that both scientists and the government address the issues of reciprocity, accountability and legitimacy when it comes to constructing and sharing climate knowledge.

In the case of the prophets, although the evidence points to the fact that they do not have the power to effectively manipulate the larger discursive configurations and meaning-making practices in which they have become embedded, some individuals do find ways of unbalancing this configuration of forces, even if temporarily. In 2004, for instance, the meteorologist slated to present in the meeting of rain prophets frustrated the audience when he affirmed that, because scientific data was still being processed, he did not have a forecast to announce. A few moments later, Chico Mariano, a prophet famous for being vocal and provocative, pointed to the meteorologist and said that he would forecast the forecast of science, and that it would announce good rains. Implied in his words was the message that if science was not yet prepared to forecast the climate, he was able to forecast the climate as well as the results of the meteorologist's scientific work. The next day, Ceará's newspapers reproduced his words, with a mixed tone of scandal and amusement. And this was exactly what he had intended.

Notes

1. The word *dotô* (*doutor,* doctor) is commonly used to refer to technicians in rural Ceará.
2. Configuring what White and Wilbert (2009, 6) termed *technonature* (see also Henne and Gabrielson, this volume).

References

Assaré, P. (1997) '*Patativa - 88 Anos de Poesia.*' Audio recording.
Bourdieu, P. (1991) *Language and Symbolic Power.* Cambridge, MA: Harvard University Press.
DaMatta, R. (1997a) *A Casa e a Rua.* Rio de Janeiro: Rocco.
———. (1997b) *Carnavais, Malandros e Heróis: Para uma Sociologia do Dilema Brasileiro.* Rio de Janeiro: Rocco.
Derrida, J. (1994) *Specters of Marx.* New York and London: Routledge.
Finan, T. J., and D. R. Nelson. (2001) 'Making Rain, Making Roads, Making do: Public and Private Adaptations to Drought in Ceará, Northeast Brazil,' *Climate Research,* Vol. 19, No. 2, pp. 97–108.
Holston, J. (2008) *Insurgent Citizenship: Disjunctions of Democracy and Modernity in Brazil.* Princeton: Princeton University Press.
Igoe, J., S. Sullivan and D. Brockington. (2010) 'Problematising Neoliberal Biodiversity Conservation: Displaced and Disobedient Knowledge,' *Current Conservation,* Vol. 3, No. 3, pp. 4–7.
Instituto de Pesquisa e Estratégia Econômica do Ceará (IPECE). (2008) *Indicadores Sociais do Ceará 2008.* Fortaleza: IPECE.
Kurtz, H. (2003) 'Scale Frames and Counter-Scale Frames: Constructing the Problem of Environmental Injustice,' *Political Geography,* Vol. 22, Issue 8, November, pp. 887–916.
Latta, A. (2007) 'Locating Democratic Politics in Ecological Citizenship,' *Environmental Politics,* Vol. 16, No. 3, June, pp. 377–393.
Lemos, M. C. (2003). 'A Tale of Two Policies: The Politics of Climate Forecasting and Drought Relief in Ceara, Brazil', *Policy Sciences,* Vol. 36, No. 2, pp. 101–123.
Lemos, M. C., et al. (2002) 'The Use of Seasonal Climate Forecasting in Policymaking: Lessons from Northeast Brazil,' *Climatic Change,* Vol. 55, No. 4, pp. 479–507.
Lipton, M. (1977) *Why Poor People Stay Poor: Urban Bias in World Development.* Cambridge, MA: Harvard University Press.
Martins, J. S. (1999) *O Poder do Atraso: Ensaios de Sociologia da História Lenta.* São Paulo: Hucitec.
Moffett, M. (2006) 'Sweaty Donkey Ears and Peeping Frogs? That Must Mean Rain,' *The Wall Street Journal,* 5 January, A1.
Orlove, B. S., and J. L. Tosteson (1999) *The Application of Seasonal to Interannual Climate Forecasts Based on El Niño-Southern Oscillation (ENSO) Events: Lessons from Australia, Brazil, Ethiopia, Peru and Zimbabwe.* Berkeley Workshop on Environmental Politics, Working Paper 99-3, Institute of International Studies, University of California, Berkeley.
Pennesi, K. (2007) 'The Predicament of Prediction: Rain Prophets and Meteorologists in Northeast Brazil,' PhD dissertation, University of Arizona, Tucson, Arizona.
Portis-Winner, I. (2002) *Semiotics of Peasants in Transition.* Durham: Duke University Press.
Scott, J. C. (1985) *Weapons of the Weak: Everyday Forms of Peasant Resistance.* New Haven: Yale University Press.
———. (1990) *Domination and the Arts of Resistance.* New Haven: Yale University Press.

Souza-Fuertes, L. (2007). 'Twentieth-Century Orientalist Re-creation in Brazil,' in I. López-Calvo (ed.), *Alternative Orientalisms in Latin America and Beyond*. New Castle: Cambridge Scholars Publishing, pp. 168–181.

Tacoli, C. (1998) 'Rural-urban Interactions: A Guide to the Literature,' *Environment and Urbanization*, Vol. 10, No. 1, April, pp. 147–166.

Taddei, R. (2005) 'Of Clouds and Streams, Prophets and Profits: The Political Semiotics of Climate and Water in the Brazilian Northeast,' PhD dissertation, Graduate School of Arts and Sciences, Columbia University, New York.

———. (2009a) 'Oráculos de Lluvia en Tiempos Modernos. Medios, Desarrollo Económico y Transformaciones de Identidad Social de los Profetas del Sertão,' *Historia y Desastres Vol. III*, La Red/CIESAS, Mexico, pp. 331–352.

———. (2009b) 'The Politics of Uncertainty and the Fate of Forecasters: Climate, Risk, and Blame in Northeast Brazil,' in V. Jankovic and C. Barboza (eds), *Weather, Local Knowledge and Everyday Life: Issues in Integrated Climate Studies*. Rio de Janeiro: MAST, pp. 287–296.

———. (2009c) 'The Pragmatics of Prognostication in Times of Climate Change: Ethnographic Notes from Northeast Brazil,' paper presented at the annual meeting of the American Anthropological Association, Philadelphia, 4 December.

———. (2011) 'Watered-Down Democratization: Modernization Versus Social Participation in Water Management in Northeast Brazil,' *Agriculture and Human Values,* Vol. 28, No. 1, February, pp. 109–121.

Taddei, R., and A. L. Gamboggi. (2009) 'Gender and the Semiotics of Political Visibility in the Brazilian Northeast,' *Social Semiotics,* Vol. 19, No. 2, June, pp. 149–164.

White, D., and C. Wilbert (2009) 'Inhabiting Technonatural Time/Spaces,' in D. White and C. Wilbert (eds), *Technonatures: Environments, Technologies, Spaces, and Places in the Twenty-first Century*. Waterloo: Wilfrid Laurier University Press, pp. 1–32.

Environmental Marginality
and the Struggle for Justice

6

Negotiating Citizenship in the Maya Biosphere Reserve, Guatemala

Juanita Sundberg

Since the mid to late 1990s, Latin American countries have witnessed new forms of environmental governance strategies (MacDonald, Nielson and Stern 1997; Roberts and Thanos 2003; Miller 2007). In particular, the number of protected areas increased significantly, prompting the creation of new environmental institutions and management rationalities (Eyre 1990; Zimmerer and Carter 2002). Given that this period coincides with the return to democratic rule in most Latin American countries, it is imperative to examine how environmental discourses and practices became articulated with processes of democratization and especially citizenship formation (García-Guadilla and Blauert 1992; Leff 1997; Wright and Wolford 2003; Castro 2006; Carruthers 2008). In this chapter, I frame environmental protection as a site of citizenship formation and contestation. My interest in citizenship is inspired by social movements in the region, many of which have challenged conventional framings of who counts as a political actor, what counts as political and where politics happens (Van Cott 1994; Alvarez, Dagnino and Escobar 1998a; Sieder 2002; Yashar 2005; Postero 2007). Analysing environmental protection in relation to who counts allows me to emphasize the ways in which citizenship is contested and therefore subject to (re)configuration.

If, and how, such transformations take place is best examined through geographically located empirical research. Hence, this chapter mobilizes my research in Guatemala's Maya Biosphere Reserve, which was created in 1990 to protect 1.6 million hectares of tropical lowland flora and fauna. Specifically, I analyse how individuals and collectives – differently situated socially, politically and geographically – conceptualized and negotiated historical patterns of exclusion in Guatemala that restricted them from embodying the category of political actor, (environmental) decision maker and therefore citizen. Interviews with key players as well as ethnographic research on the daily practices of conservation in the reserve highlight how social inequalities are (re)produced but also (re)configured in unexpected ways.

The case studies presented here draw from qualitative research conducted between 1996–1997 on the politics of conservation in Guatemala and the Maya Biosphere Reserve. In July 2000 and 2003, I conducted additional fieldwork focusing specifically on the relationship between conservation and processes of democratization.[1] The fieldwork thus captures a moment when new environmental rationalities and practices were gaining salience in Latin American political cultures. Unless otherwise noted, all quotations are taken from my taped interviews and fieldnotes, which I have translated from the Spanish. With the exception of some public officials, all names of people, villages and organizations have been omitted or changed to protect the identity of the men and women working both to protect Guatemala's biophysical landscapes and to create a more just society.

Citizenship and Socio-Natural Practices

Since the colonial era, 'rigid social hierarchies of class, race, and gender' organizing Latin American societies 'prevent the vast majority of de jure citizens from even imagining, let alone publicly claiming, the prerogative to have rights' (Alvarez, Dagnino and Escobar 1998b, 12). And yet, as noted, social movements in the late twentieth century have pursued the democratization not only of formal political institutions, but also of 'society as a whole, including therefore the cultural practices embodied in social relations of exclusion and inequality' (Dagnino 1998, 47). In this context, citizenship is (re)conceptualized to include not only a set of legal attributes, including rights and responsibilities as articulated in particular political frameworks, but also 'the [social] practices which define membership in society' (Sieder 1999, 106). From this perspective, citizenship is enacted as individuals negotiate and contest legal frameworks and daily practices in their efforts to exercise rights and responsibilities as well as belonging.

Attention to social practices necessarily foregrounds the sites of citizenship struggles, for practical hurdles to citizenship are located not only in formal political arenas, but also in various geographical sites, such as the workplace, community and home (Staeheli and Cope 1994; Blomley and Pratt 2001; Staeheli and Mitchell 2007; Sundberg 2008). Recent scholarship highlights the significance of environmental formations as sites of citizenship formation (Sundberg 2003; Castro 2006; Latta 2007; Wittman 2009). How is belonging – who 'counts' – negotiated in relation to large-scale reorganizations of space, such as that which occurs with protected areas, agrarian reform or dam building? And of particular relevance to my analysis, as well as to the analysis of others included in this volume (Grillo and Sharon; Henne and Gabrielson), is how imaginaries of place – as in the Amazon or Chilean Forest – are articulated with racial formations and social practices to exclude particular groups from embodying the category of political actor, decision maker and therefore citizen.

In what follows, I examine the articulation between citizenship and environmental formations to highlight how imaginaries and practices delimiting who counts were negotiated in Guatemala's Maya Biosphere Reserve in the late 1990s.

Environmental Mobilizing in Post–Civil War Guatemala

Guatemala returned to civilian rule in the 1980s, when the military permitted national elections in 1985 to appoint the first civilian regime since 1966, thus ending three decades of military rule (Azpuru 1998).[2] A decade later in 1995 through 1996, Peace Accords were signed between the Guatemalan government and the Guatemalan National Revolutionary Unity to end a thirty-year civil war and bring peace to a nation torn apart by violence. This period of dramatic social change prompted unprecedented national-level debates about Guatemala's 'pigmentocracy', the 'racialization of inequality' and gender politics (Casaús Arzú 1999; Gonzalez-Ponciano 1999; Blacklock and Macdonald 2000). Struggles over citizenship – or who counts as a political actor – are at the heart of such debates in a country where about 60 per cent of the population pertain to one of twenty-three indigenous or ethno-linguistic groups.[3]

Throughout the twentieth century, structural inequalities, systemic racism, judicial inequality and impunity for perpetrators of human rights abuses have meant that the majority of the population (composed of rural indigenous and ladino campesinos) has had little or no conception of themselves as citizens with rights and obligations (Seider 1999, 109). However, social activism during the civil war led to transformations in people's conceptions of citizenship, in the sense of fostering analysis and awareness of both formal political rights and responsibilities *and* of cultural imaginaries that dictate who counts.

In addition to women's and indigenous movements, the mid 1980s witnessed the emergence of an environmental movement made up of biologists, ecologists and lawyers from Guatemala's professional and elite classes (Berger 1997). In particular, the movement focused attention on deforestation in the Petén, Guatemala's northernmost department. In the popular imagination, the Petén was a heavily forested region rich in natural resources; for many it represented the country's future (Soza 1970; Schwartz 1990). However, as environmental activists revealed, the expansion of the cattle-ranching industry, logging and migrant farming had removed approximately 50 per cent of the Petén's forest cover between the 1960s and 1990s (Ponciano 1998). During this same period, the Petén's population had increased from about 25,000 people to 300,000 in 1990 (Schwartz 1990; Nations 1999).

Taking advantage of the political opening created by the return to civilian rule, environmentalists succeeded in convincing then President Vinicio

Cerezo Arévalo to sign legislation in 1989 establishing a System of Protected Areas and a new administrative agency, the Consejo Nacional de Áreas Protegidas (National Council of Protected areas, CONAP). This legislation created the Maya Biosphere Reserve in the northern Petén to protect 1.6 million hectares of tropical forest (CONAP 1996). As mandated by UNESCO (1984), the biosphere reserve model divides protected areas into different zones with varying management regimes: nuclear zones require strict protection, multiple use zones permit 'traditional' livelihood activities deemed compatible with conservation goals and the buffer zone encircles populated areas.

Although CONAP had the legal authority to implement the reserve, the Guatemalan government signed an agreement in 1990 with the United States Agency for International Development (USAID) to participate in the management of the reserve under the auspices of the Maya Biosphere Project (USAID 1989). USAID contracted three North American NGOs to carry out the project: The Nature Conservancy to strengthen the reserve's management; CARE International to carry out environmental education; and Conservation International to encourage alternative economic activities. In the next section, I examine the implementation of conservation legislation; my focus is on the first six to seven years of the project.

The Politics of Exclusionary Conservation

Implementation of the Maya Biosphere Reserve began in 1990, just four years after civilian elections and democratic reforms in Guatemala. The new civilian regimes, however, have been unable to transform the autocratic forms of governance that prevail in Guatemalan state bureaucracies. Indeed, CONAP, the new park administration, took an authoritarian stance with respect to its mandate to implement the legal statutes creating the reserve. CONAP's first executive secretary stated, 'Our first job in Petén will be to make our presence felt. Once we have laid down precedents for a strict protection of the nuclear zones, then we can negotiate with interested parties for a limited exploitation of the secondary areas' (quoted in Perera 1989). A former CONAP leader concurred, 'The approach was to impose and enforce the law.' Those implementing the Reserve, he said, 'were driven by a TNC [The Nature Conservancy] vision –this is a park and we are going to enforce the law'. Moreover, another former state official suggests CONAP did not allocate funding for the promotion and dissemination of information about the reserve to reassure the population if and under what conditions their use rights would be respected.

'The reserve was not implemented in a participatory manner,' stated the leader of a Central American sustainable development organization. However, he said, it was urgent to establish the reserve and the administration would have lost too much time trying to do it in a participatory way. Plus, he added, 'people would not have agreed to it anyway.' A senior official at CONAP also lamented the approach taken at the time, but his reasoning supported such tactics. As he stated, 'If all of the people had participated in the creation of the reserve, perhaps the reserve would not have the problems it currently faces, perhaps it would be better protected than it currently is.' 'Was this possible at that time?' I inquired. 'It was impossible,' he replied, 'because no one understood environmentalism, and no one knew what it was for.' His statement points to the ways in which environmental protection was regarded as an outside ideology.[4]

As these comments suggest, the urgent need to protect the Petén's forests was called upon to justify the use of authoritarian tactics. Although they may not have agreed in principle, U.S.-based NGOs and the USAID were complicit with CONAP's authoritarian methods in the early 1990s, because those practices accomplished desired institutional goals.

As a consequence of such attitudes, neither municipal, departmental leaders nor local residents were consulted prior to the creation of the reserve. Many individuals found out they resided within a protected area after being instructed to halt traditional practices in certain areas (collecting forest products, felling timber for housing, farming). People residing within the reserve demonstrated their disapproval of the arbitrary implementation of legislation and the potential loss of livelihood by burning several CONAP check points in 1991 (Cabrera 1991) and 1993 and a biological station in 1997. As a result of one such incident, CONAP abandoned its post in a Maya Q'eqchí agricultural settlement, although a military encampment replaced it. Indeed, the military came to be viewed as a valuable resource in the fight to protect the forest. In the words of one project director, 'The military can help give support' because, as he said, it is widely 'respected.'

Explaining Exclusionary Measures

Governmental and non-governmental personnel justified such authoritarian and exclusionary measures in a number of ways. Of particular relevance to this chapter are responses identifying the poor quality of democracy in Guatemala and the perceived cultural traits of the reserve's inhabitants. For instance, a manager at CONAP framed his answer to a request for clarification as to why inclusive decision-making processes were not part of the reserve's implementation plan as follows: 'The processes of democratization in Guatemala have been bad. It's said that there is democracy in Guatemala, but this is doubtful. I don't think there has been vision, and decision making is done at a centralized level. The Maya Biosphere Reserve's boundaries were drawn up at a desk, so there it is. This is why there are so many problems.' From his perspective, centralized decision making and authoritarian measures stem from the lack of real democracy in Guatemala. A North American NGO director also pointed to the quality of democracy as a factor influencing conservation practices. 'Guatemala is currently neither democratic nor authoritarian,' he suggested. 'If it was at least authoritarian, we could at least say, "This is the law, so obey it." We get by with negotiations, not by applying the law.'

In responses to a question about why institutions find it difficult to foster participation, the Guatemalan director of a U.S.-based NGO stated: 'The worst obstacle of all is the people themselves, the communities don't want to do it. After thirty years of non-declared war, people's psychology is affected; they make accusations like, are you a communist? Are you a *guerrillero* [guerrilla fighter]? This defines the socio-economic profile of Guatemala today. We are a country scarred by a non-declared war.' Here, the speaker is suggesting that Guatemalan culture is anti-democratic and therefore Guatemalan people are not psychologically or culturally capable of participating as decision makers in projects that affect their lives. This rationale enabled NGOs to explain why projects were announced to, not negotiated with, communities.

Highlighting the importance of exclusionary social practices are responses identifying cultural obstacles as the primary reason why institutions are unable to accomplish their goals through democratic means. From this perspective, it is people's culture or their essential nature that causes organizations to take authoritarian measures.

A CONAP official responded to a question about the social barriers to participation by pointing to education (*la misma educación*). When asked to elaborate, he responded: 'Because people don't know how to read and write, so how are we going to involve them? They are thinking principally about making sure they have food for the following day.' In this case, illiteracy and poverty are represented as obstacles to reasoning; people are deemed incapable of making decisions about their lives because they cannot read and write and because they are poor.

Along similar lines, the Guatemalan director of community development for a Latin American NGO suggested that my study of environment and democratization should begin with an analysis of *campesino* culture. There are several characteristics of campesino communities that limit both processes, he said, including 'illiteracy, culture, vices, personal interests, and limited capacity to invest [limited capital and limited ability to think ahead]'. These limitations, he suggested, 'often oblige the NGOs to act in anti-democratic or even coercive ways.' This is because, he added, 'Guatemalans have a long history of violence and we are not accustomed to acting in democratic ways.'

In the rationales outlined here, neither the biosphere reserve model nor the means by which it was implemented were mentioned as possible provocations for resistance or sabotage; rather, blame was placed on the cultural traits of poor indigenous and ladino campesinos.[5] These narratives resonate with elite ideologies, which have positioned indigenous people as the primary obstacle to modernization since the mid-nineteenth century. The rationale went, 'The government and plantation owners want to help the indigenous peoples but they resist progress' (González-Ponciano 1999, 18). Similarly, nineteenth- and twentieth-century racial hierarchies have consistently positioned indigenous and ladino campesinos as 'racially degenerate' and 'unprepared to make use of their civil liberties ... and for this reason they demand a tough hand to control them' (González-Ponciano 1999, 18; see also Taracena 2002). The metaphor of parent and child, also evoked in conservationists' narratives, has guided elite thinking about indigenous and ladino campesinos, who were seen as requiring the guidance of racially and culturally superior people. In positioning Guatemalan campesinos as obstacles to democratic process in the Maya Biosphere Reserve, conservationists reproduced long-standing racial and cultural hierarchies at the root of Guatemala's violent socio-economic and political system. In the following section, I analyze how two communities negotiated such exclusionary forms of environmental protection.

Negotiating Exclusionary Conservation

The Maya Biosphere Reserve is inhabited by indigenous communities situated along the shores of Lake Petén-Itza; ladino forest collectors who consider themselves to be native *Peteneros;* and long- and short-term migrant farmers growing maize for national markets and working as wage labourers for other farmers, ranchers, merchants, hoteliers, etc. In 1999, the population living within the Maya Biosphere Reserve was estimated to be 90,300, including both Peteneros and migrants (Grunberg 1999). Early studies revealed that the majority of migrants were ladino and Q'eqchí campesinos from the eastern and northeastern departments (SEGEPLAN 1993, 76; Grunberg 1999).[6] As mentioned, these communities were not initially consulted, nor included in the reserve's formal power structures. Individuals and collectives within these communities were differently affected by shifting management strategies; their differing experiences stem from the ways in which intersecting axes of power constituted their ability to embody the category of political actor, decision maker and therefore citizen.

In what follows, I analyze how two social groups historically excluded from citizenship negotiated the implementation of environmental protection measures. In the first ethnographic vignette, I focus on San Geronimo, a community of migrant agriculturalists who found themselves included within the reserve; here, class position and racial identity are the most salient features of analysis. In the second case, I concentrate on an indigenous women's medicinal plants group and isolate gender and race in my analysis. In each of these cases, my goal is to examine how everyday practices of conservation (re)configure citizenship.

Land and Inequality

By the mid 1990s, the eighteen to twenty ladino and indigenous families forming San Geronimo had been in the area for twenty to twenty-five years.[7] As the settlement was included in the reserve, the Center for Education and Investigation of Tropical Agronomy (CATIE) based in Costa Rica began working with community members through a region-wide conservation and sustainable development project funded by Norway, Sweden and Denmark. When CATIE personnel approached the community in 1991, many regarded them with suspicion. In part, this was because people feared they would be physically removed from the area with the declaration of the Maya Biosphere Reserve (about which they knew very little). As one man said, 'We thought that they [CATIE] wanted to trick us, that it was just government policy [*politicas del gobierno*] to get us out.' *Don* Chema[8] said he had thought 'the president had sold us to the *gringos* [North Americans]. That is why they were so interested in preventing the destruction of the forest.' Pointing to sustainable development as a peculiar social practice, Don Francisco commented, 'it's very rare that someone says they are concerned about us; it is a little strange. Then they convinced us that, yes. Although I personally don't really believe them.'

Through the project, the settlement was granted Guatemala's first community forestry concession in 1994, which gave residents the rights to manage a 7,039-hectare area zoned for agriculture, sustainable forestry and forest conservation (Gretzinger 1998). However, interviews with a majority of the adult residents suggested the community's participation in decision making was limited. For instance, the president of the concession committee indicated that the planning process did not involve locals directly. As he described it, 'We were invited to a meeting and they told us what they were doing and asked if it was good, and we approved.' Male members of the concession were involved in the project primarily as day labourers and field assistants, carrying out instructions set out by the CATIE staff. Thus, selected members earned daily wages working in demonstration plots and forest management areas; during the timber harvest, a larger number of members and non-members were employed.

Interestingly, the project director lamented the community's lack of participation; as he put it, 'They just don't have a vision of the project as their own. They just don't have an understanding of this as a business.' From his perspective, if the inhabitants of San Geronimo did not take ownership of the project then they themselves were to blame, rather than the attitudes of project personnel or the mechanisms through which the project was carried out.

In their narratives, people in San Geronimo positioned themselves as going along with the project because they obtained benefits from their participation. The principal benefit was perceived to be land tenure security and the right to plant *milpa* or cornfields. Thus, Don Andrés commented, 'The land is ours and we are paying taxes to harvest.' Similarly, Don Francisco indicated: 'The land is ours. We are paying taxes for it and the concession is for San Geronimo [and three other settlements]. So, we are the only ones that have rights to it.' Don Chema said, 'We know that we are renting this land and that they can't remove us, nor can others come in.' Don Xavier seconded this comment saying, 'No one can come and take it away or steal. Because people from other areas are not permitted to enter.'

Although people in San Geronimo may have achieved goals consistent with their desire to live a dignified life, the project positioned them, and they positioned themselves, as manual labourers. In sharp contrast, the CATIE staff members were positioned as responsible for the intellectual architecture of the project. Indeed, six years into the project, people in San Geronimo still did not see themselves as capable of managing the concession alone. When asked about CATIE's impending withdrawal, most people said that they believed the project would not continue without further assistance. As Don Juan remarked, "We need help from people that are educated [*preparado*].' This comment was seconded by Don Chema; 'No [we can't continue alone], because there are no educated people here.' 'We need advice from someone who knows about these things,' said Don Francisco. 'We work, but in written and other things, we can't do it.'

In sum, the project's daily practices (re)produced social hierarchies that positioned uneducated and economically marginalized campesinos as incapable of making decisions about their future. Community members were not able to embody or enlarge the category of environmental decision maker and therefore citizen. As such, the daily practices of conservation in San Geronimo did little to transform long-standing, exclusionary citizenship formations.

Conservation and Women's Citizenship

Although the above analysis does not point to the gendered nature of conservation, in the CATIE project, as well as the majority of other projects in the Maya Biosphere Reserve, men were positioned as the primary agents of social and environmental change. Thus, NGOs tended to work with male leaders and male heads of household. The Guatemala director of a North American NGO suggested, 'even as NGOs try to avoid it, sexism is reproduced'.

'We do marginalize the position of women. People say that this is a cultural problem, "we can't change cultural patterns". We say, "women don't want to leave their houses". Even if they don't want to, we also don't search for the mechanisms to find spaces for women.' In privileging men and effectively giving them more say over the future of decision making and land use in the reserve, conservation projects were implicated in reproducing gender-based inequalities.

And yet, the presence of conservation projects in the reserve also disrupted local power structures, thereby creating spaces for new political formations (for a discussion of how international conservation projects in Argentina's Paraná forest similarly created new opportunities, see Ferrero, this volume). In this second ethnographic vignette, I focus on alliances between a group of indigenous women and international conservation projects, which disrupted the gendered exclusions in Guatemala and permitted the women to become participants in civil society (for additional details, see Sundberg 2004).

The women live in a historically marginalized indigenous community. As was the case with others, the community was excluded from the Maya Biosphere Reserve's formal decision-making circles in the early 1990s. If and when members of the community were invited to the table, men represented the community, thereby perpetuating indigenous women's lack of representation and participation in formal political processes.

In 1996, Sam, a European botanist, was working closely with women in the community to compile basic data on indigenous plant use and collect recipes for specific remedies. In collaboration with Sam, several women started a project combining environmental and cultural conservation goals. This idea evolved into an 'ethno-pharmacy' selling traditional remedies gathered and packaged by the women. Although the primary goal was to rescue medicinal plant use, Rosalia, the group's first president, put forth a second goal: 'that women succeed in forming a group. ... Women rarely participate and when you see an organization, it is always directed by a man.'

Participation in the medicinal plants group presented most women with a constant struggle to balance their household demands with the desire to expand their reach outside the home, to participate and take responsibility in the group and to learn new things. Although many women initially saw the group as a chance to valorize or regain their knowledge of medicinal plants, the daily practices of participation had more significant effects on social relations at the level of family and community. For a number of the women, articulating a priority beyond their immediate families was a significant step. Doña Flor explains: 'At home, when you have finished the housework, you may want to go somewhere, but there is nowhere to go. If I go out in the street, people will say, "that woman just wanders around". ... But with this responsibility [in the group] I have somewhere to go.' More importantly, the group gave women the opportunity to speak their minds and to become decision makers. Several participants identified a women-only environment as critical to fostering the confidence and assertiveness needed to take such steps. In interviews, the women explained why. 'Between women we talk,' said Doña Flor. 'With a man there, we will give him the prerogative to speak and he ends up directing.' Doña Margarita, a mother of three girls, criticized parents who discouraged their daughters' participation. As she put it, 'They don't give their daughters support by saying, "Look daughter, this is good, you got involved and now you will have more opportunities and God willing, will learn things that I did not learn."' As a result, she continued, 'There are girls who do not lose their fear and embarrassment [*pena*].' Rosalia concluded, 'I think women are afraid to speak because they have never done so.' Rosalia said she accepted her nomination to the presidency of the medicinal plants group so she could encourage other women to acquire confidence.

The group chose not to work with any of the international NGOs in the Maya Biosphere Project for fear they would be co-opted and their decision-making power reduced. However, through Sam, they obtained support from the EcoLogic Development Fund, a U.S.-based NGO that offers hands-off financial assistance.[9] Support from outsiders gave the group legitimacy and status in the community that extended to the individual participants.

This case demonstrates how emergent environmental relations offer unexpected opportunities wherein the category of citizen may be enlarged and transformed. Through the women's group, individual women became participants in civil society and linked into a network of other (indigenous) women's organizations striving for a voice in the process of democratizing Guatemala. At another, more intimate level, each woman took significant steps to speak, assume responsibility and make decisions, thereby (re)configuring who counts as a political actor and decision maker in her home and community.

Environmental Protection and Citizenship Formation

In this chapter, I frame environmental protection as a site of citizenship formation. Here, the concept of citizenship includes reference to legal frameworks as well as social practices that facilitate or restrict specific groups from embodying the category of citizen and exercising rights and responsibilities. Such a conceptualization shifts the focus of analysis to the *sites* of citizenship struggles, as practical hurdles to citizenship occur in daily practices at multiple geographical scales: the home, conservation projects and environmental institutions. Ultimately, placing notions of citizenship at the centre of my analysis allows me to consider how citizens are constituted in the action of socio-natural relations, rather than presuming identities before the action gets started.

I bring this approach to bear on my research in Guatemala, conducted at the moment when new environmental rationalities and practices were introduced in the mid 1990s. As I illustrate, entrenched social hierarchies informed management decisions in the Maya Biosphere. Deemed incapable of appropriate environmental decision making, the reserve's resident population were said to *oblige* the reserve's administrators and the NGOs 'to act in anti-democratic or even coercive ways'.

Ethnographic research in two reserve communities reveals how different groups dealt with such an exclusionary social system. In San Geronimo, ladino and indigenous migrant campesinos were excluded from participating in the intellectual architecture of a sustainable development project that transformed their lives. However, community leaders went along with the project plans because it accomplished goals consistent with their wants and needs. In this case, the project reflected and reproduced exclusionary practices even as the community obtained rights to land. In contrast, my study with the indigenous women's medicinal plants group suggests that the presence of conservation projects in the area disrupted local power structures, while researchers provided access to new networks of political and financial support. In this case, indigenous women became decision makers and participants in civil society – a truly significant step in Guatemala. Just as this chapter outlines a set of outcomes in Guatemala that are not static, the approach outlined here treats citizenship as a dynamic and contested formation. Such an approach enables openness to the unexpected as individuals and collectives negotiate and (re)configure legal frameworks and daily practices.

Notes

1. This chapter is a substantially revised version of Sundberg (2003). I am grateful to the University of British Columbia for funding my research in August 2000 with an HSS grant. Support from IIE Fulbright funded my research in 1996–1997.
2. Technically, Guatemala had been ruled by the military since a coup in 1954 ousted democratically elected president Jacobo Arbenz. However, civilian Julio César Méndez Montenegro was "elected" president in 1966 – always under military rule.
3. Guatemala is a small country with incredible ethnic or racial diversity. There are twenty-one distinct Maya languages as well as Xinca and Garífuna (Afro-Guatemalan) speakers (Cojtí 1996).
4. The translation is somewhat awkward; in Spanish he replied: "Era imposible, porque nadie conocía el tema ambiental y nadie sabía para que era."
5. See Handy (2009) on the long history of framing peasants as backward and obstacles to progress.

6. Although population density is highest in Guatemala's indigenous highlands, only 15 per cent of migrants appear to have come from this region. The data cited here is gathered from a variety of sources. While the numbers may not be completely accurate, they provide an idea of population and ethnicity in the area.
7. The families in this community identified as ladino, Chorti' and Mopan; it was difficult to learn about indigenous identity as many people in Guatemala are accustomed to hiding such information.
8. The titles *Don* and *Doña* are used in Guatemala to designate respect for grown men and women.
9. Visit the EcoLogic Development Fund at http://ecologic.org.

References

Alvarez S., E. Dagnino and A. Escobar (eds). (1998a) *Cultures of Politics/Politics of Culture: Re-Visioning Latin American Social Movements*. Boulder: Westview Press.

———. (1998b) 'Introduction: The Cultural and the Political in Latin American Social Movements,' in Alvarez, Dagnino and Escobar (eds), *Cultures of Politics/Politics of Culture: Re-Visioning Latin American Social Movements*. Boulder: Westview Press, pp. 1–29.

Azpuru D. (1998) 'Peace and Democratization in Guatemala: Two Parallel Processes,' in C. Arnson (ed.), *Comparative Peace Processes in Latin America*. Stanford: Stanford University Press, pp. 97–125.

Berger, S. (1997) 'Environmentalism in Guatemala: When Fish Have Ears,' *Latin American Research Review*, Vol. 32, pp. 99–115.

Blacklock, C., and L. Macdonald. (2000) 'Women and Citizenship in Mexico and Guatemala,' in S. Rai (ed.), *International Perspectives on Gender and Democratisation*. London: Macmillan, pp. 19–40.

Blomley, N., and G. Pratt. (2001) 'Canada and the Political Geographies of Rights,' *Canadian Geographer*, Vol. 45, No. 1, pp. 151–166.

Cabrera, M. (1991) 'Informe del Viaje Realizado a la Comunidad de El Naranjo-Frontera, Municipio la Libertad, El Petén, durante las fechas 28 Febrero al 2 de Marzo 1991,' internal report. Guatemala City, Guatemala: CECON.

Carruthers, D. (2008) *Environmental Justice in Latin America: Problems, Promise, and Practice*. Cambridge, MA: MIT Press.

Casaús Arzú, M. E. (1999) 'La Metamorfosis del Racismo en la Elite de Poder en Guatemala,' in C Bianchi, C. Hale and G. Murga (eds), *¿Racismo en Guatemala? Abriendo el Debate Sobre un Tema Tabú*. Guatemala: AVANSCO, pp. 47–92.

Castro, J. E. (2006) *Water, Power and Citizenship: Social Struggle in the Basin of Mexico*. Basingstoke, England: Palgrave Macmillan.

Cojtí Cuxil, D. (1996) 'The Politics of Maya Revindication,' in E. Fischer and R. McKenna Brown (eds), *Maya Cultural Activism in Guatemala*. Austin: University of Texas Press, pp. 19–50.

Consejo Nacional de Áreas Protegidas (CONAP). (1996) *Plan Maestro Reserva de la Biósfera Maya*. Turrialba, Costa Rica: CATIE.

Cooperative for Assistance and Relief Everywhere, Inc. (CARE). (1996) *Project Description: Maya Biosphere Project,* internal report. Santa Elena, Guatemala: CARE.

Dagnino, E. (1998) 'Culture, Citizenship, and Democracy: Changing Discourses and Practices of the Latin American Left,' in S. Alvarez, E. Dagnino and A. Escobar (eds), *Cultures of Politics/Politics of Culture: Re-Visioning Latin American Social Movements*. Boulder: Westview Press, pp. 33–63.

Eyre, L. A. (1990) 'The Tropical National Parks of Latin America and the Caribbean: Present Problems and Future Potential,' *Conference of Latin Americanist Geographers,* pp. 15–33.

García-Guadilla, M., and J. Blauert (eds). (1992) 'Environmental Social Movements in Latin America and Europe: Challenging Development and Democracy,' *International Journal of Sociology and Social Policy,* Vol. 12, pp. 1–274.

González-Ponciano, J. (1999) 'Esas Sangres No Están Limpias, Modernidad y Pensamiento Civilizatorio en Guatemala (1954–1977),' in C. Bianchi, C. Hale and G. Murga (eds), *¿Racismo en Guatemala? Abriendo el Debate Sobre un Tema Tabú.* Guatemala City, Guatemala: AVANCSO, pp. 1–46.

Gretzinger, S. (1998) 'Community Forestry Concessions: An Economic Alternative for the Maya Biosphere Reserve in the Petén, Guatemala,' in R. B. Primack, et al. (eds), *Timber, Tourists, and Temples: Conservation and Development in the Maya Forest of Belize, Guatemala, and Mexico.* Washington, DC: Island Press, pp. 111–124.

Grunberg, J. (1999) 'La Intermediación Cultural como Estrategia de Consolidación Socioambiental de la Frontera Agrícola en la Reserva de la Biosfera Maya en Petén.' Paper delivered at the 'International Encounter of Scholars: New Perspectives on the Sustainable Development of the Petén,' Santa Elena, Guatemala, 2–4 December.

Handy J. (2009) '"Almost Idiotic Wretchedness": A Long History of Blaming Peasants,' *Journal of Peasant Studies,* Vol. 36, No. 2, pp. 325–344.

Latta, P. A. (2007) 'Citizenship and the Politics of Nature: The Case of Chile's Alto Bío Bío,' *Citizenship Studies,* Vol. 11, No. 3, pp. 229–246.

Leff, E. (1997) 'Cultura Democrática, Gestión Ambiental y Desarrollo Sostenido en América Latina,' in G. López Castro (ed.), *Sociedad y Medio Ambiente en México.* Michoacán, Mexico: El Colegio de Michoacán, pp. 43–57.

MacDonald, G., D. Nielson and M. Stern (eds). (1997) *Latin American Environmental Policy in International Perspective.* Boulder: Westview Press.

Miller, S. 2007. *An Environmental History of Latin America.* New York: Cambridge University Press.

Nations, J. (1999) 'The Uncertain Future of Guatemala's Maya Biosphere Reserve,' in J. Nations (ed.), *Thirteen Ways of Looking at a Tropical Forest: Guatemala's Maya Biosphere Reserve.* Washington, DC: Conservation International, pp. 10–13.

Ponciano, I. (1998) 'Forestry Policy and Protected Areas in the Petén, Guatemala,' in R. B. Primack, et al. (eds), *Timber, Tourists, and Temples: Conservation and Development in the Maya Forest of Belize, Guatemala, and Mexico.* Washington, DC: Island Press, pp. 99–110.

Postero, N. G. (2007) *Now We Are Citizens: Indigenous Politics in Postmulticultural Bolivia.* Stanford: Stanford University Press.

Roberts, J. T., and N. D. Thanos. 2003. *Trouble in Paradise: Globalization and Environmental Crises in Latin America.* New York: Routledge.

Schwartz, N. (1990) *Forest Society: A Social History of Petén, Guatemala.* Philadelphia: University of Pennsylvania Press.

Secretariat of Planning and Programming for the Presidency (SEGEPLAN). (1993) *Plan de Desarrollo Integrado de Petén: Diagnostico General de Petén.* Flores, Guatemala.

Sieder, R. (1999) 'Rethinking Democratisation and Citizenship: Legal Pluralism and Institutional Reform in Guatemala,' *Citizenship Studies,* Vol. 3, pp. 103–118.

——— (ed.). (2002) *Multiculturalism in Latin America: Indigenous Rights, Diversity, and Democracy.* New York: Palgrave Macmillan.

Soza, J. M. (1970) *Monografía del Departamento de El Petén.* Guatemala City, Guatemala: Editorial Jose de Pineda Ibarra.

Staeheli, L., and D. Mitchell. (2007) *The People's Property? Power, Politics, and the Public.* New York: Routledge.

Staeheli, L., and M. Cope. (1994) 'Empowering women's citizenship,' *Political Geography,* Vol. 13, pp. 443–460.

Sundberg, J. (2003) 'Conservation and Democratization: Constituting Citizenship in the Maya Biosphere Reserve, Guatemala,' *Political Geography,* Vol. 22, pp. 715–740.

———. (2004) 'Identities-in-the-Making: Conservation, Gender, and Race in the Maya Biosphere Reserve, Guatemala,' *Gender, Place, and Culture,* Vol. 11, No. 1, pp. 44–66.

———. (2008) 'Placing Race in Environmental Justice Research in Latin America,' *Society & Natural Resources,* Vol. 21, No. 7, pp. 569–582.

Taracena, A. (2002) *Estado, Etnicidad y Nación en Guatemala, 1808–1944.* Antigua, Guatemala: CIRMA.

United Nations Educational, Scientific and Cultural Organization (UNESCO). (1984) 'Action Plan for Biosphere Reserves,' *Nature & Resources,* Vol. 2, pp. 11–22.

United States Agency for International Development (USAID). (1989) *Project Paper: Maya Biosphere Project.* Washington, DC: USAID.

Van Cott, D. L. (ed.). (1994) *Indigenous Peoples and Democracy in Latin America.* New York: St. Martin's Press.

Wittman, H. (2009) 'Reframing Agrarian Citizenship: Land, Life and Power in Brazil', *Journal of Rural Studies,* Vol. 25, No. 1, pp. 120–130.

Wright, A., and W. Wolford. 2003. *To Inherit the Earth: The Landless Movement and the Struggle for a New Brazil.* Oakland: Food First Books.

Yashar, D. (2005) *Contesting Citizenship in Latin America: The Rise of Indigenous Movements and the Postliberal Challenge.* Cambridge: Cambridge University Press.

Zimmerer, K., and E. Carter. (2002) 'Conservation and Sustainability in Latin America and the Caribbean', in G. Knapp (ed.), *Latin America in the 21st Century: Challenges and Solutions.* Austin: University of Texas Press, pp. 207–249.

7 Peru's Amazonian Imaginary

Marginality, Territory and National Integration

María Teresa Grillo and Tucker Sharon

La montaña en sus venas guardaba el petróleo de nuestro mañana. (The mountain in its veins stored the petroleum of our tomorrow.)[1]

—Augusto Polo Campos

Official state discourse around the Peruvian Amazon has historically relied on a sort of disavowal that foregrounds otherness and waylays recognition of Amazonian voices. In contrast to the coast and coastal mestizo society, which is seen as the cradle of the nation, the Amazon has consistently been construed as a marginal and empty land in need of conquest, while the people of Amazonia have been portrayed as a problematic Other. Rather than reducing the salience of this dichotomy in the national geographic imaginary, repeated political initiatives to unify and consolidate Peruvian people and territory have in fact played into its reproduction. These political projects helped shape the context for present-day struggles of indigenous Amazonian peoples in Peru, who face increasing pressures on their territories from the advance of oil, gas and other extractive pursuits (see Baldwin and Meltzer, this volume). Their marginality to the political decisions that affect their ways of life is not merely an effect of the contemporary power of transnational corporations, but rather has its roots in this historical and geographic imaginary of difference. This chapter takes up the construction of that marginality as it is manifested within projects of national citizenship in Peru, examining the discursive elaboration of difference and otherness across the interrelated domains of geographic space and socio-cultural relations. Underlying this interpretive project is a conviction that these citizenship projects depend on the hierarchical ordering of difference within what Aníbal Quijano calls the coloniality of power (2000).

To probe the construction of marginality we track the tropes of colonial ordering in the articulation of President Fernando Belaúnde Terry's internal colonization project during his 1963–1968 term in office, along with the system of land tenure initiated under President Juan Velasco Alvarado's Gobierno Revolucionario del Perú (Revolutionary Government of Peru) from 1968–1975. We focus on the political discourses of Belaúnde and Velasco for two reasons. First, both represent an initial moment of state-orchestrated intervention into the lives and livelihoods of Amazonian peoples. Belaúnde's vision marked a moment of bifurcation in the colonization process, in which spontaneous colonization – comprised of individual migrations of *serrano* peasants – was augmented by a form of directed colonization promoted, sanctioned and implemented by the state (Chirif and García 2007). Velasco's reforms in turn represented a watershed moment, when ethnic communities were first granted collective legal recognition as landowners under the 1974 Law of Native Communities. The second reason for focussing on these two presidential terms is that the framing of the Amazon in each case was imbued with a desire for national integration, marking a clear contrast with successive administrations – including Belaúnde's second term (1980–1985). Once the Velasco regime was toppled, focus on the Peruvian Amazon became increasingly characterized by extractive policy.

We argue that, notwithstanding the undeniable intention to integrate the Amazon – and, particularly in the case of Velasco, the Amazonian peoples – into a project of national consolidation, the justifications provided in support of Belaúnde's road colonization and Velasco's land reforms perpetuated the kind of ontological separation between subject and space (alternately conceived as the distinction between citizen and territory or culture and nature) inherent in the colonizing project of the nation-state. This separation allowed the portrayal of an 'empty' territory, ready for colonization, civilization and the extraction of natural riches. Relative to this territorial vision, the cultural politics of national identity established a hierarchy of subjectivity, in which racialized divisions were impressed upon geographical imaginaries that presented the coast as the wellspring of Peruvian civilization (Orlove 1993). In this way, the national landscape was defined by both spatial and social hierarchy.

As we look more closely at the evolution of the Peruvian geographical imaginary, it is also crucial to underline how it contrasts with the way local Amazonian peoples conceptualize their ecological position. Indeed, even as part of reforms aimed at securing indigenous land tenure, territory has always been defined based on an ontological separation of nature and culture, often by only considering the economic potential of land. Yet this understanding of territory, while sometimes adopted and assimilated by Amazonian peoples, is a fundamentally foreign imposition that the Peruvian state has consistently prioritized over local knowledges (Varese 1979, 2002; Surrallés and García 2005; Chirif and García 2007). This is clearly an example of what Walter Mignolo has called the subalternization of knowledge, by which local 'knowledges and languages [are] placed in a subaltern position in the exercise of the coloniality of power' (2000, 306). Like Mignolo, Arturo Escobar (2008) and Mario Blaser (2010) have maintained that modern notions of development have adapted and internalized colonial logics of subjugation, restricting the exercise of rights and duties to the narrow and universalizing parameters of market dogma.

In what Blaser (2010, 10–13) calls the 'rupturist story' of globalization, modernity's universalizing thrust is contested in a search for 'alternatives to modernity' (Escobar 2008, 196–197) that recognize difference but without ordering it in a way that renders it subaltern. Along these lines, since the 1970s the Peruvian Amazon has become a contested space, where indigenous identity politics have confronted the extractive and/or colonizing projects of private and state-sponsored agents (Varese 2002; Yashar 2005; Greene 2006; Millones 2008). One early observer, Stefano Varese (1979, 2002), saw this conflict as rooted in the issue of land. For him, the history of the Amazon had been one of colonization, in which the chief bounty was territory, not souls. Looking at modes of production, Varese (1979) saw the social conflict engendered by colonization through an ecological lens; the way Amazonian tribal societies utilized forest resources for their survival constituted an 'ecological relation that has allowed the Peruvian rainforest tribal groups to live and prosper for centuries, perfectly adapted to an extremely delicate environment' (184). This relation was threatened by the intrusion of roads and settlers (Varese 2002). While the notion of indigenous peoples living in perfect and stable harmony with their environment has been substantially complicated (Cronon 1983; Cleary 2001; Radding 2005; Miller 2007), Varese's intervention remains important. His focus on competing modes of production underlines the alternative modes of livelihood, accompanied by alternate ontologies that are subdued as part of Peru's internal colonial project.

For close to forty years the struggle for indigenous rights in the Peruvian Amazon has focused on titling tribal territories (García, Hvalkof and Gray 1998; Hvalkof 2000). More recently the idea of individual indigenous land ownership has been pursued by neoliberal ideologues as a way to tap into the 'mystery of capital among the indigenous peoples of the Amazon' (de Soto 2010) and promote the full integration of ethnic territories into the market (Chirif 2009). The idea of territory inscribed in land titles, however, conserves the inherent modernist ontology of a separation between space and subject (Surrallés and García 2005). The different worldviews embodied in ethnic territories and titled land has been usefully theorized as a distinction between territorial space, seen as the habitat or home of communities, and space-objects, or commoditized parcels treated as little more than vessels of wealth accumulation (Chirif and García 2007; see also Escobar 2008; Gray 2009). Without a comprehensive and holistic definition of territory inscribed in the titling process, community rights have also been eroded by reforms that further atomize territories through the separation of surface and subsoil rights and the exception of forest resources from some titles (Chirif and García 2007). This market-based understanding of land contravenes the spirit and letter of international law as established in Article 13 of the International Labor Organization's Convention 169 (Surrallés and García 2005; Spelucín and Giraldo 2007) and the United Nations Declaration on the Rights of Indigenous Peoples (Gray 2009).

Clearly there are strong correlations between different forms of marginalization and the uneven reach of citizenship through the Peruvian Amazon, which others have discussed in greater detail (San Román 1975; Yashar 2005; Greene 2009). Considering the interwoven evolution of discursive and legal constructions of citizenship, our analysis contributes to evolving debates around the concept of environmental citizenship by emphasizing the importance of power relationships embedded in the socio-spatial ordering of political subjects and territory. Turning to the discourses of Belaúnde and Velasco, we show that if national territorial integration for Belaúnde rested on a plan of highway building that would tie the eastern slope of the Andes more closely to Lima, for Velasco it meant institutionalizing legal recognition of the Amazonian subject. However, even though Belaúnde's utopian project and Velasco's legal reforms began to bring the Amazon into the national fold, neither was completely able to shake the historical weight of previous conceptualizations associated with the region and its inhabitants. This was manifest in the paradox by which the Amazon-as-space quickly became part of the national territory, while the Amazonian-as-subject was left out of national debates.

The Amazon: A Space Without Citizens?

Ana Pizarro (2005) breaks down the construction of discourse on Amazonian subjects into three distinct phases. The first phase dealt with the region as 'a space of paradise and hell inhabited by beings suited for transformation into servants of the Catholic Church, inhabiting a space full of richness to be considered' (66). The chronicles of the first European explorations in the Amazon depicted the region as a mythic universe, rendering its inhabitants savages and cannibals. Native women were represented as warriors and amazons and the remote lands where they lived hid the treasures of El Dorado and The Cinnamon Land (63–66).

A second phase corresponded with the eighteenth and early nineteenth centuries, a period characterized by 'reasoned' scientific travel, in which discourse was marked by attempts to categorize the unknown world through empirical observation (Stepan 2001; Raffles 2002; Pizarro 2005). However, despite recourse to the new discursive tools of enlightened Europe this second phase was not lacking in negative stereotypes of the natives. For instance, the French scientist-explorer de La Condamine (1981) described the Amazonian peoples he encountered as apathetic and stupid, with 'a short number of ideas, which do not extend further than their needs' (62). During the nineteenth century a new internal colonizing impulse was being sanctioned by the fledgling nation-state, when immigration to the jungle was spurred as local political authorities were named and fluvial navigation was expanded (San Román 1975). Depictions of the native peoples continued to replicate the old tropes of barbarity, although no longer in the form of ferocious cannibals (Pizarro 2005). Instead local indigenous peoples were seen as backwards, 'naked, resigned to laziness and to the most horrible misery, which originated in their complete lack of civilization', and according to Article 17 of the 1830 Reglamento para gobernadores de la Provincia de Maynas, such characteristics were the cause that 'governors will ensure the provision ... of labourers to the city' (San Román 1975, 118–119). Thus, during this second phase of Amazonian discourse, a transition between the discursive practice of the prior century and the construction of a subject available for exploitation took place. By transforming from cannibal to backward sloth, the Amazonian became a member of the national body who, by his or her very nature, was incapable of decision making and therefore exempt from the exercise of rights and responsibilities. Indeed, the backwards, uncivilized native was converted into a ward of the nation-state, to be tutored in Western ways and put to work.

These ideas of the Amazon as inhabited by lazy backwards wretches reached their apogee in what Pizarro (2005) identifies as a third phase of discourse, marked by the rubber boom of the late nineteenth and early twentieth centuries. In Peru, the rubber boom inaugurated a clear envisioning of the Amazon as a cache of natural resources for the rest of the country. This period brought narratives created by observers such as Roger Casement, who exposed the tragic conditions in which indigenous peoples were enslaved and massacred in the Putumayo to serve the goal of extraction. The native depicted here is a savage turned into an exploited victim by rubber traders. During this period, the state limited its role to collecting taxes, financing local authorities and creating infrastructure to facilitate trade (Barham and Coomes 1994), showing little concern for the Amazonian peoples' situation.

This discursive progression by which the Amazonian subject went from ferocious cannibal to lazy, exploitable worker and finally mistreated ward of the state stands out for the conspicuous absence of talk about the rights of the indigenous peoples in decisions about their own lives and livelihoods. While the indignation expressed by figures like Roger Casement lamented indigenous victimization, the spectre of indigenous citizenship still remained a distant afterthought. Meanwhile, these kinds of representations of Indians corresponded with geographical imaginaries that portrayed the Amazon as a promised land resting just over the troublesome peaks of the Andes. As Benjamin Orlove (1993) suggests, the tripartite spatial arrangement – coast, sierra, jungle – now so commonly associated with the national territory became more than a topographical snapshot; it was read as a narrative of national progress – achieved on the coast, destined for the jungle, yet impeded by the highlands. As geographical and racial imaginaries often do, ideas about the Amazon as promised land and Amazonian peoples as non-citizens painted indigenous subjects as obstacles to national progress. Thus, while the early twentieth century saw increased attention paid to indigenous subjects, represented by the *indigenismo* movement, for example, 'the spatialization of the Indian became a way to speak safely of race in an era of citizenship' (Orlove 1993, 328), thereby perpetuating colonial racial hierarchies based on difference.

It was this racialized geographic imaginary that presidents Fernando Belaúnde Terry and Juan Velasco Alvarado inherited and redefined as they envisioned the need to integrate the Amazon into the nation. Their discourses did not describe the natives as barbarians; but for all the rhetorical styling aimed at incorporating their territory into the space of the nation, the idea of the Amazon as a space full of wealth yet devoid of any recognizable citizenry remained constant.

Belaúnde Terry: Road Colonization and the Silencing of the Colonized

Belaúnde was not the first Peruvian politician to promote colonization of the Amazon. The area, which covers roughly 60 per cent of the national territory, had long been seen by coastal elites as a space of great potential, even as they fretted over the need to provide greater assurance of possession by increasing settlement in the region. Thus, during the late nineteenth and early twentieth centuries a small number of colonies were established, largely as private endeavours involving the settlement of European immigrants, with the aim of securing national borders and setting up farming *latifundia* (Dean 2002; Varese 2006). Belaúnde, however, elevated this colonization agenda to make it a key component of his political platform, proposing construction of a vast road network that would tie the eastern alluvial valleys of the Andes to coastal markets through the establishment of agrarian settlements. The cornerstone of this effort was to be the Carretera Marginal de la Selva (Marginal Jungle Highway, hereafter *la Marginal*), a 1,000-km-long highway spanning the eastern flank of the Andes, which Belaúnde saw as the next step in the advance of Peruvian progress. In a simplified graphic that appeared on the back cover of *Peru's Own Conquest*, Belaúnde's 1959 book, *la Marginal* took the shape of the nation's backbone, cast as the solution to a growing crisis of food scarcity and economic balkanization. By 1960, Peru had one of the worst land ratios on the planet, at about 0.21 hectares of arable land per person (Klarén 2000). At the same time, most of that land was highly concentrated in the hands of a few ruling families. Indeed, in 1961 Peru's Gini Index of land distribution was one of the most concentrated of fifty-four countries studied and 19 per cent of the national income was shared by 1 per cent of the populace (Yashar 2005). Belaúnde's attempts to assuage these issues politically were largely unsuccessful, but he did succeed at reshaping the national geographic imaginary, with the land as the colonial Other, unruly and in need of pacification: 'The great battle in the conquest of Peru by Peruvians will be the one that completes our taming of the mountain range that defines the country' (1959, 114).

Road colonization was meant to tame nature and balance what was called by Belaúnde the 'man-land' relationship. With the continual rise in population along the coast and in the foothills, there would be an ever-more-crucial need to increase the amount of land under cultivation, thus prompting the need for more agrarian colonies. Yet colonization on the scale needed would require a revolution in infrastructure planning, 'a new road philosophy', as he called it (1959, 94). Whereas the objective of prior road schemes was to connect cities by way of the shortest distance possible, Belaúnde's road colonization took an entirely new look at road construction in the Andes. The route, length and therefore cost of roads were all to be determined by where the most land could be cultivated. The other fundamental innovation in road design had to do with orientation. To maximize access to useful land, the roads built under Belaúnde's colonization of the interior would no longer aim to traverse the Andes, as all roads of jungle penetration had done in the past. Instead, Belaúnde (1959) proposed the creation of 'our *marginal de la selva*' (104), a *carretera troncal* (trunk highway) that would run parallel to the eastern slope of the Andes along the *ceja de selva* (jungle brow), providing potential access to all of the eastern mountain valleys by way of community or investor initiative to build branch roads. Through the promise of this synergy of efforts between state and people, Belaúnde (1959, 105) enticed the electorate with a vision of opening the 'land without men for men without land'.

In a simplistic form of environmental determinism, Belaúnde explained how Peruvian topography conditioned what he saw as a Peruvian national subjectivity. He posited that during the conquest, contact between conquerors and the conquered was limited by altitude across Spanish America. Thus, he suggested that from Peru's two 'fundamental habitats', the coast and the sierra, had grown a unique cultural heterogeneity, consisting of three basic ethnic categories: one of a 'Spaniloide' cultural-linguistic nature; one that is 'basically indigenous' – that is Quechua- or Aymara-speaking; and one inhabiting that space to which subjects from both of the other two camps would supposedly gravitate, simply referred to as the 'mestizo – or *cholo* – stratum' (Belaúnde and Belaúnde 1962). While this third so-called *cholo* stratum alluded to a very basic notion of cultural hybridity, this formula itself represented another iteration of what Shane Greene (2006) has called the 'Inca slot', the tendency to portray Peruvian history as a clash between a 'deep' highland culture and a Europeanized coastal one, casting aside most ecological and cultural nuance while leaving out non-Andean indigenous peoples altogether. According to this cultural mapping of the nation, the Amazon of Belaúnde's Peru was *res nullius,* empty and there for the taking. Indeed, the only Amazonian subjects mentioned in Belaúnde's (1959) campaign essays were the so-called pioneers already engaged in spontaneous colonization of the area, 'good Peruvians ... that struggle in the jungle for the greatness of the *patria*' (129).

Mestizaje, however, was not just a simplified rubric of cultural integration; it also posed as a framework for financing internal colonization. In what he called 'economic miscegenation' Belaúnde proposed a fusion of the Incan systems of communal development with a modern economy of financial capitalism. Indeed, it was to be a *mestizaje* – or miscegenation – of the economy, which Belaúnde hoped would result in the burden of development being distributed between the central state and communities; it was to be a system in which the government in Lima would respond to the need for external financial capital, while communities would take on the challenge of supplying labour. In one noteworthy metaphor, nature served as a model of this economic miscegenation, when he described the joint task of strengthening Peru's road network. The central government – with the (presumably foreign) financial capital it had secured – would build the trunks of major highways, while the communities would collectively build the branches of the highway, from which the fruit of development would come (Belaúnde 1963).

Belaúnde's ideology was presented as the result of miscegenation and thus as uniquely Peruvian, a rhetorical strategy that also revealed a unique political positionality.

> To those who can't understand the vigorous currents that emanate from our very own land, it has seemed strange that a movement such as Popular Action has arisen without foreign influences and that, instead of hoisting its sails to float effortlessly on the winds of capitalist or Marxist extremism, it would choose the winds that blow from the Plaza of Wacaypata, that receptacle of thousand-year-old experiences and traditions, heart of an arterial system whose pulse was felt in the most remote regions of Peru. (1959, 17)

By positioning the Popular Action party (AP), and by extension himself, as the valiant patriots willing to brave the winds of Wacaypata, Belaúnde suggested that any Peruvian willing to rest on capitalist or Marxist ideologies was not interested in true progress. Wacaypata, the central plaza of Cuzco and centre of the Inca Empire, was synecdochically imbued with all the meaning of Peru's Inca heritage, particularly the ingenuity manifest in the pre-Columbian empire's vast infrastructure network.

The opposition posed between internal and external ideologies thus reinforced the centrality of road colonization in the AP platform, as Belaúnde was able to frame infrastructure projects like *la Marginal* as continuing a legacy of rule inherited from the Incas. Belaúnde (1959) stressed how the Inca were able to tame the harsh Andean topography and unite all the territories under their reign through a vast and intricate network of roads. Moreover, he argued that this Inca heritage would be the primary motor capable of pushing Peru forward into modernization. At the same time that he portrayed road construction as a uniquely Peruvian development strategy, Belaúnde also sought recourse in the common metaphor of the nation as body. Roads became more than mere conduits of commerce; they were the arteries through which the blood of Belaúnde's mestizo Peru pulsed. Of course, Belaúnde's evocation of the Inca legacy as bridging the external and autochthonous ideologies of progress was very much rooted in a particular notion of development from his mid-twentieth-century global economic present.

By the time of his ouster in 1968, Belaúnde's administration had only completed some 30 per cent of *la Marginal,* originally planned to be more than one thousand kilometres. The symbolic implications of this project, however, were palpable from the start. In his portrayal of what road colonization was to offer the nation, Belaúnde fashioned a narrative of national unification rooted in the conquest of land. And by bringing this narrative to the forefront of national politics he reinforced long-standing tropes of the Amazon as *terra nullius* and Peruvian history as a story of highland-coastal mestizaje.

Velasco Alvarado: The Ambiguity of Legal Inclusion

When he was overthrown by Peruvian Army General Juan Velasco, Belaúnde's administration had already been discredited. Discrepancies had emerged over a deal with the Canadian-owned Standard Oil subsidiary, the International Petroleum Company (IPC), and his administration was seen to be favouring the foreign oil firm (Marett 1969; Cotler 1988; Contreras and Cueto 1999). Thus, the window was opened for Velasco's October 1968 coup. However, though the coup indeed marked a point of rupture on the Peruvian political scene, Velasco's 'Peruvian National Revolution' shared a lot of continuity with the modernizing project embraced by Belaúnde. This was especially clear along the eastern slopes of the Andes, where Velasco's administration advanced an extractive agenda, while also laying the groundwork for indigenous rights.

During Velasco's time in office, the Advisory Committee for the Presidency of the Republic issued a collection of documents and speech excerpts that were meant to communicate the goals and achievements of the Revolution (Velasco 1972). When juxtaposed against the two primary legal accomplishments of his regime – the Agrarian Reform Law of 1969 (Legal Decree 17716) and the 1974 Law of Native Communities (Legal Decree 20653) – fissures and ambiguities emerge regarding the place of the Amazon in Velasco's revolutionary program.

The revolutionary process was presented to Peruvians as a singular – noncommunist, non-capitalist – nationalist experience, one that would peacefully transform Peru into a more just and prosperous country. This nationalism represented the main strength of the revolution, which was seeking 'Peruvian solutions to Peruvian problems' (Velasco 1972, 266). One of its main features was the call to end Peru's economic dependency on foreign countries, in particular the United States, which Velasco framed as a fight against imperialism. While his nationalist vision shared some features with Belaúnde's discursive positioning, Velasco asserted that his predecessor had failed to carry through with the project of national consolidation and had lacked the fortitude to stand up to foreign imperialists. Velasco (1972) denounced 'the ineptitude, the senselessness, the corruption and the insensitivity of poor leaders that made us understand that it was our responsibility to assume the task which their cowardice and complicity rendered impossible' (27–28).

At the same time, there were other more substantive differences between Belaúnde and Velasco; in particular, the latter emphatically defined his revolution as pluralist and inclusive, using his public addresses to encourage the participation of all Peruvians in the revolutionary process and designing policies aimed at reducing socio-economic inequality. In July 1970, he called upon all citizens: youth, students, mothers, peasants, workers, clergy, professionals, employees, intellectuals and new businessmen, giving details on the way each of them should and could play a role in the revolution. Only one great absence was clear in this integrating speech: the indigenous Amazonian peoples (Velasco 1973).

In Velasco's discourse, the term *peasants,* in spite of its relation with the land, did not apply to Amazonian inhabitants, and they were not contemplated in the 1969 Agrarian Reform Law, which only regulated the lands of the coast and the highlands. In fact, the category of peasant was to be used as a way of integrating indigenous peoples (primarily in the Andes) into the fold of national citizenship. When promulgating the law, Velasco (1995) announced in a televised speech on 24 June 1969 that 'the Agrarian Reform Law gives its support to the great multitude of peasants who today belong to indigenous communities and from this day forward – abandoning from this day forward unacceptable racist habits and prejudices – will be called peasant communities' (267–268). The banning of the terms *indigenous* and *indian* implied 'a shift from an ethnic to a socio-economic category' (Gelles 2002, 247), opening the way for the extension of rights via the creation of workers' cooperatives, a collective legal subject organized around the economic relations of peasants as labourers.

While coastal and Andean indigenous peoples were being incorporated into the revolution as peasants, Amazonian peoples remained invisible. When Velasco spoke of the Amazon he did so not in terms of its inhabitants but rather as land and resources to be exploited for national development. Examples of this discourse can be traced to 1970, when Velasco announced the start of an ambitious program of oil and gas exploration (1973), as well as in a speech delivered by Velasco (1972) on the Day of the Army, 9 December 1971: 'A short time ago the economic situation of Peru greatly improved with the discovery of oil in the Northern jungle region. This, too, is a conquest of the revolution. Because if the revolution had not occurred, the vast oil riches of our Amazon would surely today be in the hands of that International Petroleum' (297). Velasco portrayed the discovery of oil as an achievement of his government by stressing the nationalist purpose of the legal measures that his regime had inaugurated. At the same time, he framed it as a conquest, embracing once more the extractive discourse that linked the Amazon (minus its inhabitants) to the wealth of the nation. The intention to extract oil from the Amazon was confirmed on 28 July 1972, in a speech addressed to the nation:

> The new oil richness found in the jungle opens unsuspected possibilities for our economy and for the development of the Peruvian Northeast. The realization of these possibilities implies executing the ambitious and complex task of building an oil pipeline with the effort of the whole country. … It is foreseen that towards the end of 1975 the oil of the Peruvian jungle will reach our coast in order to satisfy the needs of the internal market and for its exportation to the international market (Velasco 1973, 232–233).

It is remarkable that Velasco's political discourse, even when referring to the Amazon region, did not address the people of the Amazon, let alone include them as citizens. On the other hand, there is evidence of a concern about Amazonian natives that runs parallel to the regime's extractive goals. In the early 1970s Stefano Varese was selected by General Velasco to carry out research on the Amazon and its inhabitants in preparation for what would become the 1974 Law of Native Communities. When explaining the circumstances of his work, Varese (2006, 63) admitted his group's research was a 'small and still precarious body of knowledge on the Amazon region's indigenous communities'. Yet the Law of Native Communities drew from this research to define indigenous territories in the Amazon based in part on traditional hunting, fishing and gathering activities (Chase Smith et al. 2003). Moreover, it institutionalized the indigenous community as a collective legal subject, endowed with the right of ownership and organized around communal ties (Chirif and García 2007). The law followed the model set for Andean and coastal communities in the 1969 agrarian reform, but was ambiguous in terms of determining the quantity of land to be recognized by the state, while also fragmenting common property (Dean 2002). Likewise, it affected the ways of life of native peoples, limiting the extension of the lands they could occupy, requiring them to settle and forcing them to accept Western forms of authority (Yrigoyen 2002; Yashar 2005; Chirif and García 2007).

Looking at the Law of Native Communities alongside the 1969 agrarian reform, one can conclude that Velasco's attempt to broaden the scope of Peruvian citizenship so as to include collective subjects like the workers' cooperative and the native community rested on an ontological separation of nature from culture, a necessary legal abstraction in order to systematize land rights in relation to the Western institution of property. The 1969 agrarian reform, which applied to the coast and sierra, was more about reorganizing ownership of land than redistributing it. As Enrique Mayer points out, quality arable land was scarce, and it was very rare that peasant families were actually given land. Instead the agrarian reform aimed to redistribute the proceeds of exploiting land by shifting ownership from individual *hacendados* to collectives (Mayer 2009); however, few new land titles were created and existing titles were transferred to a new collective legal subject. In the Peruvian Amazon, however, the Law of Native communities was as much about creating new titles as it was about generating new owners. Land was considered to be *res nullius* and thus under the sole dominion of the state. To properly distribute it, the Law of Native Communities laid out the parameters by which land was to be defined, divided and owned. In Article 26 the law defined land based on the economic uses to which it could be put, distinguishing between land apt for agriculture, ranching or forestry (Legal Decree 20653 1974). The law also identified how parcelling was to take place, how territorial delineations would be conducted and how territorial conflicts would be resolved. Finally the law designated both private, individual owners and the new collective subject of the Native Community. Where it did not conflict with communal indigenous territories, individual tenure was allocated based on the time and 'improvement' dedicated to a lot. If an individual lot was found to be within the space encompassed by the territory of a Native Community, however, collective title would take precedence and individuals were to be compensated based on the value of the resources present and improvements made to the land.

What can be inferred from Velasco's legal measures and political speeches is that, although his regime's initiatives sought national integration, the revolutionary government could not avoid the persistence of deeply ingrained conceptualizations of the Amazon and its inhabitants. This is partly reflected in his discursive silence about Amazonian subjects during discussion of his economic vision for the region. It is also revealed in the lexicon for speaking about the Amazonian peoples in the context of the Law of Native Communities. The 'native' denomination underlined the difference between Amazonian and Andean indigenous peoples, as well as between the Amazonian subject and the Peruvian citizen. In a different way than *peasant,* the term *native* attached the collective subjects of Amazonian communities to the nation without conferring them citizenship – or even an actual role in the economy of the new society that the government intended to create. Perceived as unfamiliar, distant, almost unknown, the Amazonian native became a subject that was difficult for the national society to identify, even in the 1970s, when there was a strong effort to study the lives of indigenous Amazonian peoples to facilitate their incorporation into the nation (Chirif and García 2008).

The ambiguity of the 'native' subject was also manifest at a deeper level in the tensions between indigenous notions of community and territory and the legal measures purporting to institutionalize and protect them (Chirif and García 2007; Gray 2009). Indeed, it is clear that indigenous ways of life were a complex problem for the corporatist regime envisioned by Velasco (Chirif 2009; Greene 2009). On the one hand, through recognizing the Amazonian communities as collective subjects, while also seeking to protect their ways of relating to the land – gathering, hunting, fishing – the Law of Native Communities challenged the universalizing tendency of liberal citizenship. On the other hand, granting land-ownership rights to Amazonian communities relied on a view of territory as property, separated from the human beings that occupied it – a different view from indigenous conceptions of human-land relations. This last aspect of the law renders indigenous subjects vulnerable to the destructive pursuits of extractive industries (Chirif and García 2007). For instance, while the territory of a Native Community was 'inalienable and imprescriptable', a clause in Article 29 left it open to the free passage of infrastructure such as roads, telecommunications and works related to oil and gas exploration.

Conclusion

If the Amazon did not make it into Belaúnde's idea of Peruvian history it certainly became at least a liminal space in his politics. As part of his campaign essays the Amazon underwent a fetishistic disavowal; it loomed large at the edge of his mestizo Peru, useful yet negated. In the articulation of his political platform, he worked the Amazon's margins into the conceptual territory of the nation, but only to the extent that it was land to be conquered. As the nation grew, so too did the tree-like reach of *la Marginal,* bringing more and more space into the national fold to compensate for population spikes on the coast and in the highlands. Yet if the Amazon slowly crept into national discourse through Belaúnde's road colonization, Amazonian peoples were still not recognized as forming part of the national community. As the jungle went from *res nullius* to colony, the concerns of its original inhabitants went unnoticed.

Under Velasco's military revolutionary government, the legal recognition of Amazonian inhabitants was a first step towards their incorporation into Peruvian citizenship, yet it also underlined a fundamental misrecognition that effaced/displaced indigenous subjectivities and ontologies of territory. This ambiguity stemmed from the fact that his government's corporatist idea of citizenship attempted recognition of Peru's heterogeneous socio-cultural landscape while failing to abandon a homogenous conception of land and territory. By recognizing Amazonian communities as collective legal subjects based on communal ties, the Law of Native Communities respected difference. Yet, by institutionalizing territory as property, articulated to human subjects through bonds of alienable ownership, indigenous ontologies of environment were subverted and submitted to the rules of a market cosmology.

The process of clarifying indigenous land tenure that Velasco initiated began to be reversed by his successor General Francisco Morales Bermúdez Cerutti (1975–1980), as Peru was steered towards an even more fulsome embrace of market-oriented economic policies. In 1978 the Law of Native Communities was modified to open up sub-soil and forest resources to extraction (Chirif and García 2007, 2008), putting the Peruvian Amazon on a course of exploitation that was further emphasized by following administrations, particularly that of President Alberto Fujimori in the 1990s (Dean 2002; Yashar 2005).

Paradoxically, their legal incorporation as 'native communities' allowed indigenous peoples to relate with the state while at the same time maintaining a level of autonomy, enabling them to organize themselves in a much more effective way than Andean peasants (Yashar 2005; Greene 2006, 2009). Such organizing was focused on territorial autonomy and self-determination, and involved 85 per cent of the Amazonian indigenous population (Yashar 2005). When indigenous autonomy was seriously challenged by the aggressive colonizing projects of later administrations – like that of Belaúnde's second term (1980–1985) – those communities were in a better position to defend their territory against attempts to limit their rights (Yashar 2005; Chirif and García

2007). Indeed, these precedents reflect directly on the incidents of violence in Bagua in 2009, in which thousands of indigenous Amazonian protesters were able to organize against governmental measures to increase the rate of oil and gas exploration and development in their territories, leading to a deadly standoff on a stretch of Belaúnde's symbolic and transformational highway, *la Marginal* (see Baldwin and Meltzer, this volume).

Despite efforts to bridge the social, economic and political gaps that keep the Amazon at the margins of the nation, successive Peruvian governments have retained deeply ingrained discursive constructions of the native Other, along with unwavering commitment to a path of modernization and development that hinges on reaping the wealth locked in the resources of the region. Such ambiguity has manifested itself in a mode of territorial integration that emanates from the state's civilizing project, where human subjects and the landscapes they inhabit are parsed into the separate legal abstractions of citizens and property. Historically rooted discursive constructions of the Amazon remain a part of the collective imaginary, and they complicate the prospect of a non-subalternizing corporatist citizenship, one which conserves Amazonians' ties to their environment and simultaneously brings them into the national society. Whether indigenous Amazonian peoples will be able to negotiate a form of citizenship that can reconcile forms of indigenous land tenure with the legal subjectivities endowed by the state remains to be seen. In the meantime, the discursive tropes that perpetuate myths of the Amazon as a land without people, full of oil and timber to fuel the nation's growth, will most certainly serve to perpetuate the misrecognition and confrontation that increasingly mark the Peruvian State's troubled relationship with Amazonian peoples.

Notes

1. From 'Y se llama Perú', a song composed by Polo Campos at the request of General Juan Velasco Alvarado. All translations from the original Spanish are our own.

References

Barham, B., and O. Coomes. (1994) 'Reinterpreting the Amazon Rubber Boom: Investment, the State and Dutch Disease,' *Latin American Research Review*, Vol. 29, No. 2, pp. 73–109.

Belaúnde Terry, F. (1959) *La conquista del Perú por los Peruanos*. Lima: Ediciones Tawantinsuyu.

———. (1963) 'El Mestizaje de la Economía,' *Journal of Inter-American Studies*, Vol. 5, pp. 545–549.

Belaúnde Terry, F., and Francisco Belaúnde Terry. (1962) 'Idearium Peruano,' *Journal of Inter-American Studies*, Vol. 4, No. 3, pp. 421–425.

Blaser, M. (2010) *Storytelling Globalization from the Chaco and Beyond*. Durham: Duke University Press.

Chase Smith, R., et al. (2003) 'Mapping the Past and the Future: Geomatics and Indigenous Territories in the Peruvian Amazon,' *Human Organization*, Vol. 62, No. 4, pp. 357–368.

Chirif, A. (2009) 'El otro sendero (¿despistado?) de Hernando de Soto,' online report, http://www.servindi.org/actualidad/opinion/16603 (accessed 8 August 2010).

Chirif, A., and P. García Hierro. (2007) *Marcando Territorio: Progresos y Limitaciones de la Titulación de Territorios Indígenas en la Amazonía*. Copenhagen: International Working Group for Indigenous Affairs.

Chirif, A., and P. García Hierro. (2008) 'Peruvian Amazon Indigenous Organization: Challenges and Achievements,' *Indigenous Affairs*, Vol. 3, pp. 36–47.

Cleary, D. (2001) 'Towards an Environmental History of the Amazon: From Prehistory to the Nineteenth Century,' *Latin American Research Review*, Vol. 36, pp. 65–96.

Contreras, C., and M. Cueto. (1999) *Historia del Perú Contemporáneo*. Lima: Instituto de Estudios Peruanos IEP.

Cotler, J. (1988) *Clases, Estado y Nación en el Perú*. Lima: Instituto de Estudios Peruanos.

Cronon, W. (1983) *Changes in the Land: Indians, Colonists, and the Ecology of New England*. New York: Hill and Wang.

Dean, B. (2002) 'State Power and Indigenous Peoples in Peruvian Amazonia: A Lost Decade, 1990–2000,' in D. Maybury-Lewis (ed.), *The Politics of Ethnicity: Indigenous Peoples in Latin American States*. Cambridge, MA: Harvard University Press, pp. 199–238.

de La Condamine, C. M. (1981 [1745]) *Voyage sur L'Amazone*. Paris: Librairie François Maspero.

de Soto, H. (2010) 'La Amazonía no es Avatar,' report. Lima: Institute for Liberty and Democracy.

Escobar, A. (2008) *Territories of Difference: Place, Movements, Life*. Redes. Durham: Duke University Press.

García, P. H., S. Hvalkof and A. Gray. (1998) *Liberation Through Land Rights in the Peruvian Amazon*. Copenhagen: International Working Group for Indigenous Affairs.

Gelles, P. H. (2002) 'Andean Culture, Indigenous Identity, and the State in Peru,' in D. Maybury-Lewis (ed.), *The Politics of Ethnicity: Indigenous Peoples in Latin American States*. Cambridge, MA: Harvard University Press, pp. 239–261.

Gray, A. (2009) 'Indigenous Peoples and Their Territories,' in A. De Oliveira (ed.), *Decolonising Indigenous Rights*. New York: Routledge, pp.17–44.

Greene, S. (2006) 'Getting over the Andes: The Geo-Eco-Politics of Indigenous Movements in Peru's Twenty-First Century Inca Empire,' *Journal of Latin American Studies*, Vol. 38, No. 2, pp. 327–354.

———. (2009) *Caminos y Carretera: Acostumbrando la Indigenidad en la Selva Peruana*, Translated by P. Rodríguez. Lima: Instituto de Estudios Peruanos.

Hvalkof, S. (2000) 'Outrage in Rubber and Oil: Extractivism, Indigenous Peoples, and Justice in the Upper Amazon,' in C. Zerner (ed.), *People, Plants, and Justice: The Politics of Nature Conservation*. New York: Columbia University Press. pp. 83–117.

Klarén, P. (2000) *Peru: Society and Nationhood in the Andes*. New York: Oxford University Press.

Legal Decree 17716. (1969) 'Nueva Ley de Reforma Agraria: Promulgada el 24 de junio de 1969,' *El Peruano*, 25 June.

Legal Decree 20653. (1974) 'Gobierno Revolucionario Promulga Ley de Comunidades Nativas y de Promoción Agropecuaria de Regiones de Selva y Ceja de Selva,' *El Peruano*, 26 June.

Marett, R. (1969) *Nations of the Modern World: Peru*. New York: Praeger Publishers.

Mayer, Enrique. (2009) *Cuentos feos de la reforma agraria peruana*. Lima: Instituto de Estudios Peruanos.

Mignolo, W. (2000) *Local Histories / Global Designs: Coloniality, Subaltern Knowledges, and Border Thinking*. Princeton: Princeton University Press.

Miller, S. W. (2007) *An Environmental History of Latin America*. Cambridge: Cambridge University Press.

Millones, L. (2008) *Perú indígena: poder y religión en los Andes centrales*. Lima: Fondo Editorial del Congreso del Peru.

Orlove, B. (1993) 'Putting Race in Its Place: Order in Colonial and Postcolonial Peruvian Geography,' *Social Research*, Vol. 60, No. 2, pp. 301–336.

Pizarro, A. (2005) 'Imaginario y discurso: la Amazonía,' *Revista de Crítica Literaria Latinoamericana*, Vol. 31, pp. 59–74.

Quijano, A. (2000) 'Colonialidad del poder, eurocentrismo y América Latina,' in Lander, E. (ed.), *La colonialidad del saber: eurocentrismo y ciencias sociales*. Perspectivas latinoamericanas. Buenos Aires: CLACSO.

Radding, C. (2005) *Landscapes of Power and Identity: Comparative Histories in the Sonoran Desert and the Forests of Amazonia from Colony to Republic*. Durham: Duke University Press.

Raffles, H. (2002) *In Amazonia: A Natural History*. Princeton: Princeton University Press.

San Román, J. (1975) *Perfiles históricos de la Amazonía Peruana*. Lima: Ediciones Paulinas.

Spelucín, J., and V. H. Giraldo. (2007) *Minería y salud ambiental en Camisea*. Lima: Economic and Social Research Consortium (CIES) and Centro Bartolomé de Las Casas.

Stepan, N. L. (2001) *Picturing Tropical Nature*. Ithaca: Cornell University Press.

Surrallés A., and P. H. García (2005) *The Land Within: Indigenous Territory and the Perception of Environment*. Copenhagen: International Working Group for Indigenous Affairs.

Varese, S. (1979) 'Notas sobre el colonialismo ecológico,' in A. Chirif (ed.), *Etnicidad y Ecología*. Lima: Centro de Investigación y Promoción Amazónica, pp. 177–186.

———. (2002) *Salt of the Mountain: Campa Asháninka History and Resistance in the Peruvian Jungle*. Norman: University of Oklahoma Press.

———. (2006) *Witness to Sovereignty: Essays on the Indian Movement in Latin America*. Copenhagen: IWGIA.

Velasco Alvarado, J. (1972) *La Revolución Nacional Peruana*. Lima: Comité de Asesoramiento de la Presidencia de la República.

———. (1973) *La Revolución Peruana*. Buenos Aires: Editorial Universitaria de Buenos Aires.

———. (1995) 'The Master Will No Longer Feed Off Your Poverty,' in O. Starn, C. I. Degregori, and R. Kirk (eds), *The Peru Reader. History, Culture, Politics*. Durham: Duke University Press, pp. 264–269.

Yashar, D. J. (2005) *Contesting Citizenship in Latin America: The Rise of Indigenous Movements and the Postliberal Challenge*. New York: Cambridge University Press.

Yrigoyen, Fajardo, R. (2002) 'Peru: Pluralist Constitution, Monist Judiciary – A Post-Reform Assessment,' in R. Seider (ed.), *Indigenous Rights, Diversity and Democracy*. Houndmills, Basingstoke, Hampshire and New York: Palgrave MacMillan.

Citizenship Regimes and Post-Neoliberal Environments in Bolivia

8

Jason Tockman

Amid a neoliberal project in crisis, turbulent relations between state and society in Bolivia have combined with a rapid pace of social and political change since 2000, propelling a dramatic transformation in both the contemporary citizenship regime and the character of inclusion for marginalized groups, especially indigenous peoples (Roberts 1996; Yashar 2005; Kohl and Farthing 2006; Albro 2010). The contest over citizenship is, of course, a long-standing question that involves the nature of state-society relations and how these intersect with diverse social and territorial identities in Bolivia. However, the country's recent constitutional change, approved by popular referendum in January 2009, signals an important shift in the formal rules of citizenship. The 2009 Constitution codifies new individual and collective rights – in the latter case to territory, natural resources and autonomous development – which had been a central demand of social movements that sustained mass mobilizations against the country's neoliberal project between 2000 and 2005. But emanating from the demonstrations and road blockades, a second demand also rang out: nationalize the country's crucial oil and gas sector, the centrepiece of contemporary economic development in Bolivia. In a subsequent development, the 'Plurinational' Legislative Assembly passed in December 2010 a law that endows the cycles and processes of nature (i.e. air, water, biodiversity) with rights, which may provide Bolivian citizens and communities with a new legal mechanism by which to shape or prevent development projects, both private and public. These discourses and programmatic changes illustrate how the emergence of a more inclusive and participatory citizenship regime is closely related to the modification of social relations vis-à-vis the country's natural resource endowment.[1]

This chapter begins with an overview of how the transformation of citizenship in Bolivia has been shaped by, and has in turn influenced, the country's natural resource policy. It then probes more deeply into Bolivia's historical and ongoing struggles over the content and form of citizenship since 1952, emphasizing the expansion of citizenship rights and the changing character of interest intermediation and illustrating how the broad promise of citizenship has proved elusive. Next, I analyse how citizenship rights and forms of participation have unfolded during the administration of Evo Morales since 2006 and the period of constitutional transformation. I assess the extent to which Bolivia's present citizenship regime can be considered to be post-neoliberal, and find that while the concept is useful for understanding contemporary Bolivia, post-neoliberal Bolivian citizenship is complicated and contradictory, and far from post-capitalist. I argue that the post-neoliberal ambitions of Bolivian social movements, which have significantly informed official state policy, remain tethered by the market- and natural resource endowment-based path dependencies born of the neoliberal era. While the emerging citizenship regime will have varying effects on natural resource policy, it is clear that the new framework of rights will enable more voices to articulate claims with regard to natural resources, which will in some cases constrain state development plans.

The Mutual Constitution of Environment and Citizenship

Although other factors are relevant in explaining the transformation of citizenship regimes and natural resource policy (such as position in the global economy and ethno-cultural demographics), Bolivian rights of citizenship and the ways in which the state has shaped civil society participation have been substantially shaped by regional natural resource endowments and the extraction and development strategies successive regimes have used to exploit the country's natural wealth. Conversely, as I elaborate below, the character and form of citizenship have significantly influenced the human relationship with the environment and natural resource policy.

The history of natural resource exploitation in what is now known as Bolivia principally involved raw material extraction for wealth accumulation by a colonial regime, and later by a mining oligarchy, which scarcely benefited a general population whose labour power was extracted to further that accumulation. Prior to the establishment of the Republic in 1825, large-scale resettlement (of as many as 1.5 million people), tax collection and forced indigenous labour in Potosí's silver mines were the foundation of Spanish colonialism, transforming the city of Potosí into one of the world's largest commercial centres of its day (Klein 1992; Moore 2010). Indeed, Jason Moore (2010, 46) argues that the 'diaspora' of Potosí's silver pioneered the dramatic expansion of commodity production not only in what was then called the Viceroyalty of Peru, but more broadly the ascendant world capitalist system in a 'highly prefigurative moment of capitalism's audacious mixing of *productivity* and plunder … [following] the basic socio-ecological pattern of metallurgical commodity frontiers'. Put otherwise, silver mining transformed labour and land in the service of capital, breaking human bodies as it deforested the landscape (2010).

Silver mining declined during the post-independence period of military *caudillos*, but revived after the War of the Pacific against Chile (1879–1883), developing into what Dunkerley (1984, 7) describes as a political 'hegemony of the silver mine owners', only to be eclipsed by tin mining around the turn of the century. Throughout this era, politics remained an elite affair that was neither democratic nor participatory for the indigenous majority, and the 10–20 per cent of the population that was permitted to contribute in some manner of politics functioned principally as 'participant observers' (Klein 1992, 154). Indeed, by the 1920s, the tin-mining oligarchy, known as the 'Rosca', came to so completely dominate the country's politics that the term *superestado minero* (mining super-state) was applied (Dunkerley 1984, 6). Three tin-mining families accounted for 80 per cent of a sector that comprised 80 per cent of Bolivia's exports, representing the primary source of both foreign exchange and tax revenues; of these, mining magnate Simón Patiño, one of the richest men in the world at the time, controlled 40 per cent of the country's production and 10 per cent of tin output globally (Dunkerley 1984). But reliance on a single commodity inevitably proved unsustainable; by the end of the 1920s much of Bolivia's highest quality tin had been exhausted, and when global real prices for tin declined in the early 1940s, the Bolivian state found itself progressively deprived of revenues (Malloy 1977; Dunkerley 1984).

Although a world leader in mining and mineral exports, Bolivia's internal economic development was sparse and highly uneven. The country's high levels of political exclusion and social and economic inequality in the early twentieth century is evidenced by most socio-economic indicators: on the eve of the 1952 revolution, the country's GDP per capita was $119, 31 per cent of the population was literate, 8 per cent completed secondary education, 3 in 10 children died in their first year, only 706 doctors practiced in the country and only 132 degrees were granted by all Bolivian universities combined in 1950 (Dunkerley 1984, 5). Amid this poverty and exclusion, the oligarchy increasingly came under pressure from a range of social forces: reformist, democratic, nationalist and proletarian. One expression of this was the 'Thesis of Pulacayo', the Union Federation of Bolivian Mine Workers' (FSTMB) radical manifesto, which denounced the Rosca, U.S. imperialism and Bolivia's 'backwards' capitalism and called for mass direct action to bring about a workers' revolution (FSTMB 1946).

Mineworkers formed a central pillar of the National Revolutionary Movement's (MNR) successful armed insurrection in 1952, and their demands after the Revolution spurred the state's takeover of the sector. These miners, much like all subaltern sectors at the time, had been politically excluded by the oligarchic regimes. But employment in the extraction of minerals had constituted mineworkers as a discrete group, inculcating a self-aware social class with profound grievances and some resources with which to mobilize. Yet miners found themselves constrained by a political system that refused any real political agency. Gradually, through collective organization and radicalized mobilizations, mineworkers achieved a socio-political subjectivity that politicized natural resource policy and played a central role in transforming the sector when the MNR came to power mid century. Although prior to 1952 nationalization of the mines had not been a part of any MNR platform, this achievement became one of the Revolution's central legacies (Dunkerley 1984).

The mutual constitution of political subjects and natural resource policy is also apparent in contemporary struggles, as evident in the 'wars' over water privatization in Cochabamba and El Alto and, more significantly, in contestation over the development of the hydrocarbon sector (oil and gas). As I elaborate below, between 1985 and 2005, neoliberal governments' hydrocarbon policies – first, minimizing state control over the sector; then privatizing it ('capitalization' in the Bolivian variant); and finally planning to export gas through Chile to the U.S. and Mexico – significantly shaped the character of social movement mobilization and of social and political relations in general. As Brent Kaup (2008) asserts, leaders of social movements were able to convince the masses to take to the streets by successfully employing a critical discourse that constructed Bolivian gas as their own, even if they lived far from any actual reserves. In this way, Denise Humphreys Bebbington and Anthony Bebbington (2010, 145) argue grievances over gas became 'bundled with the identity of citizenship'.

In the discourse and demands of the mobilizations of 2003 to 2005, including the 'Gas War' of 2003, one can observe how both the proposed changes to hydrocarbon development and the broader legacy of mineral extraction shaped particular demands for citizenship, and how the call for the nationalization of oil and gas was intertwined with the demand for a new constitution. This was expressed by indigenous leader Japth Mamani Yanolico, from the Omasuyos Province near Lake Titicaca, who, speaking during a 2005 mass mobilization, asserted, 'We want our oil and gas nationalized, so that our children can have them one day... and we want a Constituent Assembly' (Tockman 2005). During the same week of protests, Santo Anagua, of the National Council of Ayllus and Markas of Qullasuyu (CONAMAQ), then in his fourth week of a hunger strike, explained: 'We have not been able to participate during the 180 years of the republic. Throughout this time, we have been battered in this country. There is poverty and discrimination, and now the indigenous people as a civil society have put forward that things cannot continue as they are' (Tockman 2005). These popular mobilizations were the impetus for President Carlos Mesa's July 2004 referendum that asked Bolivians if they supported the recovery of state ownership of oil and gas – to which 92 per cent voted 'yes' (Gordon and Luoma 2008). This was translated into law by President Morales in his May 2006 Decree Law 28701, 'Heroes of the Chaco', which 'nationalized' the country's hydrocarbons. The role of miners in the street protests is significant, illustrating Bolivia's history of natural resources both shaping and becoming a central object of social struggle. Having lost their jobs through neoliberal restructuring in the 1980s, many miners migrated to the *coca*-growing region of the Chapare and the booming urban expanse of El Alto, bringing with them a radical politics that would resurface in 2000. The miners' dynamite that punctuated the mobilizations around hydrocarbon policy contributed to the departure of two presidents committed to a neoliberal program, and the subsequent calling of a Constituent Assembly.

Finally, regional cleavages between eastern and western Bolivia factor significantly into the debate over hydrocarbon policy, and more generally the history of Bolivian citizenship and resource exploitation. Through a mix of sustained investment by the central government and private entrepreneurism, the departments of Santa Cruz and Tarija have for decades been the centres of economic development in agriculture and hydrocarbons, respectively; together with the Pando and Beni departments, they comprise the *media luna* (half-moon) of eastern Bolivia, which has emerged as the locus of opposition to the Morales government. When in 2006 the newly elected Morales proposed to rewrite the constitution, 'nationalize' the hydrocarbon sector and initiate a new agrarian reform, political and business leaders of the *media luna* responded with secession-tinged demands for regional autonomy in an effort to retain their comparatively advantageous economic position, and based on fears that citizenship gains by the largely indigenous western highlands would come at their expense. Although their privileged economic position has hardly waned, large segments of the *media luna* have come to see themselves as excluded in a manner that parallels past marginalization of subaltern groups and, in fact, their sustained opposition has drawn on the very protest tactics previously employed by left-wing social movements. Moreover, autonomist 'civic committees' in these departments have discursively exploited the geographic cleavage by asserting themselves to be the defenders of modernity and democracy against illiberal 'ethnic fundamentalists' based in the west (Gustafson 2010, 49).

From National to Plurinational Revolution

To understand the regional tensions that emerged in response to Morales's political project we need to double back in this historical account to take a closer look at the events of 1952, when revolution and agrarian reform – the latter of which transformed agrarian relations in the west but not the east –

radically recast both the country's citizenship regime and its relationship with the natural world. Beginning with these landmark reforms we can trace a chain of developments in the relationship between state, socio-ecological relations of production and citizenship that leads up to the present day. The Revolution of 1952 was a critical juncture in state-society relations in Bolivia, marking a transition from a neocolonial era of extreme exclusion of the country's majority to the incipient and incomplete extension of citizenship rights. Consistent with Bryan Roberts's (1996) observation about the Latin American region in general, formal citizenship rights in Bolivia have not translated into meaningful political or economic power for most of the country's inhabitants, principally serving elite interests in the construction of a 'modern' nation. As the following discussion outlines, the contradictions that arose in the 1950s, though they have undergone numerous transmutations, continue to hinder the emergence of the broadly inclusive and participatory sociopolitical order outlined by the 2009 Constitution.

At the time of the Revolution, Bolivia was still a largely rural country. Though mining had long been central to the economy, over 70 per cent of the population worked in agriculture in 1950 (Malloy 1977, Dunkerley 1984). Between 1953 and 1974, agrarian reform appropriated and redistributed 30 per cent of the country's agricultural land, largely to rural collectives (Dunkerley 1984, Sobhan 1993) throughout the western highlands and central valleys – but not in the eastern lowlands. One of the most significant in Latin America, Bolivia's agrarian reforms constituted an important deepening of social and economic citizenship, putting land in the hands of those that worked it and organizing them into unions within a corporatist structure (Van Cott 2005). Although indigenous peoples remained excluded from representative politics, the Bolivian state provided for the first time mechanisms, however limited, by which indigenous actors, as campesinos, could pressure the state to respond to their interests and grievances.

Another major MNR reform was the significant expansion of the educational system, including into rural areas, which served to inculcate indigenous peoples as part of the party's nation-building project. The MNR's 'national populism' demanded allegiance to the state, combining a discourse of *lo popular* with a singular *mestizo* identity. The ideology of *mestizaje* sought to mask Bolivia's ethnic diversity, eliding the identities of the thirty-seven indigenous groups living within the country's geographic boundaries. Concomitantly, the MNR attempted to implement a form of interest intermediation based on corporatism, instituting a system of officially sanctioned associations that linked society's principal interest groups – business, labour, miners, the peasantry – to ministries of successive MNR administrations, serving both as conduits of support and channels for making demands on the state.

Indigenous peoples, who, then as now, constituted around 60 per cent of the population, were profoundly affected. While on the one hand they gained entry into the public realm and a role in national politics, on the other hand the MNR's project of modernization attempted to recast all indigenous peoples under a new identity – campesinos – with the principal goal of institutionalizing rural support for the party (Yashar 2005). Much as Grillo and Sharon (this volume) describe the national popular discourse of Peruvian President Juan Velasco (1968–1975), the MNR sought to unify the nation with the 'common people' as its symbols: 'Any organisation on the basis of ethnic or cultural identity was ruled out … indigenous people had a place in the nation only insofar as they fit into the broader social categories of peasants or workers' (Schaefer 2009, 402). Yet in many parts of the country, behind a discursive acquiescence designed to secure resources – access to land, discounts on price-supported goods and arms and bullets – indigenous communities sustained a high degree of autonomy that took 'a form of syncretism – an accommodation of union nomenclature and a displacement of "indigenous leaders as interlocutors" but a basic maintenance of indigenous customs and practices at the local level' (Xavier Albó, quoted in Yashar 2005, 161).

The corporatist arrangement eroded during the military dictatorships from 1964 to 1982. The prevailing citizenship regime during those years was one of diminished autonomy and rights, both collective and individual, which, as Deborah Yashar emphasizes, served as the impetus for the first generation of indigenous mobilization, as expressed by the Kataristas, a class- and ethnicity-based movement that developed strong local networks with other social actors during the 1970s and 1980s (Yashar 2005). Yet the military's 'pact' with indigenous and campesino communities was sustained through the continuation of agrarian reform and basic education programs (Gray Molina 2003), surviving until 1974, when General Hugo Banzer ordered the massacre of between eighty and two hundred peasants protesting in Tolata (Kohl and Farthing 2006).[2] The killings generated a surge in campesino mobilization, increasingly inflected with a discourse of indigenous identity. In 1979, this crystallized in the formation of Confederation of Peasant Workers' Unions of Bolivia – Tupak Katari (CSUTCB-TK), Bolivia's foremost peasant and indigenous organization (Van Cott 2005).

If dictatorship fractured the corporatist citizenship regime, neoliberalism dismembered what remained. Shortly after the resumption of electoral democracy, Bolivia responded to extreme economic crisis (uncontrolled inflation, balance of payment problems and budget deficits) by embarking on one of Latin America's most radical neoliberal restructuring programs. In 1985, President Victor Paz Estenssoro introduced the New Economic Policy (Decree Law 21060), a series of reforms that fundamentally reorganized Bolivian politics, the economy and state-society relations (Gamarra 2003). Through privatization and free trade, the private sector was granted primacy in economic affairs, while the state apparatus surrendered the resources and capacity to respond to the demands of civil society. The 'neoliberal citizenship regime' followed the liberal logic of laissez faire: rights and responsibilities were bestowed on the freely competing individual, deliberately undermining the collective organization that had undergirded society and politics (Yashar 2005). Corporatist interest intermediation was replaced with a privatized and individualized system, which entailed the closure of mines and attendant lay-off of more than 22,000 state mining employees, elimination of programs to support rural communities and diminished access to policy makers (Yashar 2005). Formal rights of citizenship – civil, social and economic – were modified in various ways. Indigenous peoples living in rural areas suffered from a range of austerity measures, including cuts in social services, wage freezes and the withdrawal of subsidies for and price controls on agricultural goods and gas; meanwhile, closure of tin mines put heavy pressures on rural communities, which were suddenly forced to accommodate an influx of mine workers, many of indigenous origin (Yashar 2005). States of emergency were declared to control the grievances of newly alienated sectors, and numerous labour leaders that challenged the new model were imprisoned or exiled to far reaches of the country.

President Gonzalo Sánchez de Lozada's 1994 Law of Popular Participation (LPP) was an attempt to contend with indigenous and peasant movements' demands for greater participation, especially in local-level decision making, and reincorporate large segments of the population that had been cast out of the political system by neoliberal restructuring. Expanding on previous legislation, the LPP legally recognized indigenous and campesino communities, granting them certain territorial rights; significantly increased municipal governments' authority; deepened participatory planning (albeit unevenly across the country); and increased the share of the national revenues disbursed to rural areas. To be sure, Sánchez de Lozada's principal aim was to decentralize power in a manner advantageous to the MNR, circumventing department-level prefects (governors) and creating municipalities in which the party could better contain civil unrest. Though initially criticized by social movements, municipal elections and governance provided a critical testing and training ground for a new generation of politicians, many indigenous, who emerged from and maintained strong ties to social movements. It is from this group that the Movement Toward Socialism (MAS) would build its base and gain power under Morales's leadership.

When the MAS came to power in 2006 it again modified the country's citizenship regime through constitutional and legal reforms that have expanded institutional mechanisms of public participation, as well as the ability of indigenous peoples to autonomously exercise collective citizenship rights, including control over natural resources. These developments, which are described in greater detail below, represent both continuity and a pronounced break with the incremental expansion of citizenship as a result of the 1952 Revolution and the LPP. In terms of continuity, the MAS has sought to marshal constituent power towards a hegemonic project, incorporating and at times co-opting social-movement energies according to the logic of the state. This has had a demobilizing effect on many social movements of the left, diminishing their capacity for autonomous action (Dangl 2010) – at least until the passage of the new Constitution. Since that time, one can discern in social movements' expanding protests against the MAS's policies an echo of the gradual disenchantment of peasant and labour groups to the increasing clientelism and policy moderation of the MNR in the late 1950s.

But where the MNR became increasingly dependent on the U.S. to address its budget deficit, ceding sovereignty to the priorities of foreign interests (Malloy 1977), the MAS is better equipped in terms of resources and foreign reserves to forward an endogenous project. This modest degree of state autonomy notwithstanding, the MAS has not freed itself from the constraints of global capitalism, or the particularities of Bolivia's path dependencies associated with the neoliberal turn. As explicated by Kaup (2010), the capacity of Morales or any government to institute significant socio-economic change is still limited by the prior restructuring of the hydrocarbon sector, most notably the terms of pre-existing contracts, the established distribution of rents, lack of capacity of state-owned enterprises (SOEs), lack of exploration and existing transportation infrastructure. These factors militate against radical change, which helps explain why Morales's hydrocarbon 'nationalization' program falls well short of the expropriation or confiscation conventionally associated with the term – leading Kaup (2010, 130, 135) to characterize the action as a 'free-market buyout' and 'neoliberal nationalization'.

On the other hand, the contemporary socio-ecological context has permitted changes in citizenship rights – in particular, collective rights extended to indigenous peoples – significantly departing from the old scripts, which can be attributed to a region-wide dissatisfaction with the outcomes of neoliberalism, a shift in regional geopolitics in which Venezuela's oil-based diplomacy and discourse of a 'socialism of the twenty-first century' bolsters other governments of the left – both materially and ideologically – and high prices for primary commodity exports. Under these conditions, Morales has maintained sufficient autonomy to respond to social-movement demands for greater rights, participation and access to state resources; the resulting citizenship regime is more inclusive and participatory than the post-1952 reforms and the LPP. As I elaborate in the following section, the 2009 Constitution grants novel rights to indigenous peoples, defining the country as 'plurinational'; reserving seats in the legislature, constitutional court and other key governmental bodies for indigenous representatives (although less seats than proposed by some indigenous groups); and enabling indigenous communities to exercise collective rights by asserting autonomy within the state. The degree of participation has also expanded in terms of increased use of mechanisms of democratic participation (recall and referendum); greater representation of historically marginalized groups, especially women and indigenous peoples; and an unprecedented level of access to government officials at all levels.

Post-Neoliberal Citizenship in Contemporary Bolivia

A growing body of literature points to pushback against neoliberal policies across Latin America, positing the emergence of some type of 'post-neoliberal' era (Sader 2008; Grugel and Riggirozzi 2009; Macdonald and Ruckert 2009; Beasley-Murray, Cameron and Hershberg 2010; Gustafson 2010). While this scholarship highlights the significant role that social movements have played in constructing post-neoliberalism in terms of citizenship, the Bolivian case also illustrates how this transition has both been influenced by, and in turn, modified the human relationship to natural resource endowments. This section employs a post-neoliberal lens to trace the key events in this evolution, and describes the relationship between an ensuing citizenship regime and natural resource policies.

But how should Latin America's incipient post-neoliberalism be conceptualized in terms of its influence on changing regimes of citizenship and the role of natural resources in shaping patterns of development? It is important to first clarify that post-neoliberalism should generally not be conflated with post-capitalism, as the slogan 'socialism of the twenty-first century' suggests; rather, it emerges as a response to a discrete period of global capitalism characterized by an ideology of free-market fundamentalism, and a corresponding project of social engineering that involves reconstructing the institutional foundation of society (Taylor 2009). The policies that flow from this logic are fiscal austerity, open capital flows, privatization of SOEs, deregulation, liberalized trade and export-oriented growth.

Emerging from this context, post-neoliberalism posits that there *is* an alternative to the existing economic architecture; however, as Laura Macdonald and Arne Ruckert (2009, 6) argue, post-neoliberalism appears to be less of a clean break with neoliberalism than a 'discontinuity within continuity' in which the pursuit of progressive policies has arisen from neoliberalism's own contradictions, yet these alternative policies usually contain remnants of the neoliberal program. Thus, rather than a singular program, post-neoliberalism may be expressed as a variant of Keynesianism, social democracy, the welfare state, or a path to socialism. Externally, it entails a range of measures, such as imposing capital controls, restricting trade flows, defaulting on or renegotiating debt payments on more favourable terms, 'nationalizing' foreign-owned property and withdrawing from international trade and investment accords. On the domestic front, this involves the reassertion of greater state control over certain economic and natural resource sectors and increased state support for social programs, as well as efforts to reverse the institutional restructuring that took place under neoliberalism, challenging market relations, private property and individualism as the primary loci of social organization (Taylor 2009). In contrast with previous citizenship regimes, post-neoliberal citizenship signifies expanded political and social rights – both individual and collective – and greater opportunities for direct participation at both the national and local level, including in decision making around natural resource policy, in which the state itself is an increasingly important player.

To a significant extent, a post-neoliberal shift is underway in Bolivia. The Bolivian government has reasserted a moderate, but important, degree of state control over the hydrocarbon sector (the so-called 'nationalization'), which involved the renegotiation of several of the largest oil and gas contracts so as to secure majority ownership and between 50 and 80 per cent of revenues (Gordon and Luoma 2008). In a 2009 referendum, Bolivians approved a constitutional change to limit the size of new agricultural land holdings to five thousand hectares, and the administration has implemented an agrarian reform.

Underpinning these policy changes, a sustained struggle against neoliberalism has been waged by a wide range of social movements, including not only the *coca* growers of the Chapare region, but also indigenous peoples and campesinos across the country, water users in Cochabamba and El Alto, urban neighbourhood associations, women's organizations, miners and other sectors that resisted free-market reforms. In other words, the primary carrier of expanded citizenship in contemporary Bolivia is not the late-arriving political vehicle of a party (the MAS), but the country's social movements, which Roberts (1996, 39) asserts are ordinarily the 'most visible signs of the struggle to define and redefine citizenship' in Latin America. Interrogating why these mobilizations happened when they did, Yashar (2005) compellingly argues that the surge of indigenous mobilization against neoliberalism resulted from three factors: (1) the shift in citizenship regime, from corporatist to market-based and individualist, which constrained indigenous autonomy during the military dictatorships and neoliberalism; (2) expansion of political associational space; and (3) flourishing of trans-community social networks.

The precise spark that set off the rebellion against neoliberalism came in 2000, when, under pressure from the World Bank, the government of Hugo

Banzer privatized Cochabamba's municipal water system, turning it over to a U.S.-European consortium led by the San Francisco-based Bechtel Corporation. Residents of Cochabamba revolted when water rates increased, in some cases significantly. The subsequent 'Water War' entailed a series of escalating blockades, strikes and popular assemblies, as well as a referendum that rejected the privatization, culminating in the April 2000 cancellation of the water contract. Many have pointed to this successful mobilization as the key point at which the greater part of Bolivian civil society turned against neoliberalism, setting in motion a half-decade progression of demonstrations and road blockades that increasingly pressured the political establishment to accept a more statist system in which citizens and communities have broader rights. Among the most notable events of this period are land takeovers by landless peasants in 2001; the January 2002 protests against closure of legal *coca* markets; the February 2003 'Tax War' over increased tax rates; the October 2003 'Gas War' over the exportation of natural gas, which prompted the resignation of President Sánchez de Lozada; and mass protests in 2005 that led to the fall of President Mesa (Kohl and Farthing 2006).

In the course of confronting the neoliberal program, social movements became powerful political agents in setting the country's political agenda, and they experienced important political gains. The *coca* growers' political party, the Assembly for Sovereignty of the People, experienced increasing success in getting representatives elected to Congress in 1997, culminating with the election of Evo Morales to the presidency in 2005 (then with the MAS). One of the key demands of social movements was for a new constitution that would provide a foundation for enhanced social and economic rights and greater political inclusion. The MAS embraced this demand as a central plank of its agenda, navigated a contentious course of convening a Constituent Assembly (CA), and oversaw a process which enabled individuals and groups across Bolivia's political spectrum many opportunities to provide input into the Constitution's drafting. This was both more participatory than past constitutional reforms in Bolivia, and, as Maxwell Cameron (2010) notes, was more inclusive of the diversity of opinions than the constitutional reforms recently undertaken by other countries in the region, including Colombia, Venezuela and Ecuador. However, social movement representation in the CA did not fulfil the platform that emanated from the country's leading indigenous groups, who proposed that twenty-six Assembly members be directly selected by indigenous communities according to indigenous *usos y costumbres* (customs and traditions) and one from the Afrobolivian community (Centro de Comunicación y Desarrollo Andino et al. 2004; Hochstetler and Friedman 2008). The CA process was often difficult. Some social organizations decried that Assembly candidates were required to compete via political parties rather than other forms of organization, such as unions, citizens groups, or indigenous communities, and that too many concessions were made to appease the opposition (such as lack of retroactivity in agrarian reform). Meanwhile, business and autonomist groups in the eastern departments of the *media luna* charged that the CA's drafting and ratification process was illegal. In the end, a compromise was struck between the MAS and opposition members of the Congress, and the Constitution was approved by 61 per cent of voters on 25 January 2009, with 90 per cent of eligible voters casting ballots (Carvalho and Mejía 2009). In addition to establishing a new framework for the exercise of citizenship rights, the constitutional reform process and outcome also signified a crucial stage in the consolidation of both the MAS's power and the reconfiguration of relationships between the central and regional governments.

The 2009 Constitution significantly modified the country's citizenship regime, both in form and content.[3] In Part 1, Articles 13–29, individual persons receive the 'negative' rights familiar to many constitutions, including the right to life, liberty, personal security, physical and psychological integrity, privacy, thought, self-identification, association, the freedom to participate politically, to vote and to access information. This section also creates numerous 'positive' rights that are less common in constitutions: the right to food, water, health, education, adequate housing, utilities, communication and dignified work. In terms of collective rights of indigenous peoples, the Constitution elaborates rights to cultural identity, language, beliefs, traditions, institutions, territorial autonomy, self-determination, cosmovision, practices, customs and protection of sacred sites and collective intellectual property, as well as the right to live in a healthy natural environment and to receive an education that is intercultural, intracultural and plurilingual. Articles 190–192 describe indigenous nations' right to exercise their own systems of authority and justice, based on customary norms and procedures, although the Constitution states that these must respect the rights and guarantees outlined elsewhere in the document. The Constitution specifies that indigenous nations' institutions will factor into the state's general structure, including reserved seats in the legislature and an unspecified number of representatives from communal systems of justice in the new 'Plurinational Constitutional Tribunal' – the highest state organ responsible for overseeing constitutional matters (Article 197). Article 352 guarantees that prior to the exploitation of natural resources on indigenous territory, the state will undertake free and informed consultation with affected indigenous communities, respecting their varying conventions of norms and procedures for decision making, although the degree to which this will enable communities to refuse consent for projects they oppose is uncertain.

The Constitution has a high degree of specificity, clarifying questions many countries leave to the legislature to sort out; however, the Legislative Assembly still needed to pass a series of laws to implement the Constitution (Solón 2010). Various implementing laws have already been approved, including an Electoral Law which reserves seven seats of the 130-member 'Plurinational Legislative Assembly' (formerly the Congress) for indigenous representatives chosen by indigenous peoples. While this signifies an important gain in terms of collective representation of indigenous communities, it is well below the eighteen seats for which indigenous groups including the Confederation of Indigenous Peoples of Eastern Bolivia (CIDOB) campaigned (EFE 2010). Moreover, many of the positive rights the Constitution delineates, such as access to clean water and dignified work, remain out of reach for many citizens, and may continue to be an unfulfilled promise for generations.

During Morales's presidency, space for political participation has expanded in several respects. The government has made liberal use of referenda and recall procedures. In addition to approving the Constitution, Bolivians have also voted on departmental autonomy in 2006, on whether to recall Morales and the sitting departmental governors in 2008 and on the size limit of agricultural holdings in 2009. Morales's 2006 intervention into the hydrocarbon sector can be viewed as a response to the 2004 referendum on that question. Social movements have also achieved extensive and unprecedented access to ministers and other state officials (Tockman 2008). Several social movement leaders and activists have assumed posts with the government, including ministerial positions, fostering open channels of communication; however, the close relationship between the MAS and social movements has, according to numerous observers, raised the spectre of clientelism (e.g. Dangl 2010).

In terms of regional and local-level autonomy, the Constitution includes provisions by which departments, regions, municipalities and indigenous communities (Autonomías Indígenas Originarias Campesinas, AIOCs) can secure autonomy over various functions and resources. All nine departments have now voted in favour of autonomy, decentralizing many administrative powers from the central state, as have eleven indigenous AIOCs[4] (CNE 2010). Where indigenous communities occupy ancestral territory and vote for autonomy, Article 304 provides them with *exclusive* jurisdiction over the management of economic, social and political development, administration of renewable natural resources and protected areas, taxation, housing, road maintenance and the application of justice. It remains to be seen, however, how community regulation of natural resources will be reconciled with government resource development objectives, in the case that the Morales administration prioritizes the 'nationalization' of a hydrocarbon field on autonomous indigenous territory. In the April 2010 elections for departmental, regional and local representatives, indigenous people were directly chosen by indigenous communities to twenty-three positions, scattered across the country's nine departmental assemblies (CNE 2010).

As John Cameron (2010) observes, Bolivia's new Constitution arguably goes beyond any other country's constitution in extending to indigenous nations the right to self-governance. However, although it was the MAS that drafted the Constitution and passed the subsequent Framework Law on Autonomy and Decentralization of 2010, MAS activists campaigned *against* indigenous autonomy initiatives in December 2009, and the party subsequently ran its own candidates against those selected by local indigenous peoples in the April 2010 elections – in the communities that had approved autonomy. In 2010, the government's preliminary draft of the autonomy law was rejected by CIDOB, which organized a 1500-kilometer 'March for Territory, Autonomy, and Defense of Indigenous Peoples' Rights' from Trinidad to La Paz. Eventually, a compromise was negotiated between the administration and CIDOB; modifications were made to the autonomy law, and the remaining segment of the march was called off.

The complex intersection of nature, citizenship and local sovereignty is perhaps best illustrated by the struggle over Guaraní territory in the Alto Parapetí of southeast Bolivia, where until contemporary times indigenous communities endured feudal relations described by international observers and the Morales administration as 'slavery' and 'various forms of debt bondage analogous to slavery' (IACHR 2007). Central to its effort to 'decolonize the state,' the MAS has attempted to transform social relations in the Alto Parapetí by reconstituting the Guaraní's ancestral territory under provisions of a 2006 agrarian reform law (Gustafson 2010). However, the Alto Parapetí is also significant in that it sits atop the massive Inkawasi gas reserve, controlled by the French firm Total. Before changes in land tenure took effect, royalties accrued to local municipalities and departments which opposed the central government (Gustafson 2010). Returning the land to indigenous control thus had the double effect of undermining those opposed to the MAS and generating MAS support among the Guaraní. With respect to citizenship, Bret Gustafson (2010, 48, 62) argues that whereas previous governments had enacted violence against this highly marginalized population, the new 'sovereignty-making practices' of the MAS have converted the Guaraní into 'collective socio-territorial formations' that have been validated by the MAS's calls for decolonization in the framework of a 'plurinational' state. In the discursive battles that ensued, the MAS claimed to be defending the human rights of highly exploited Guaraní communities, while the local political elite alleged the government was motivated by control of the gas reserves. Violent confrontations escalated, which the central government was unable to control due to its weak capacity, especially in the eastern departments. By February 2009, however, the government expropriated 36,425 hectares of *latifundios,* which were subsequently redistributed to Guaraní families (Bolpress 2009). Thus, while struggle in the Alto Parapetí demonstrates how the MAS has taken steps to enhance economic and social citizenship at the country's margins through land redistribution and constitutional recognition of indigenous rights to territory, it concomitantly showcases how weak state capacity attenuates the delivery of citizenship rights.

Conflicts over natural resources have not gone away during Morales's presidency; rather, the lines of debate over natural resource policy have shifted from those of Bolivia's neoliberal period. The state's exertion of greater control over natural resources on behalf of the 'common good' has certainly enhanced revenues for the central government, enabling it to expand social programs; however, as a consequence, communities may find themselves less able to articulate positions against MAS proposals related to natural resource development.[5] This is likely to become an increased source of tension where the resource-related policies of the MAS conflict with local socio-ecological realities. An additional twist was added to the relationship between nature and citizenship when in December 2010, President Morales signed a law that provides rights to the cycles and processes of nature – air, water, biodiversity and so on – recognizing nature as a 'collective subject of public interest'. It remains to be seen how extensively Bolivia will comply with this extension of rights to a subject-bearing natural world; however, it should not be long before comparisons can be drawn between the new law and the comparable provisions of Ecuador's 2008 Constitution. In the later case, Pinto (this volume) indicates that nature's newfound rights have not meaningfully factored into President Rafael Correa's policies, as he has pushed through legislation to greatly expand resource extraction, among other measures that could significantly damage natural processes.

Post-Neoliberal Environments and Citizenships in Bolivia

What are the implications of Bolivia's post-neoliberal citizenship regime for natural resource exploitation, and the processes by which natural resource policies are negotiated? The question is relevant not only for established hydrocarbon, mineral and agricultural sectors; it takes on new dimensions in light of plans for extraction and development of the extensive lithium deposits located in the Salar de Uyuni region of southwest Bolivia, which are estimated to contain more than half of the world's reserves and are now being targeted by foreign automakers for use in electric car batteries (Friedman-Rudovsky 2009). It is too early to discern the varied ways in which the reconstitution of state-led development strategies under the MAS are compatible with new citizenship rights, such as those related to indigenous autonomy; however, there is little reason to think that conflicts between resource development and indigenous rights are likely to disappear with post-neoliberalism. It also remains to be seen how the rights of nature afforded by the 2010 Law of the Rights of Mother Earth will alter the environment-citizenship relationship, although it is plausible that the law's provisions will provide indigenous communities with a novel tool with which to prevent unwanted development projects. That said, neither the enhancement of citizenship rights nor new rights of nature associated with the post-neoliberal turn have broken free from the shackles of global capitalism, or Bolivia's dependence on markets and natural resources as drivers of development.

Morales and the MAS have expanded the conception and practice of citizenship in ways that are both qualitatively and quantitatively significant. If these do not always go as far as social movements demand, the degree of participation in Bolivia's unfolding citizenship regime stands in sharp contrast with the clear narratives of contemporary exclusion that appear elsewhere in this volume, as in the cases of the Mapuche in Chile and Amazonian peoples in Peru, described in the chapters by Henne and Gabrielson, and Grillo and Sharon. The refounding of Bolivia as plurinational, the provision of autonomy to indigenous communities that opt for it and the new state structures that ensure reserved seats for indigenous representation all signify advances in the inclusion of previously marginalized sectors. The deepening of citizenship will have varying and sometimes unanticipated effects on natural resource policy, but it will almost certainly entail more voices challenging the dominant mode of economic development and questioning the legitimacy of specific projects. In some cases, this may slow down or impede state development plans, which helps explain why elements of the MAS, after having constitutionally expanded citizenship rights and avenues for participation, subsequently moved to limit the exertion of indigenous autonomy. In that step, one can hear a ricochet of the constraints to citizenship that followed the Revolution of 1952: the form and practices of citizenship have been enhanced, but its exercise may be impeded where it conflicts with the ruling party's hegemonic ambitions. The task the MAS faces now is to ensure that its natural resource policies enacted on behalf of a putative 'common good' do not trammel on indigenous rights, not merely because the party attempts to take indigenous concerns into consideration when developing policy, but because indigenous communities – and social movements more generally – are being included in the process of formulating the natural resource program, and enjoy the autonomous capacity to direct or prevent development plans that affect their territories. The 2009 Constitution's bold promise of collective indigenous rights comes close to requiring that the government secure prior and informed consent for any natural resource projects advanced in autonomous indigenous territory. In practice, Bolivia's unfolding post-neoliberal citizenship regime and natural resource program remain beset by contradictions – creative and sometimes violent tensions that will continue their mutual constitution in the years to come.

Notes

1. Many thanks to Hannah Wittman and Alex Latta, both of whom provided extensive comments on early drafts of this chapter.
2. Reports vary on the number of campesinos killed; no military deaths occurred (Dunkerley 1984).
3. Unless otherwise noted, the source for this section is the *New Political Constitution of Bolivia* (2008), published by the government in the lead-up to the national referendum in which the constitution was approved.
4. John Cameron (2010) notes that eighteen indigenous communities sought to hold autonomy referenda; however, only twelve were able to comply with the bureaucratic restrictions established under Morales's interim framework for indigenous autonomy, which was in force between August 2009 and July 2010.
5. The tension between the MAS's development plans and the natural resource policy preferences of local indigenous peoples is perhaps best illustrated by the case of a proposed highway that would bisect the Isiboro-Sécure Indigenous Territory and National Park (TIPNIS) in the departments of Cochabamba and Beni. This major infrastructure and development project emerged as one of the country's most significant and contentious political issues in late 2011.

References

Albro, R. (2010) 'Confounding Cultural Citizenship and Constitutional Reform in Bolivia,' *Latin American Perspectives,* Vol. 37, No. 3, pp. 71–90.

Beasley-Murray, J., M. Cameron and E. Hershberg. (2010) 'Latin America's Left Turns: A Tour d'Horizon,' in M. Cameron and E. Hershberg (eds), *Latin America's Left Turns: Politics, Policies, and Trajectories of Change.* Boulder: Lynne Rienner Publishers, pp. 1–20.

Bolpress. (2009) 'El INRA Revertirá 10 Haciendas que Mantienen en Condición de Servidumbre a Medio Centenar de Familias Guaraníes,' *Bolpress,* 5 February.

Cameron, J. (2010) 'Is this What Autonomy Looks Like? Tensions and Challenges in the Construction of Indigenous Autonomy in Bolivia.' Paper prepared for the Latin American Studies Association Conference in Toronto, Canada, 8–9 October.

Cameron, M. (2010) 'The State of Democracy in the Andes: Introduction to a Thematic Issue of *Revista de Ciencia Política,*' *Revista de Ciencia Política,* Vol. 30, No. 1, pp. 5–20.

Carvalho, E., and A. Mejía. (2009) *Bolivia Update: Working with a New Constitution,* online report, http://as.americas-society.org/article.php?id=1505 (accessed 12 April 2010).

Centro de Comunicación y Desarrollo Andino et al. (2004) *Hacia una Asamblea Constituyente Soberana y Participativa.* Cochabamba, Bolivia: Centro de Comunicación y Desarrollo Andino et al.

Corte Nacional Electoral (CNE). (2010) 'Que Elegiremos el 4 de Abril: Elecciones Departmentales y Municipales 2010.' Public Information Document #3, La Paz, Bolivia: Corte Nacional Electoral.

Dangl, B. (2010) *Dancing with Dynamite: Social Movements and States in Latin America*. Oakland: AK Press.

Dunkerley, J. (1984) *Rebellion in the Veins: Political Struggle in Bolivia, 1952–1982*. London: Verso.

EFE. (2010) 'Cocaleros Amenazan con No Dejar Pasar Marcha de la CIDOB,' online report, http://www.jornadanet.com/n.php?a=49611-1 (accessed 21 May 2011).

Friedman-Rudovsky, J. (2009) 'For Lithium Car Batteries, Bolivia Is in the Driver's Seat,' *Time Magazine*, 22 January.

Gamarra, E. (2003) 'Political Parties since 1964: The Construction of Bolivia's Multiparty System,' in M. Grindle and P. Domingo (eds), *Proclaiming Revolution: Bolivia in Comparative Perspective*. London: Institute of Latin American Studies, pp. 289–317.

Gordon, G., and A. Luoma. (2008) 'Oil and Gas: The Elusive Wealth beneath Their Feet,' in J. Shultz and M. Draper (eds), *Dignity and Defiance: Stories from Bolivia's Challenge to Globalization*. Berkeley: University of California Press, pp. 77–116.

Gray Molina, G. (2003) 'The Offspring of 1952: Poverty, Exclusion and the Promise of Popular Participation,' in M. Grindle and P. Domingo (eds), *Proclaiming Revolution: Bolivia in Comparative Perspective*. London: Institute of Latin American Studies, pp. 345–363.

Grugel, J., and P. Riggirozzi (eds). (2009) *Governance after Neoliberalism in Latin America*. New York: Palgrave Macmillan.

Gustafson, B. (2010) 'When States Act Like Movements: Dismantling Local Power and Seating Sovereignty in Post-Neoliberal Bolivia,' *Latin American Perspectives*, Vol. 36, No. 4, pp. 48–66.

Hochstetler, K., and E. Friedman. (2008) 'Can Civil Society Organizations Solve the Crisis of Partisan Representation in Latin America?' *Latin American Politics and Society*, Vol. 50, No. 2, pp. 1–32.

Humphreys Bebbington, D., and A. Bebbington (2010) 'Anatomy of a Regional Conflict: Tarija and Resource Grievances in Morales's Bolivia,' *Latin American Perspectives*, Vol. 37, No. 4, pp. 140–160.

Inter-American Commission on Human Rights (IACHR). (2007) *Access to Justice and Social Inclusion: Strengthening Democracy in Bolivia*. Washington: Organization of American States.

Kaup, B. (2008) 'Negotiating through Nature: The Resistant Materiality and Materiality of Resistance in Bolivia's Natural Gas Sector,' *Geoforum*, Vol. 39, pp. 1734–1742.

———. (2010) 'A Neoliberal Nationalization? The Constraints on Natural-Gas-Led Development in Bolivia,' *Latin American Perspectives*, Vol. 37, No. 3, pp. 123–138.

Klein, H. (1992) *Bolivia: The Evolution of a Multi-Ethnic Society*. New York: Oxford University Press.

Kohl, B., and L. Farthing. (2006) *Impasse in Bolivia: Neoliberal Hegemony and Popular Resistance*. New York: Zed Books.

Macdonald, L., and A. Ruckert. (2009) 'Post Neoliberalism in the Americas: An Introduction,' in L. Macdonald and A. Ruckert (eds), *Post-Neoliberalism in the Americas*. New York: Palgrave Macmillan, pp. 1–20.

Malloy, J. (1977) 'Authoritarianism and Corporatism: The Case of Bolivia,' in J. Malloy (ed.), *Authoritarianism and Corporatism in Latin America*. Pittsburgh: University of Pittsburgh Press, pp. 459–485.

Moore, J. (2010) '"Amsterdam is Standing on Norway" Part I: The Alchemy of Capital, Empire and Nature in the Diaspora of Silver, 1545–1648,' *Journal of Agrarian Change*, Vol. 10, No. 1, pp. 33–68.

New Political Constitution of Bolivia. (2008) Vice-Presidency of the Republic of Bolivia and the Constituent Assembly's Presidential Representative. October.

Roberts, B. (1996) 'The Social Context of Citizenship in Latin America,' *International Journal of Urban and Regional Research*, Vol. 20, No. 1, pp. 38–65.

Sader, E. (2008) *Posneoliberalismo en América Latina*. Buenos Aires: CLACSO-CTA Ediciones.

Schaefer, T. (2009) 'Engaging Modernity: The Political Making of Indigenous Movements in Bolivia and Ecuador, 1900–2008,' *Third World Quarterly*, Vol. 30, No. 2, pp. 397–413.

Sobhan, R. (1993) *Agrarian Reform and Social Transformation: Preconditions for Development*. London: Zed Books.

Solón, P. (2010) 'Bolivia's New Political Space: An Interview With Ambassador Pablo Solón,' *North American Congress on Latin America*, 15 March.

Taylor, M. (2009) 'The Contradictions and Transformations of Neoliberalism in Latin America: From Structural Adjustment to "Empowering the Poor",' in L. Macdonald and A. Ruckert (eds), *Post-Neoliberalism in the Americas*. New York: Palgrave Macmillan, pp. 21–36.

Tockman, J. (2005) 'Bolivia Pulls Back From The Brink Of Civil War,' online report, http://www.zcommunications.org/bolivia-pulls-back-from-the-brink-of-civil-war-by-jason-tockman (accessed 8 January 2011).

———. (2008) 'An Analysis of Bolivia's New Framework for Social, Political and Economic Regional Integration.' Master's thesis, Latin American Studies, Simon Fraser University.

Union Federation of Bolivian Mine Workers (FSTMB). (1946) *Thesis of Pulacayo*. Pulacayo, Bolivia: FSTMB.

Van Cott, D. L. (2005) *From Movements to Parties in Latin America*. New York: Cambridge University Press.

Yashar, D. (2005) *Contesting Citizenship in Latin America: The Rise of Indigenous Movements and the Postliberal Challenge*. New York: Cambridge University Press.

Chile is Timber Country

Citizenship, Justice and Scale in
the Chilean Native Forest Market Campaign

Adam Henne and Teena Gabrielson

Quien no conoce el bosque chileno no conoce este planeta.

—Pablo Neruda, 1974

Neruda's famous claim, 'Anyone who hasn't been in the Chilean forest doesn't know this planet', is used widely in Chile by environmentalists, travel agents and chambers of commerce. In its simplicity, the line is appealing, but also deceptive. 'The Chilean Forest' is not by any means a single entity, and attempts to cast it in that light are deeply political projects, with serious implications for citizenship and social natures. As Bruce Braun (2002) noted in the context of Canadian forestry, the forest that is an object of forest conflicts is actually an assemblage of shifting discourses and political practices. What piece of landscape can even be considered as 'forest' is in part a product of the political activity of variously situated actors. At the same time, different political actors are constituted out of conflicts over forest landscapes. In this way, timber companies, international environmental NGOs and indigenous activists are all part of a larger Chilean social ecology. Moreover, the forest is an assemblage of people, non-human nature, artefacts and technologies within larger ecological, economic, cultural, discursive and political networks. In conceptualizing the Chilean forest as a technonature, we draw on the recent work of Damian White and Chris Wilbert (2009, 6) to examine the diverse social natures of the forest and the extent to which these natures are 'technologically mediated, produced, enacted, and contested'. By attending to the mediation and production of the forest, we highlight the ways in which specific forms of knowledge are bound to particular scale-frames. Thus, they come to serve as axes of inclusion and exclusion within the discourses of citizenship that are articulated in and through the construction of specific technonatures.

In particular, we are concerned with the implications for citizenship and justice that are written into forest conflicts, often elided in nature discourse like that of Neruda's poem. What version of 'Chilean' do we understand when we speak of 'the Chilean forest'? Somewhat surprisingly, academic studies of environmental citizenship and environmental justice have not been well integrated (Dobson 2003; Agyeman and Evans 2006), although a number of recent normative and empirical works seek to bridge this gap (Kurtz 2005; Latta 2007a, 2008; Sandler and Pezzullo 2007; Smith and Pangsapa 2008; Sze et al. 2009; see also de Castro, this volume). The concept of scale emerges in these studies as a particularly trenchant means of examining the complex power dynamics of environmental conflict. As Erik Swyngedouw (2007, 24) explains, 'socio-environmental projects are predicated upon scalar tactics and strategies.'

In what follows, we envision the Chilean forest as a 'technonature' open to diverse but unequal constructions of citizenship subjectivity, socio-spatial relations, political economies and environmental value. Using the Chilean Native Forest Market Campaign as an example,[1] we turn to the concept of scale to illuminate the ways in which discourses of citizenship come to articulate logics of inclusion and exclusion through the construction of 'environmental formations' or the 'historically contingent articulations between environmental imaginaries, natural resource allocations, and political economies' (Sundberg 2008, 569). In our analysis, both Chilean environmental NGOs and the timber industry construct environmental formations that bind scale and science to legitimate the exclusion of the Mapuche. In contrast, the Mapuche articulate an understanding of citizenship that draws together community self-determination with a traditional concept of territory that includes both humans and non-humans. Our 'technonatural' analysis shows the pivotal role of scale in negotiating the claims of justice within competing discourses of citizenship.

The Technonatural Assemblage

White and Wilbert (2009) propose 'technonatures' as a concept that captures the increasing extent to which technologies saturate the everyday experience of socially produced natures. The authors use the term to highlight

> a growing range of voices ruminating over the claim not only that we are inhabiting diverse social natures but also that knowledges of our worlds are, within such social natures, ever more technologically mediated, produced, enacted, and contested, and, furthermore, that diverse peoples find themselves, or perceive themselves as ever more *entangled* with things – that is, with technological, ecological, cultural, urban, and ecological networks and diverse hybrid materialities and non-human agencies. (6)

Such entanglements are deeply political in that technonatures both articulate and embody social, cultural, economic and political power relations. Thus, the construction of any particular technonature relies on the mobilization of power networks or 'allied group[s] of social elites, together with particular discursive and material enrolments of nature, around a distinct socio-environmental project' (Swyngedouw 2007, 10). While 'technonatures' can describe the co-constructive action of subalterns as well as social elites, as becomes clear with the case of the Mapuche, elites often dominate the political process. At the time of the Chilean Native Forest Market Campaign, the dominant voices in the technonatural construction of the Chilean Forest belonged to the Chilean state and timber industries.

It would be difficult to overstate the importance of the forest industry to the Chilean economy. Wood products have been a major growth industry for decades; export volume has grown from 2.2 billion dollars in 2002 to 5.5 billion dollars in 2008 (falling to 4.2 billion dollars with the downturn in 2009). This growth puts the forest product industry second only to copper mining in terms of contribution to the Chilean economy (INFOR 2010). Driven by this overwhelming profitability, the plantation sector has expanded rapidly. Chile's forestry agency calculated that plantations, overwhelmingly made up of exotic Monterey pine (*Pinus radiata*), covered more than 14 per cent of Chile's total forested land for a total of more than 2.3 million hectares (INFOR 2010). This marks a staggering increase from fifteen thousand hectares in 1940 and only eighty thousand hectares even into the 1980s (Clapp 1998). Supporters of the plantation model of forestry production describe plantations as *replacement* forests, taking harvesting pressure off native forests (Hartwig 1994; Sedjo and Botkin 1997); at least in Chile, though, research suggests that the lack of incentive to conserve native forest continues to promote their exploitation and eventual conversion to plantation (Clapp 2001).

Most of the remaining native forests in Chile are temperate rainforests, an increasingly threatened ecotype. Chile possesses about a third of the world's remaining intact temperate rainforest (Wilcox 1996; Neira, Verscheure and Revenga 2002). While not as rich in biodiversity as their tropical cousins due to their geographic isolation, Chilean forests show a very high degree of species endemism (Aagesen 1995). Twenty-eight out of eighty-four plant species are endemic, as well as eleven species of mammals, twenty-four species of amphibians and thirteen species each of birds and fish (Neira, Verscheure and Revenga 2002, 13). In addition to their biodiversity, Chilean forests serve important ecosystemic functions, maintaining hydrological cycles and soil stability, protecting watersheds and even acting as a carbon sink due to their exceptionally large standing biomass (Neira, Verscheure and Revenga 2002).

Native forest cover is currently being lost at a rate of 120,000 to 200,000 hectares each year; at this rate, all native forest throughout the central region of the country could be gone within twenty-five years (Echeverria et al. 2006; Wilcox 1996). A number of factors are at work in this deforestation process, including agricultural clearing, firewood harvesting and forest fires. The greatest single factor driving the loss of native forest, however, is the growth of the plantation timber industry (Catalán 1999) – an industry deeply indebted to technological innovation, largely through the support of the Chilean state.

Dating back to the Pinochet regime, the state has used a variety of mechanisms to support the timber industry. The state funds research into silvicultural chemicals, harvest and management modelling and tree improvement, including quite advanced biotechnology via Chile's Instituto Forestal *and* well-funded university forestry departments, which were notably immune to criticism during the dictatorship's purging of universities. Management research includes social as well as biological technologies: integrative modelling software that can simulate forest growth and harvest patterns alongside labour cycles and transportation costs (Bluth 2002; Camus 2006). The state has also provided and/or protected land for forestry to the extent of confiscating it from indigenous or campesino cooperatives, while providing significant tax incentives to cover land purchases and other start-up costs of timber production (Hartwig 1994; Aylwin 2001; Frias 2003; Quiroga 2003; Camus 2006). Finally, the state has prevented the interference of organized labour or indigenous claims through a variety of union-busting actions, typically framed as 'anti-terrorist' police actions (McFall 2001; Frias 2003; Klubock 2004; Ray 2007).

Unlike forest conflicts in Southeast Asia or the Amazon, which revolve around multinational timber companies, the Chilean Native Forest Market Campaign targeted domestic companies. The owners of Compañía Manufacturera de Papeles y Cartones (CMPC) and Arauco (Grupo Matte and the Angelini family, respectively) constitute some of the greatest concentrations of wealth in Chile, with extensive holdings in manufacturing, petrochemicals, mining and hydroelectric generation. These industry leaders make political capital from their dominant position in the Chilean economy, maintaining a great deal of influence in parliamentary politics. While the military dictatorship made this influence most explicit, Matte and Angelini have had a hand in the crafting of state economic policy since their emergence among the small group of families in Chile's socio-economic elite in the early twentieth century (Fazio 2005). Post-dictatorship governments have grappled with this legacy of interventionist capital, with varying degrees of commitment and limited success at insulating themselves from its influence (Carruthers 2001; Ffrench-Davis 2002; Silva 2002). It is the thorough and persistent intermingling of state and capital that has underwritten the economic and political projects linked to the plantation sector's dramatic expansion.

Chile's environmental movement, as noted, has framed the issue of forest protection and loss primarily around the conversion of native forest to timber plantation. At stake in that conversion is the national patrimony of biodiversity that native forests represent. Biodiversity as a concept in forest conflicts has global resonance and a thorny history (Zerner 1996; Escobar 1998; Braun 2002); some have suggested that the quantitative underpinnings of biodiversity conservation serve as a sort of scientific proxy for fuzzier notions like wilderness or the sublime landscape that drove earlier periods of nature conservation (Song and M'Gonigle 2001; Whitten, Holmes and Mackinnon 2001; Carolan 2006). The Chilean movement does not carry the history of colonial preservationism that characterizes the field in North America and Europe; the birth of the movement is often dated to the founding of the Comité Pro-Defensa de la Fauna y Flora (Fauna and Flora Defence Committee, or CODEFF) in 1968, when many of the current leaders were graduate students in the biological sciences (CODEFF 2005). Current efforts to protect Chile's forests draw discursively and materially on biodiversity conservation as a global and highly technology-mediated phenomenon:

> The global significance of Chile's forests has been recognized by multiple well-known international conservation organizations such as World Wildlife Fund, Conservation International and the World Conservation Union. WWF, for example, has catalogued Chile's temperate forests as one of the top conservation-priority forest ecoregions in the Southern Hemisphere [Global 200], while CI and IUCN have identified Chile's forests as one of the 25 'hot spots' for biodiversity conservation in the world. (Neira, Verscheure and Revenga 2002, 18)

'Biodiversity hot spots' and the 'Global 200' are systems developed by the largest international environmental NGOs for setting biodiversity priorities at a global scale. This view from above is accomplished via a complex array of species population algorithms, satellite imaging and GIS modelling. Ecoregional planning as a conservation and management strategy is explicit about its commitment to visualizing and acting upon biodiversity across national borders, despite the political and epistemological problems this entails (Brosius and Russell 2003; Brosius 2004). For Chilean NGOs to cast their national patrimony, the 'Chilean forest', in this global technocratic frame is a tense but unambiguous statement about what sort of technonature they aim to defend.

Where environmentalists are concerned with the threat plantations pose to biodiverse native forests, the establishment of new plantations on *non*-forested land is not without controversy. The majority of pine plantations are located in Chile's VIII, IX and X regions, an area that corresponds closely to the territory recognized by the Spanish crown during the colonial period as belonging to the indigenous Mapuche. While population and land tenure have of course shifted dramatically in the three hundred years since that recognition, more than 200,000 Mapuche, or nearly a third of those living in Chile, still live in the rural areas of these three regions (INE 2003). With a large and marginalized indigenous population already confined to small *reducciones* (reservations) and facing population pressure on their lands, the arrival of a land-hungry new industry was bound to lead to conflict.

Mapuche activists and community leaders argue that the expansion of the plantation sector comes at the expense of their territorial, environmental and political rights. Many of the properties currently being converted into plantations are located within territory returned to the Mapuche under Spanish 'títulos de merced', or claimed by Mapuche cooperatives under the socialist Allende administration and ratified according to the agrarian reform laws. These lands became available to timber companies only after having been taken by force during the military dictatorship's 'rollback' of the land reform (Bengoa 1999; Frias 2003). Even in cases where rights to the lands themselves are not in question, activists claim that the environmental impacts of industrial tree farming on neighbouring properties are threatening the health and livelihoods of indigenous communities. This may take the form of pesticides, erosion, floods, drought, or the lack of access to firewood and wild plants (Catalán 1999; McFall 2001; Rohter 2004). Mapuche concerns overlap with a variety of expert domains and technologies – hydrology and geomorphology in terms of flooding and drought, forest ecology in terms of the extirpation of native food and medicinal species, toxicology in terms of the leaching of pesticides into community water tables and so on. Measuring the extent of these impacts scientifically becomes a challenge to the resources, flexibility and interdisciplinary expertise of researchers and community advocates. As a result, the process of evaluating and documenting impacts and introducing them to public-policy arenas has called for alternative models of doing science, integrating expert research with community monitoring, participatory methods and public activism. Through activist bodies including the Latin American Observatory of Environmental Conflicts (OLCA) and the Institute for Indigenous Studies, Mapuche organizations are attempting to build a network of scientists to document the impact of plantations on their communities by incorporating participatory community research and the first-hand accounts of individuals who have been dislocated or injured (see, for example, Frias 2003; Catalán et al. 2006). This model of 'citizen science' (Irwin 1995; Corburn 2005; Leach, Scoones and Wynne 2005) resonates with the network of expertise and activism familiar to environmental justice circles in North America and also with similar kinds of emerging activism in other parts of Latin America (see Merlinsky and Latta, this volume).

Significantly, however, citizenship discourse as such does not appear in the repertoire of the Mapuche organizations engaged with this campaign. For these activists, as for many contemporary Mapuche, the term *Chilean* refers specifically to non-Mapuche – to *white* Chileans, a category from which they are excluded a priori. Rather than appeal to their rights as citizens of Chile, these activists frame the forest conflict in terms of autonomy and territory. In particular, the concept of *wallmapu*, usually translated as 'territory', explicitly refers to *all* traditional Mapuche territory on both sides of the Chile–Argentina border (Toledo 2006). With equally subversive implications, *wallmapu* also includes non-human persons: animals, trees, rivers and soils, the spirit world. Contemporary activists invoke traditions of solidarity building through reciprocal exchanges of tobacco, dyes, foodstuffs and sacrificial offerings; these circuits historically extended from Pacific to Atlantic coasts, and incorporated mountains, rivers and animal spirits as well as neighbours and extended kin groups (Coña 1930; Hilger 1966). By renovating a territorial principle outside the Chilean state on so many levels, Mapuche activists critique Chile's nexus of state and capital, while positioning themselves as historically and culturally privileged environmental subjects.

As these rich and differing understandings of the Chilean forest suggest, forest landscapes are neither homogeneous entities nor abstract spaces, but spaces of technonature open to multiple imaginings and discursive constructions that bind together non-human nature, citizen subjectivities, artefacts, socio-spatial relations and technological understandings within larger networks of cultural and material flows. In what follows, we demonstrate the centrality of a politics of scale to the different political fortunes of these alternate technonatures in the context of a conflict over the future of Chile's forests in the Chilean Native Forest Market Campaign.

Citizenship, Justice and the Politics of Scale

Originating in the fields of political and radical geography, the concept of scale refers to a fragment of landscape that is understood to be socially produced (Agnew 1997). While conceptions of scale may overlap with ontologically defined geographical boundaries, as in the familiar conceptions of local, urban, regional, national and global, scale is the product of social relations and political contestation. The politics of scale, or the 'production, reconfiguration, or contestation of particular differentiations, orderings and hierarchies among geographical scales', permeates discussions of environment (Brenner 2001, 600). Questions of scale are critical to understanding the discursive framing of environmental problems and solutions, the mobilization and counter-mobilization of constituencies and the construction and adoption of political strategies by various parties to environmental conflict (Williams 1999; Towers 2000; Kurtz 2003; Bickerstaff and Agyeman 2009; Sze et al. 2009). In an effort to identify how activists contend with the 'social complexity and spatial ambiguity inherent in environmental justice disputes', Hilda Kurtz (2003, 892, 894) turns to 'scale frames' or 'the discursive practices that construct meaningful (and actionable) linkages between the scale at which a social problem is experienced and the scale(s) at which it could be politically addressed or resolved'.

The frame of particular interest here is scale as means of inclusion/exclusion, primarily because of its bearing on questions of citizenship. As critics often note, as much as citizenship defines a community of equals empowered to engage in decision making regarding collective welfare, it also establishes the boundaries of that community and marks those excluded. It should come as no surprise, then, that actors in environmental conflict often draw on discourses of citizenship to articulate scale frames of inclusion and exclusion so as to advance their own interests. Such frames can integrate aggrieved parties into larger social movements, or they may legitimate the exclusion of the aggrieved by marginalizing and circumscribing their claims (Towers 2000; Kurtz 2003, 2005; Sundberg 2008; Sze et al. 2009).

The processes by which exclusionary scale frames become legitimized are often deeply intertwined with processes of racialization. It seems wise to approach this point with caution, as Latin America's racial regimes do not map neatly onto the models of racial discrimination developed by environmental justice scholars in North America. Nonetheless, if we consider race as an historical process rather than a demographic category (Pulido 1996), the relevance to the Chilean context becomes clearer. As Juanita Sundberg (2008, 571) explains, 'White supremacy and white privilege inform legal systems, and everyday understandings of self and other, as well as the organization of space, place, and, I argue, conceptions of appropriate natural resource management.' Drawing upon several distinct historical examples from Latin America, Sundberg shows the intertwining of processes of racialization and the construction of environmental formations. In the modern era, such articulations are often central to defining the boundaries of citizenship (see also Sundberg's contribution to this volume).

In the environmental formations that emerge, the ideal citizen is often depicted as one who is positioned to know or imagine, and potentially engage in, a very particular green 'good life' that draws heavily on Western conceptions of the non-human natural world and humans' appropriate relation to it (Gabrielson and Parady 2010). With an intellectual history based in colonialism and industrial urbanization, such green ideals often depend upon a deeply entrenched nature/culture dualism, a vision of the non-human natural world as either ripe for development or as pristine nature to be protected and defended (Latta 2007b). As it travels from Global North to Global South, or from affluent white Chile to marginal indigenous Chile, the dualistic ethics resonate with existing hierarchies of value. Across these formations, expert, abstract and scientific forms of knowledge often come to legitimate exclusions rooted in misrecognition (Kurtz 2009). In a discussion of the racialized state, Kurtz (2009) explains how the particular and experiential knowledge of environmental justice activists is often pitted against the more abstract, scientific and expert knowledge of the state that reinforces a 'liberal universality that does no small disservice to non-white populations' (693).

Exclusionary discourses that privilege expert forms of knowledge are often central to the construction of specific environmental formations and deeply bound up with a politics of scale. Scale is not ontologically given, but constructed through political conflict and articulated discursively, politically and geographically. These articulations are key in constituting the environmental imaginary or discursive ideal that defines a particular environmental formation; from them emerge the networks necessary to mobilize a constituency that can institute and maintain that particular ideal. Further, 'these relational scalar networks articulate with produced *territorial* or geographical configurations that also exhibit scalar dimensions' (Swyngedouw 2007). In the case of the Chilean Native Forest Market Campaign, the politics of scale reveal an underlying consensus between the Chilean timber industry and environmental NGOs. On the face of it, the two groups' environmental formations would seem to pit preservation against development. However, underlying this surface conflict exists a shared reliance on an international scalar dimension that includes networks of transnational environmental NGOs, North American consumers and an international timber market. Attending to the conflicting scalar dimensions at work in this case illuminates the ways in which the geo-political networks binding the Global North and South prompt a construction of Chilean citizenship conducive to the interests of both native forest preservation and plantation development. This underlying consensus develops at the expense of the community autonomy and territorial sovereignty of the Mapuche.

The Chilean Native Forest Market Campaign

The roots of the campaign lie in earlier attempts to pressure wood retailers in the United States to raise their environmental standards for wood products. Beginning in 1997, Rainforest Action Network (RAN) launched a campaign against Home Depot and other United States retailers of forest products. The campaign consisted of boycotts and letter writing, as well as dramatic street theatre events involving banner hangings, lockdowns, a giant inflatable dinosaur and so on. A number of celebrities, including R.E.M. and the Dave Matthews Band, added to the pressure. In 1999, Home Depot responded to the extended campaign by announcing a commitment to stop selling wood from 'environmentally sensitive areas'. The home improvement megastore denied that they were responding to pressure from environmentalists, and described the policy change as the result of lengthy consideration of their 'responsibility as a global leader to help protect endangered forests' (Hagerty 1999). Nonetheless, environmental activists used this victory as a point of leverage to encourage Home Depot to pursue more proactive policies and to pressure other retailers to follow their example.

In 2002, Chilean environmental NGOs (Defensores del Bosque Chileno, CODEFF and Fundación Terram, among others) began writing letters to 'more than 100 forestry businesses speaking of the necessity of putting an end to the replacement of native forests by forest plantations' (Sanger, in Anderson 2003). Only one responded, in the negative, and indeed there had been precious little dialogue in Chile at that point on the subject of more sustainable logging practices. Another controversial aspect of the campaign at this point was the participation of famed Chilean novelist Isabel Allende, who joined Defensores del Bosque Chileno in encouraging Chilean producers to harvest more sustainably, and called on North American consumers to purchase only sustainable wood products. Allende's participation was decried as treason (González 2002).

On 13 September 2002, North American NGO ForestEthics, cosponsored by a large alliance of environmental groups, placed a full-page advertisement in the *New York Times* asking North American consumers to avoid buying wood products unsustainably harvested in Chile. While the environmentalists were at pains to point out that the ad was calling for educated consumerism rather than an outright boycott of Chilean wood (Anderson 2003), this did little to protect them from criticism. Chilean timber companies were outraged, lambasting the Chilean cosponsors of the advertisement as traitors to Chile. As anthropologist Julia Paley (2001) points out, such attacks are a common strategy used against critics of government or corporate policy in post-dictatorship Chile; any form of dissent is seen as a threat to fragile democratic and development projects.

Before the end of 2002, however, the tide began to turn. At the request of Aaron Sanger of ForestEthics, Home Depot officially approached their suppliers in Chile asking them to reconsider their position. After the original RAN Old Growth Campaign against them, the North American corporation had learned its lesson about environmental politics. Newly appointed 'environmental global project manager' Ron Jarvis was explicitly tasked with the mission of maintaining the corporation's credibility as an environmentally sound retailer. He had demonstrated the ability to negotiate complex environmental issues in earlier work with Indonesian suppliers, and led Home Depot to take a principled stand against that country's unsustainable logging practices (Carlton 2004).

At Jarvis's urging, and with the threat of a pullout by Home Depot hanging over them, Chile's two largest timber companies, CMPC and Arauco, agreed to meet with the coalition behind the market campaign. The first set of meetings took place at Home Depot's main offices in Atlanta, with Ron Jarvis as mediator. Representatives from United States groups ForestEthics, RAN and American Lands Alliance joined Chilean environmentalists from Defensores del Bosque Chileno, Greenpeace Chile and Instituto del Ecología Política in pressing CMPC and Arauco for dramatic changes in their practices. According to several of the representatives present, the companies surprised the environmentalists with their willingness to discuss sustainable harvesting. The principal of non-substitution (that is, not converting native forest to plantation) became central to the discussion. The companies claimed not to have been engaged in substitution for many years, a claim the environmentalists contested vigorously, but both parties agreed that eliminating substitution was a positive goal. No documents were signed at this point, and all parties seemed to agree that the discussions were tense, productive, but largely preliminary. Towards the end of the meetings, the timber companies proposed that the second round of discussions take place in Chile, along with a visit to their properties to demonstrate their conservation and sustainable harvest practices.

Thus in July 2003, North American environmentalists joined their Chilean counterparts on a walking tour of CMPC and Arauco's forestry operations. Jason Tockman, taking part as a representative of the American Lands Alliance, later described the event as a 'dog and pony show'. The other environmentalists generally agreed that the event was a careful public relations operation, and that the private parks and selective harvest experiments on display were not representative of the companies' practices in general. Nonetheless, the discussions established the grounds for compromise. While the content remained uncertain, it was clear that both sectors would at some point sign an agreement putting an end to the campaign and committing the companies to more sustainable practices. Negotiations over the content of the agreement continued by email and teleconference for several months.

Significant differences of opinion appeared among interview subjects as far as when and to what extent the interests of Mapuche activists entered into the campaign. Mapuche activists argued that they had lent information and support to the campaign from the beginning. Chilean environmentalists say that from the start, the campaign was based on native forests and never addressed issues of Mapuche territorial rights. As the negotiations towards a final agreement progressed, the contested role of Mapuche activists in the campaign became more salient. In September 2003, ForestEthics and American Lands Alliance invited Alfredo Seguel, of the Mapuche organization Konapewman, to speak about Chilean forest issues at the counterforum outside the WTO ministerial in Cancún. Jason Tockman of American

Lands Alliance accompanied Seguel and handled his travel arrangements; in the process, the two became friends. Towards the end of the forum, Seguel expressed his concern to Tockman that the environmentalists in the campaign were negotiating with the timber companies. How, he asked, could environmentalists sign deals regarding the sustainable use of territories that by right belonged to the Mapuche, especially when the timber companies at the table were primary actors in the repression of those rights? Tockman took this concern very much to heart, and brought the issue back to his colleagues in the United States. While all agreed that the issue was important, Tockman says he was the only one who felt that it might require calling off negotiations.Towards the end of September, American Lands Alliance invited Pablo Huaiquilao, another member of Konapewman, to take part in a speaking tour of the United States. Huaiquilao travelled the Southeast with Tockman and an indigenous Mexican activist, speaking about the impact of pine plantations on Mapuche communities. He was also concerned about the negotiations still taking place, and asked Tockman to pressure his colleagues to withdraw. So late in the game withdrawal seemed improbable, but Tockman encouraged Huaiquilao and others in Konapewman to put their concerns in writing as soon as possible. The North American environmental activists emphasized that they were anticipating a written intervention from the Mapuche activists and further dialogue from their Chilean NGO counterparts; unfortunately, neither of these written communiqués appeared until after the agreement was signed.

In November 2003 the environmentalists and the timber companies (along with Home Depot) signed an agreement. CMPC and Arauco committed to end substitution on their properties, to end the promotion of substitution by other contracted parties and to refuse to purchase timber from lands converted after a given period of time. In return, the environmentalists lent their support to the companies' harvesting practices and private conservation on their own properties. According to many of the environmentalists interviewed, the content had been agreed on from the early stages of negotiation; the remaining contention revolved around the language of the agreement: 'It's just a matter of working out the details, just a few words of disagreement. Of course the companies wanted us to sing praises of them and talk about how wonderful their forest operations were, where environmentalists, their objective was to get as many commitments and statements out of the company, so we both had an agenda. ... So the objective was to find common ground.' The language of the agreement is indeed quite non-specific, including statements such as 'NGOs recognize the leadership that CMPC and Arauco have in the Chilean forestry industry' and 'Companies recognize that collaborating with NGOs on the Conservation Assessments can help them continue their commitment to environmental responsibility.' Echoing the language of Home Depot's concessions in 1999, the timber companies gave no indication that they were pressured into signing the agreement by the campaign: 'These initiatives reflect CMPC's and Arauco's interest in protecting Chile's native forests' (Defensores del Bosque Chileno 2003).

The environmental organizations announced the agreement as a victory for Chile's forests, and put an end to the more visible aspects of their campaign against the timber industry. The signing of the agreement, however, marked a transitional rather than a final phase of the campaign. Defensores del Bosque Chileno began describing the new phase of the campaign as the 'Chilean Joint Solutions Process'; as their communications director described it, the 'campaign *with* the timber companies, together'. The companies are collaborating with university researchers to define maps of conservation targets within their properties, while the environmental organizations prepare local 'community monitoring' groups to oversee compliance with the standards of the agreement.

As the timber companies and the environmental movement formalized this new stage of their relationship, the Mapuche activists finally went public with their complaints. An open letter to the NGO members of the campaign appeared in a number of print and online venues, in which a Mapuche coalition (the Coordination of Mapuche Organizations and Territorial Identities, CITEM) denounced the agreement and called for a new and more critical wave in the campaign *against* the timber companies:

> To establish any negotiation with these companies is to contribute to the washing of their image, to continue consolidation of the international wood export markets, and to continue to ignore the fundamental problems that exist in these territories. ... Our spirit and interest is to stop the forestry expansion for the protection of the natural resources in these areas and to transform the current social, political and legislative relationships that the Mapuche communities face with the Chilean State. ... We believe in the path that you had shown, involving a campaign of criticism and awareness that you generated in the US. Therefore, we encourage you to continue in that way, and not to negotiate, and we urge you to engage in strategies that can be taken accordingly. (CITEM 2003)

Inclusion and Exclusion in the Chilean Native Forest Market Campaign

In the realm of public discourse, timber companies present themselves as benevolent caretakers of the Chilean landscape, transforming degraded pastures and 'wasted space' into productive forests that benefit all citizens. Particularly noteworthy here are the advertising campaigns, including the aforementioned billboards, '*Chile: País Forestal*' (Chile: Timber Country) and the more recent campaign, '*Bosques para Chile*' (Forests for Chile). In a series of TV and radio spots, a child asks her doting father how plants grow in their garden. The father describes how a good gardener nurtures plants and soil, stepping in at just the right time to lend nature a helping hand. A kindly voiceover completes the analogy between forestry and gardening, explaining that timber companies nurture the forests to help nature provide her bounty to all of Chile.

In spite of intensive state investment in the industry, timber companies continue to argue that private property is the paramount value of democracy; as in most liberal discourses, the role of the state is to empower individuals. This is best illustrated by the production of Chile's 'weak or absent regulation'; as Alex Clapp (1998) notes, there is persistent political pressure against regulating the forest industry in any way that might threaten this critical source of revenue. The 2007 Native Forest Law was the product of fifteen years of bitter debate and backroom dealing; many of Chile's environmentalists consider it already dangerously compromised (Firmani 2008). In summary, a discourse of benevolent private interests is mobilized to cover the intervention of a cronyist state in support of a high-tech, rationalized industry. The timber industry cultivates natural resources to provide for all Chilean citizens and thereby fulfils both a paternalistic and nationalist role. But, in doing so, we see here that cutting-edge forest technologies are just one part of a citizenship model that Neil Harvey (2001) refers to as neoliberal or market citizenship, 'in which subjects are created by the extension of individual property rights and capitalist rationality' (1046; see also Schild 1998; Baldwin and Meltzer, this volume). As the campaign and its outcome suggest, Chilean environmentalists have mostly been willing to engage with the model of market-based citizenship that the timber companies promote. The communications director of Defensores del Bosque told me, when I asked about the organization's strategies towards government environmental regulation, 'We believe that the international market generating conscience in the consumers, generating pressures on the distributors of Chilean wood, can serve someday to change the situation within Chile.' As noted, environmentalists actively rejected any reference to the earlier boycott campaign as a campaign 'against' the timber companies: 'No no, this is a campaign *with* the timber companies, together.'

The campaign itself cast the fundamental conflict between environmentalists and timber companies in a shared conceptual language with an agreed-upon technonatural object – the fate of the Chilean forest – that enabled explicit disagreement, negotiation, agreement and subsequent collaboration. Linked to this shared vision of the forest was a citizenship discourse that made Mapuche claims latent to the negotiation over its future, their place within the campaign marginal and easily erased. Consistent with the Chilean state's long-standing commitment to an 'ideology of national homogeneity' (Latta 2007a, 232), both the timber companies and Chilean environmental NGOs involved in the campaign constructed environmental formations that tied the future of Chile's forests to the good of all of its citizens. This nationalist environmental imaginary, whether it privileged economic development or the preservation of native forests, became projected into international networks of power in such a way as to discredit the more local and culturally specific claims of the indigenous Mapuche. Thus, while North American consumers are empowered to pressure the Chilean timber industry, the distributional inequities in the treatment of the Mapuche are obscured by removing from discussion the question of timber plantations' encroachment on Mapuche lands. More pointedly, the Mapuche's deeply political claims for community, autonomy and territorial sovereignty are bracketed from a negotiation in which the key players share a common understanding of the forest as a technonature to be managed and administered by political elites and technological experts.

While environmentalists in Chile and elsewhere described the agreement as a historic breakthrough, it corresponds to a familiar pattern in Chilean politics known as '*democracia de acuerdos*' (democracy by agreement), also known as 'gentleman's democracy', 'democracy from above' or 'democracy behind closed doors' (Paley 2001). The irony of these qualified 'democracies' is not lost on the Chileans who use the terms. And yet environmental organizations have represented themselves as spokespeople for all of Chile in this sort of negotiation, without seeking to engender a process for broader democratic participation or representation. When asked why the Mapuche did not have an active stake in the campaign, environmental activists frequently replied, 'We are protecting biodiversity for all Chileans, not just one class.' This is a complex situation with multiple implications for who counts as Chilean at all; statements like these clearly cast the Mapuche as not *part* of 'all Chileans', while simultaneously promoting negotiations over the protection of biodiversity as a legitimate venue for that decision. The conflicting scalar dimensions at work in this process of marginalization reveal the extent to which neoliberal frameworks, universal conceptions of citizenship and preservationist objectives can become articulated through scientific discourse. Such discourse, in turn, effectively depoliticizes nature, further delegitimizing community claims to autonomy and calls for more participatory democratic process.

The story of Mapuche involvement with the Chilean Native Forest Market Campaign demonstrates that while collaborations between indigenous activists and environmentalists can be rhetorically powerful in some settings, they can run aground in a number of ways. Potential problems include not just the incommensurable views of nature noted by environmental anthropologists (see, for example, Brosius 1997; West 2006) or the structural conflicts of interest debated by conservationists (Redford and Sanderson 2000; Berkes 2004; also compare Chapin 2004). Equally salient are the mundane and often unintentional issues of who is invited to which meetings and what types of organizations and leaderships should be consulted – everyday forms of racism and exclusion.

Notes

1. The material on the Chilean Native Forest market campaign is based on ethnographic interviews with Mapuche activists and Chilean and North American environmental activists conducted by Adam Henne in 2003. Unless otherwise cited, quoted statements are drawn from these interviews.

References

Aagesen, D. (1995) 'On the Northern Fringe of the South American Temperate Forest,' *Environmental History*, Vol. 3, No. 1, pp. 64–85.

Agnew, J. (1997) 'The Dramaturgy of Horizons: Geographical scale in the 'Reconstruction of Italy' by the New Italian Parties, 1992–95,' *Political Geography*, Vol. 16, pp. 99–121.

Agyeman, J., and B. Evans. (2006) 'Justice, Governance, and Sustainability: Perspectives on Environmental Citizenship from North America and Europe,' in A. Dobson and D. Bell (eds), *Environmental Citizenship*. Cambridge: MIT Press, pp. 185–206.

Anderson, S. (2003) 'Aaron Sanger's El Mercurio Interview,' *Santiago Times*, 11 December.

Aylwin, J. (ed.). (2001) *Políticas Públicas y Pueblo Mapuche*. Concepción: Ediciones Escaparate.

Bengoa, J. (1999) *Historia de un Conflicto: El Estado y los Mapuches en el Siglo XX*. Santiago: Planeta.

Berkes, F. (2004) 'Rethinking Community-Based Conservation,' *Conservation Biology*, Vol. 18, No. 3, pp. 621–630.

Bickerstaff, K., and J. Agyeman. (2009) 'Assembling Justice Spaces: The Scalar Politics of Environmental Justice in North-east England,' *Antipode*, Vol. 41, No. 4, pp. 781–806.

Bluth, A. (2002) *Chile, País Forestal*. Santiago: Corporación Nacional de la Madera.

Braun, B. (2002) *The Intemperate Rainforest: Nature, Culture and Power on Canada's West Coast*. Minneapolis: University of Minnesota Press.

Brenner, N. (2001) 'The Limits to Scale? Methodological Reflections on Scalar Structuration,' *Progress in Human Geography*, Vol. 25, No. 4, pp. 591–614.

Brosius, J. P. (1997) 'Endangered Forests, Endangered Peoples: Environmentalist Representations of Indigenous Knowledge,' *Human Ecology*, Vol. 25, No. 1, pp. 47–69.

———. (2004) 'Seeing Natural and Cultural Communities: Technologies of Visualization in Conservation.' Paper presented to the Berkeley Environmental Politics Working Group, 2 February.

Brosius, J. P., and D. Russell. (2003) 'Conservation from Above: Transboundary Protected Areas and Ecoregional Planning,' *Journal of Sustainable Forestry*, Vol. 17, No. 1/2, pp. 39–65.

Camus, P. (2006) *Ambiente, Bosques y Gestión Forestal en Chile, 1541–2005*. Santiago: LOM.

Carolan, M. (2006) 'The Value and Vulnerabilities of Metaphors within the Environmental Sciences,' *Society and Natural Resources*, Vol. 19, No. 10, pp. 921–930.

Carlton, J. (2004) 'Once Targeted by Protesters, Home Depot Plays a Green Role,' *Wall Street Journal*, 6 August, pp. A1, A6.

Carruthers, D. (2001) 'Environmental Politics in Chile: Legacies of Dictatorship and Democracy,' *Third World Quarterly*, Vol. 22, No. 3, pp. 343–358.

Catalán, R. (1999) *Pueblo Mapuche, Bosque Nativo y Plantaciones Forestales.* Temuco: Ediciones Universidad Católica.

Catalán, R., et al. (eds). (2006) *Bosques y Comunidades del sur de Chile.* Santiago: Editorial Universitaria.

Chapin, M. (2004) 'A Challenge to Conservationists,' *Worldwatch Magazine* November–December, pp. 17–31.

Clapp, R. A. (1998) 'Waiting for the Forest Law: Resource-Led Development and Environmental Politics in Chile,' *Latin American Research Review*, Vol. 33, No. 2, pp. 3–37.

———. (2001) 'Tree Farming and Forest Conservation in Chile? Do Replacement Forests Leave any Originals Behind?' *Society and Natural Resources*, Vol. 14, pp. 341–356.

Coordinación de Identidades Territoriales Mapuche (CITEM). (2003) 'Carta de las Organizaciones Mapuches,' online report, http://www.wrm.org.uy/paises/Chile/articulo3.html (accessed May 2011).

Comité pro Defensa de la Fauna y Flora (CODEFF). (2005) *Ciudadanos de la Tierra: Construyendos Sueños 1968–2005.* Santiago: CODEFF.

Coña, P. (1930) *Vida y Costumbres de los Indígenas Araucanos en la Segunda Mitad del Siglo XIX.* Santiago: Imprenta Cervantes.

Corburn, J. (2005) *Street Science: Community Knowledge and Environmental Health Justice.* Cambridge, MA: MIT Press.

Defensores del Bosque Chileno. (2003) 'Documento de Acuerdo,' online report, http://www.mipapel.cmpc.cl/mipapel69/p2.html (accessed May 2011).

Dobson, A. (2003) *Citizenship and the Environment.* New York: Oxford University Press.

Echeverria, C., et al. (2006) 'Rapid Deforestation and Fragmentation of Chilean Temperate Forests,' *Biological Conservation*, Vol. 130, No. 4, pp. 481–494.

Escobar, A. (1998) 'Whose Knowledge, Whose Nature? Biodiversity, Conservation, and the Political Ecology of Social Movements,' *Journal of Political Ecology*, Vol. 5, pp. 53–82.

Fazio, H. (2005) *Mapa Actual de la Extrema Riqueza en Chile al año 2005.* Santiago: LOM Ediciones.

Ffrench-Davis, R. (2002) *Economic Reforms in Chile: From Dictatorship to Democracy.* Ann Arbor: University of Michigan Press.

Firmani, C. (2008) 'El Bosque Nativo Tiene Ley,' *Biblioteca de Congresa Nacional de Chile*, 4 April, online report, http://www.bcn.cl/carpeta_temas_profundidad/ley-bosque-nativo (accessed May 2011).

Frias, G. (2003) *Invasión Forestal: Khla Nagnegai taiñ Weichangepan.* Toronto: IDRC.

Gabrielson, T., and K. Parady. (2010) 'Corporeal Citizenship: Rethinking Green Citizenship through the Body,' *Environmental Politics*, Vol. 19, No. 3, pp. 374–391.

González, G. (2002) 'Isabel Allende Helps Defend Native Forests,' *Environment Chile*, 24 July, online report, http://www.mapuche-nation.org/english/html/news/n-50.htm (accessed May 2011).

Hagerty, J. (1999) 'Home Depot Vows to Change Policy on "Sensitive" Wood Use,' *Wall Street Journal*, 27 August.

Hartwig, F. (1994) *La Tierra que Recuperamos.* Santiago: Editorial Los Andes.

Harvey, N. (2001) 'Globalization and Resistance in Post-Cold War Mexico,' *Third World Quarterly*, Vol. 22, No. 6, pp. 1045–1061.

Hilger, I. (1966) *Huenun Ñamku: An Araucanian Indian Remembers the Past.* Norman: University of Oklahoma Press.

Instituto Nacional de Estadísticas (INE). (2003) 'Censo 2002: Síntesis de Resultados.' Santiago: INE Chile.

Instituto Nacional Forestal (INFOR). (2010) 'Estadísticas Forestales 2009,' Boletín Estadístico 126. Santiago: INFOR.

Irwin, A. (1995) *Citizen Science: Studies of People, Expertise and Sustainable Development.* London: Routledge.

Klubock, T. M. (2004) 'Labor, Land, and Environmental Change in the Forestry Sector in Chile, 1973–1998,' in P. Winn (ed.), *Victims of the Chilean Miracle.* Durham: Duke University Press, pp. 337–388.

Kurtz, H. (2003) 'Scale Frames and Counter-Scale Frames: Constructing the Problem of Environmental Injustice,' *Political Geography,* Vol. 22, pp. 887–916.

———. (2005) 'Alternative Visions for Citizenship Practice in an Environmental Justice Dispute,' *Space and Polity,* Vol. 9, No. 1, pp. 77–91.

———. (2009) 'Acknowledging the Racial State: An Agenda for Environmental Justice Research,' *Antipode,* Vol. 41, No. 4, pp. 684–704.

Latta, P. A. (2007a) 'Citizenship and the Politics of Nature: The Case of Chile's Alto Bío Bío,' *Citizenship Studies,* Vol. 11, No. 3, pp. 229-246.

———. (2007b) 'Locating Democratic Politics in Ecological Citizenship,' *Environmental Politics,* Vol. 16, No. 3, pp. 377–393.

———. (2008) 'The Ecological Citizen,' in E. Isin (ed.), *Recasting the Social in Citizenship.* Toronto: University of Toronto Press, pp. 239–260.

Leach, M., I. Scoones and B. Wynne. (2005) *Science and Citizens: Globalization and the Challenge of Engagement.* London: Zed Books.

McFall, S. (ed.). (2001) *Territorio Mapuche y Expansión Forestal.* Temuco: Ediciones Escaparate.

Neira, E., H. Verscheure and C. Revenga. (2002) *Bosques Frontera de Chile: Un Patrimonio Natural a Conservar.* Santiago: Instituto de Recursos Mundiales.

Paley, J. (2001) *Marketing Democracy: Power and Social Movements in Post-Dictatorship Chile.* Berkeley: University of California Press.

Pulido, L. (1996) 'A Critical Review of the Methodology of Environmental Racism Research,' *Antipode,* Vol. 28, No. 2, pp. 142–159.

Quiroga, R. (2003) *Comercio, Inversiones y Sustentabilidad: El caso de Chile.* Santiago: LOM.

Ray, L. (2007) *Language of the Land: The Mapuche People in Argentina and Chile.* Copenhagen: IWGIA.

Redford, K., and S. E. Sanderson. (2000) 'Extracting Humans from Nature,' *Conservation Biology,* Vol. 14, No. 5, pp. 1362–1364.

Rohter, L. (2004) 'Mapuche Indians in Chile Struggle to Take Back Forests,' *New York Times,* 11 August.

Sandler, R.,. and P. Pezzullo (eds). (2007) *Environmental Justice and Environmentalism: The Social Justice Challenge to the Environmental Movement.* Cambridge: MIT Press.

Schild, V. (1998) 'Market Citizenship and the 'New Democracies': The Ambiguous Legacies of Contemporary Chilean Women's Movements,' *Social Politics,* Vol. 5, No. 2, pp. 232–249.

Sedjo, R., and D. Botkin. (1997) 'Forest Plantations to Spare Natural Forests,' *Environment,* Vol. 39, No. 10, pp. 14–20.

Silva, E. (2002) 'Capital and the Lagos Presidency: Business as Usual?' *Bulletin of Latin American Research,* Vol. 21, No. 3, pp. 339–357.

Smith, M., and P. Pangsapa. (2008) *Environment and Citizenship: Integrating Justice, Responsibility, and Civic Engagement.* London: Zed Books.

Song, S., and R. M'Gonigle. (2001) 'Science, Power, and System Dynamics: The Political Economy of Conservation Biology,' *Conservation Biology,* Vol. 15, No. 4, pp. 980–989.

Sundberg, J. (2008) 'Placing Race in Environmental Justice Research in Latin America,' *Society and Natural Resources,* Vol. 21, No. 7, pp. 569–582.

Swyngedouw, E., 2007. 'Technonatural Revolutions: The Scalar Politics of Franco's Hydro-Social Dream for Spain, 1939–1975.' *Transactions of the Institute of British Geographers,* Vol. 32, 9–28.

Sze, J., et al. (2009) 'Defining and Contesting Environmental Justice: Socio-natures and the Politics of Scale in the Delta,' *Antipode,* Vol. 41, No. 4, pp. 807–843.

Toledo, V. L. (2006) *Pueblo Mapuche, Derechos Colectivos y Territorio.* Santiago: LOM Ediciones / Chile Sustentable.

Towers, G. (2000) 'Applying the Political Geography of Scale: Grassroots Strategies and Environmental Justice,' *The Professional Geographer,* Vol. 52, No. 1, pp. 23–36.

West, P. (2006) *Conservation is Our Government Now: The Politics of Ecology in Papua New Guinea.* Durham: Duke University Press.

White, D., and C. Wilbert. (2009) 'Inhabiting Technonatural Time/Spaces,' in D. White and C. Wilbert (eds), *Technonatures Environments, Technologies, Spaces, and Places in the Twenty-first Century.* Waterloo: Wilfrid Laurier University Press, pp. 1–32.

Whitten, T., D. Holmes and K. Mackinnon. (2001) 'Conservation Biology: A Displacement Behavior for Academia?' *Conservation Biology,* Vol. 15, No. 1, pp. 1–3.

Wilcox, K. (1996) *Chile's Ancient Forest: A Conservation Legacy.* Redway: Ancient Forests International.

Williams, R. (1999) 'Environmental Injustice in America and its Politics of Scale,' *Political Geography,* Vol. 18, No. 1, pp. 49–73.

Zerner, C. (1996) 'Telling Stories about Biological Diversity,' in S. B. Brush and D. Stabinsky (eds), *Valuing Local Knowledge.* Washington, DC: Island Press, pp. 68–101.

Citizens, Environmental
Governance and the State

Access Denied

Urban Highways, Deliberate Improvisation and Political Impasse in Santiago, Chile

Enrique R. Silva

Starting in the mid 1990s, the Chilean state began an entrepreneurial approach to public works planning in the Ministry of Public Works' (MOP) infrastructure concessions system. In a relatively short period of time, the concessions system – a franchise model that allows private capital to build, operate and profit from large public works – endowed the country and its cities with thousands of kilometres of state-of-the-art highways, among other major works. Unwittingly, the concessions system also provided Chileans opportunities to practice insurgent citizenship (Holston 2008) vis-à-vis their built environment, engaging in acts of counter-politics that destabilized the socio-political order that shapes city space. In the Chilean capital, Santiago, anti-highway protests emerged as one of several forms of popular protest that tested the elite's guarded process of democratization (Garretón 2003) and planning (Zunino 2006), challenged governmental visions of the sustainable city and threatened the viability of an internationally acclaimed public works development model (Gómez-Lobo and Hinojosa 2000).

One such protest in southern Santiago has stood out above all the others. Between 2004 and 2010, a loose coalition of low-income residents in Santiago's southern periphery blocked the completion of the Acceso Sur a Santiago (Southern Access to Santiago) highway by denying it an entry point into the capital, effectively undermining its utility. The protests and blockade were triggered by the flawed and under-regulated construction of the highway through the densely populated Avenida La Serena sector of the municipalities of La Granja and La Pintana. Along most of the construction site, the work of the highway franchise company damaged homes and businesses, and created hazardous environmental conditions for local residents and passersby. The damage and pollution, however, were not the sole drivers of the protests. According to area residents, the MOP, which sponsored the highway and was responsible for the oversight of its construction, had done more than jeopardize the safety of local residents.

Beyond noting the poor application of construction mitigation measures, residents along Avenida La Serena reproached the MOP for having little control over a project it had franchised and awarded to private investors for construction and operations. A more serious set of rebukes focused on the MOP's exploitation of and perceived indifference towards the plight of the poor. At one level, the MOP was accused of undermining collective action by negotiating compensations for damages on a household, rather than community-wide, basis. At another, more symbolic level, the MOP was seen as immune to the demands of the poor, but not to those of wealthier and politically well-connected Chileans who had managed to force the redesign of another urban highway, the Costanera Norte[1] in the mid 1990s (Alvarez 2005).

The Acceso Sur protests also pointed to flaws in the country's nascent environmental protection system, which was cast as too weak to regulate even minimal mitigation measures.[2] Together, these claims were meant to point out the uneven playing field between the state and the poor, as well as the state's purposeful deflection of a discussion of relevant policy issues that ranged from the right to housing and private property to the disparity of environmental mitigation measures between rich and poor neighbourhoods.

Although the highway was eventually completed and inaugurated by 2010, the obstruction of a state project by the poor is a telling act of denial, a citizens' rejection of the state's will and planning mode. The significance of this act not only rested on the nature and form of the critique against the state, but also on the original act of denial that triggered the conflict, the state's initial rebuff of citizen consultation and socio-economic considerations in Chile's public works planning process. These two intertwined acts of denial speak to current debates about the roles that democracy and the environment, citizenship and planning megaprojects play in mediating the relationship between the three (Sabatini 1998; Roberts and Portes 2006; Merlinsky and Latta, this issue). As presented in this chapter, a primary lesson from the Acceso Sur case is that the expansion of state capacity to plan and shape the urban environment necessitates an expansion of the capacity to negotiate the social contracts embedded in each step and site of the planning process. This particular kind of negotiation shows how battles over the environment, land use and property double as contestations over the notion and practices of citizenship. More importantly, I argue that these denials and the processes they triggered are rooted in the mode of governance the Chilean state used to manage its infrastructure concession system.

In the eyes of the government officials who designed the concessions system in the early 1990s, its strength rested on a set of mechanisms meant to cater to investor needs, including financial and political risk mitigation and contract transparency. The system was purposefully designed to minimize the need to consider and address social and environmental issues associated with public works projects. Despite awareness that a host of non-technical aspects of franchised public works were not being directly addressed and planned for, government officials proceeded with the concessions system, confident in their capacity to address unplanned social and environmental components of the projects (Silva 2011).[3] Ultimately, the absence of plans that would minimize risk and provide transparency at the neighbourhood level forced the MOP to improvise the management of public outcries over unplanned and poorly handled aspects of the projects it commissioned.

What emerges from the battle over the Acceso Sur are not just insights into neighbourhood-level collective action, which echo those of several other contributions in this book, most notably Merlinsky and Latta's work on industrial development and environmental contamination in Argentina, and Richard's analysis of Mexico's food sovereignty movement. The Acceso Sur illustrates the privileged, intransigent, power of the state and its agencies to manage people, place and the public debate around the environment and citizenship. Inspired by a Foucauldian analysis of power and governmentality (Foucault 1991), this chapter is not meant to assess whether the Chilean state's power to shape environmental issues and notions of citizenship is inherently regressive or coercive. Rather, the emphasis is on how the state's logic and strategies of governance both engender and constrain the very processes and relationships that shape formal and lived notions of citizenship.

To this end, I analyse the Acceso Sur case and its relevance to debates on citizenship and the urban environment through the lens of the concept I call 'deliberate improvisation' (Silva 2008, 2011). Deliberate improvisation is the purposeful strategy of governments to 'plan without a plan' as a response to neoliberal imperatives of capital accumulation, restrictive institutional-legal conditions and complex social-political dynamics. It is a manifestation of sovereignty, the power to 'determine the state of exception' (Roy 2005) and to hold on to the 'monopoly to decide' (Ong 2006). Deliberate improvisation is in essence a modality of flexibility in the realm of public policy and city building, which in turn affects broader processes of citizenship construction (Ong 1999, 2006). In this light, deliberate improvisation is a political choice that signals the power of the state to define what should be planned, how, when and for whom. In the Chilean context, this concept highlights three key aspects of that country's mode of development and domestic debates around citizenship: the state's belief in its own power to manage people and place; the privileged position of markets in urban development; and the political vulnerability of communities directly affected by large projects.

As a logic of governance, deliberate improvisation purposefully avoids addressing a given set of policy issues unless someone raises them. In the planning realm, it creates a context that allows the state to exclude issues and certain stakeholder groups from public debate, which means deliberation about projects and their socio-environmental impact has to be raised by territorialized communities that might or might not have the resources to articulate and press issues of concern against the state. Deliberate improvisation is critical of the ways that this mode of governance conditions the construction and practice of democratic citizenship in a country that has re-embraced democracy.

Contemporary theorization on citizenship (Ong 2006) underlies my use of the term *deliberate* as a key qualifier of the logic of governance that emerged with Chile's concessions system. In her work on neoliberalism as exception (the power to decide what counts or does not count in the public realm), which explores mutations of citizenship and modes of governance in the Global South, Aihwa Ong states:

> I conceptualize ... exception ... broadly, as an extraordinary departure in policy that can be deployed to include as well as to exclude. As conventionally understood, the sovereign exception marks out excludable subjects who are denied protections. But the exception can also be a positive decision to include selected populations and spaces as targets of 'calculative choice and value-orientation' associated with neoliberal reform. ... We need to explore the hinge between neoliberalism as exception and exception to neoliberalism, the interplay among technologies of governing and disciplining, of inclusion and exclusion, of giving value to human conduct. (2006, 5)

Thus, there is a crucial link between understanding how the state of exception manifests itself and the degrees of vulnerability (material, political, psychological) experienced by groups of people affected by decisions that consider what is and what cannot be planned and by whom. Conversely, these conditions offer an opportunity to see when and how the excluded become part of the public agenda. Under conditions of deliberate improvisation, the state plays a subtle, yet important, hand in the construction of citizenship, the relation between state and society that generates particular attributes of belonging in society (Holston 2008, 9–14).

An analysis of the Chilean state's logic of governance as manifested through its concessions-based planning process is helpful to fully understand the political impasse over the Acceso Sur and its contributions to current debates on the liberalization of markets, insurgent planning and citizenship (Ong 1999, 2006; Holston 2008; Miraftab 2009), as well as the free market city and collective action (Sabatini 1998; Roberts and Portes 2006). By focusing on the relationship between policy choices and collective action at the neighbourhood level, this chapter speaks not only to the concessions systems as an innovation in planning, but also to citizenship as a field of struggle under conditions of economic and political liberalization (Ong 2006; Holston 2008). Closely linked to such struggle, the Acceso Sur provides a grounding for the Lefebvrian (1996) notion of the right to the city, which advocates for a concept of rights that are territorialized and linked to one's participation in systems of production and reproduction.

As demonstrated in the pages that follow, the Acceso Sur and its focus on deliberate improvisation is a lesson on the context that shapes logics and strategies of governance, and by extension, struggles over notions of citizenship and the environment. With regard to the latter, the chapter concludes with a series of reflections on the scalar limitations of territorialized struggles, as well as the need for researchers to better conceptualize and study their mid- to long-term legacies.

Concessions and the Stage for Insurgent Citizenship in Santiago

Chile's infrastructure concessions system, as a venture into the privatization of public works, was a state response to a deficit of road, port, airport and energy infrastructure that purportedly threatened the viability of the country's growing export-led economy and development goals. The three democratically elected governments that followed the military regime of Augusto Pinochet (1973–1989) consistently argued that the state could not significantly move beyond the maintenance of the existing infrastructure grid without private investment (MOP 1997). Launched in the mid 1990s, Chile's concessions system is a build-operate-transfer model of development, whereby the state auctions off the right to build and manage public works projects to private investors. The system was designed, implemented and managed largely by the country's MOP (Rufián 1999).

Inter-urban and urban highways have been a central component of the MOP's concessions project portfolio. Once franchised, the investors build and operate the project over a determined period of time while recuperating costs from tolls. After a project is auctioned off, the MOP's role is to enforce the terms of the concessions contract with the private investors. What makes highway concessions different from other public works projects is that the state turns highways into commodities, a product with an exchange value that can be franchised and whose relevance is based on their capacity to generate returns on investments. This has forced public works planning to accommodate econometric and marketing criteria alongside technical criteria in the different stages of project development. To plan and oversee a concessions project is therefore not just a political transaction that must serve and be justified by some defined public interest; a concessions project is also, and perhaps more importantly, a business. Because the concessions turned public works into a business transaction, the dictum in the MOP was 'time is money'. In planning terms: 'auction off the project and build first, all else can wait' (Silva 2008).[4]

To function properly, proponents of the concessions system insisted that it not only have projects that generated a timely return on investment, but that it also be flexible and endowed with clear regulations to manage financial risk and establish private sector confidence in the new infrastructure market.[5] To ensure this clarity and hasten private investment in the construction of much-needed projects, the MOP officials responsible for the launch of the system adopted a multi-pronged policy design and planning strategy. First, the concessions system was treated as a financial mechanism rather than an infrastructure planning process or, more importantly, a fundamental change in the mission and structure of the MOP. The system was thus cast as a means to an established end, the construction of public works projects to facilitate Chile's economic development (Cruz 1999). From that perspective, MOP officials felt they could design the system with little public consultation and few changes to the organic structure of the MOP or other relevant legal structures such as Chile's laws on expropriations or environmental protection.

The concessions system was also designed in ways that would insulate it and private investors from social and political concerns. Each concession project would be subject to a stand-alone contract between the MOP and the private investor which shielded aspects of the project such as design changes or liability from public scrutiny. Moreover, the MOP developed an arbitration mechanism, the Conciliatory Commission, which would function outside of the traditional local and national court system in case of conflicts between the private sector investors and the state (Cruz 1999). Together, these strategies of political insulation effectively meant that the domestic and international private sector investors that would build and operate public works projects were conspicuously absent from most public debates around the concessions system and its projects. In the Acceso Sur, for example, the MOP absorbed most of the critiques and responses raised by the public, which essentially rendered the franchise owner invisible.

Tactically, the decision to go simple and clear for investors also meant that the political and environmental dimensions of infrastructural development and the role of social actors in project identification, design and implementation would be downplayed or deferred until after the projects were auctioned off (Silva 2008, 2011). Downplaying the social took several forms, from an abstraction of what is considered public to proceeding with the minimal requirements for public review and mitigation of project impacts. With regard to the former, MOP officials considered that the social dimension of public works projects was represented by the government's participation in the concessions contract. This assumed that the public good was embedded a priori in anything that was labelled 'public', as in 'public works.' A more systematic review of social and environmental impacts of concessions projects would only come into play if and when the concessions project was subject to public review under Chile's fledgling environmental review system, the Sistema de Evaluación de Impacto Ambiental (SEIA) set up in Law No. 19.300. Under the 1994 Law, highways and plans that displace or disrupt human settlements, among other projects and impacts, are required to undergo the state-run environmental review and permitting process. The process not only necessitated an account of the project's impacts and proposed mitigation measures, but also a single public review and comment period.[6]

Although Chile had its environmental protection laws on the books by 1994, the actual environmental review process only became legally binding in 1997. By 1997, however, most of the major inter-urban and urban highway projects had been designed and franchised, thus missing any legal requirement to undergo an environmental review process. Some projects, such as the Costanera Norte, were submitted for an environmental review by the MOP in the mid 1990s on a 'voluntary' and experimental basis, as a response to political pressure by neighbourhood groups to open up the planning process to the general public (Irizarri 1997; Cruz 1999).

Government officials and planners rationalized this approach to the design and implementation of the concessions system and its projects on two levels: thorough deliberation on anything other than the technical and financial dimensions of concessions risked delaying the implementation of the system and the construction of much-needed infrastructure; and the political costs of not delivering infrastructure would be higher than the costs associated with any political fallout linked to concessions and its projects. This perspective, moreover, was built on the assumption that if and when unforeseen consequences arose, the government would have the capacity to manage them (Silva 2008, 2011). While this approach ensured private sector participation in public works and the construction of projects at an unprecedented scale and speed, it necessitated a conscious decision by planning authorities to adopt improvisation as a planning strategy: issues or aspects of the concessions project that fell outside of the realm of the project contract would be dealt with on a case-by-case basis and without clear contingency plans. I call this choice and mode of planning deliberate improvisation. In Santiago, the pitfalls of deliberate improvisation would become apparent and ultimately challenged.

Access Denied: The Propertied Poor versus the MOP

The Acceso Sur to Santiago is the urban portion of a 266-kilometer inter-urban highway designed to provide a shorter high-speed access to Santiago from the South and an alternative to commercial and private traffic bound for the eastern and northeastern suburbs of Santiago by allowing commuters to bypass the city centre. In May 1998, the MOP adjudicated the highway,

formally known as the Santiago-Talca-Acceso Sur Highway, to a Limited Liability Corporation owned in large part by the Spanish construction conglom-
erate Cintra. In 1999, after Chile's SEIA became legally binding, the MOP
filed its environmental impact report for Acceso Sur, primarily because it displaced and disturbed human settlements along portions of its route, most
notably in Southern Santiago (Servicio de Evaluación Ambiental 1999).

With specific regard to human settlements, Chile's environmental protection legislation required the MOP to identify and describe the 'groups of human beings' that would be displaced or affected to secure the highway's right
of way (Republic of Chile 1997–2001, 13). Despite this requirement, which
includes the identification of land tenure and housing patterns, the environmental protection legislation does not specify the approach a project propo-
nent should take to catalogue and compensate the impacted community. In
its Environmental Impact Report (MOP 1999), the MOP interpreted this
requirement in three ways. First, it catalogued the community as a collection of properties (titled parcels of land) that would be impacted. Second, it
recognized that the impact on a parcel did not simply affect the property title
holder, but possibly renters. Third, in the case of properties used as homes
(owner-occupied or rented), the impact was considered to be on the entire
household, including extended family members.

Within this framework, a compensation package would have to be offered
to each impacted household, which could include, but not necessarily have
to be, the expropriation of private property. For those households considered
in the plans and environmental reports for the Acceso Sur, the MOP offered
two impact mitigation measures (COREMA 1999; MOP 1999, Addendum
No. 1): (1) *Improved Home Solutions* consisted of a government-sponsored
transfer to a new home or property within the project area, of equivalent or
better conditions than the one expropriated, in lieu of payment for the expropriated property; (2) *Expanded Compensation Packets (Vouchers)* were offered by the MOP in lieu of a property transfer because land for new homes
near the project area was limited. Under the first voucher option, property
owners would receive market value for the property plus an additional one-
time payment (at the time, the equivalent of $8500 USD) to cover relocation
expenses. Under the second option, oriented towards renters, each person
living in the home at the time of expropriations would receive an $8500
payment. To be eligible for a voucher, the individuals would have to register
with the MOP.

Voucher allocations to both owners and renters were contingent upon
proof of purchase or intent to buy a home. The MOP listed 465 properties
that would be displaced or impacted by the Acceso Sur project, the majority of which were located in the Municipalities of La Pintana and La Granja
(COREMA 1999; MOP 1999, Addendum No. 1). The state would expropri-

ate some of these 465 properties and offer one of the two financial compensation packages to the rest. By September 1999, the state agency responsible for the review and permitting of the environmental impact report approved the project via Environmental Resolution No. 380 (Resolución Calificada Ambiental, RCA). With the RCA in hand, construction on the project began that same month.

The first serious signs of conflict between residents and the MOP did not emerge when the highway project was announced or when the original 465 homes were identified as impacted in 1999; tensions mounted when it became clear that the MOP had underestimated the number of households and property that would be affected by the project, especially in the route's final path into Santiago. In the rural portions of the highway, minimizing the impact on human settlements was relatively easy compared to the urban portions of the route. For the MOP, fewer impacted properties meant a faster planning and construction process, which obeyed a key principle of the concessions system. In the portion where the Acceso Sur enters the Santiago Metropolitan Region and meets the emerging system of urban highways, the need to minimize the number of impacted properties intensified and the planning process became much more complex for the MOP, which was responsible for clearing and ensuring the highway's right of way.

The MOP focused on those areas where it needed the most room to build and stage construction, primarily at the entrance and exit of the proposed tunnel. For those areas, the MOP planned compensation packages for the affected properties. Under the approved project plans, the properties and households *between* the tunnel's egress and exit, however, would not receive compensations or considerable attention by the MOP since that would require a financial and time investment that could undermine the feasibility of the concession. To avoid additional costs and delays, the MOP planned the tunnel under an existing public street that was approximately thirty metres wide, Avenida La Serena. The idea was to excavate the street, create a trench and build the tunnel within that trench. In this manner, there would be no need to consider the homes facing the avenue since the MOP, seeking to maximize economy and efficiency, calculated that the construction could be done without any impact to the abutters of the construction site.

This plan and the tunnel's design would prove to be the project's Achilles' heel. The MOP and the highway franchise not only miscalculated the technical challenges of building a tunnel within a densely populated area, but also the social and political dynamics of the entire neighbourhood through which it would pass. The MOP's strategy for Acceso Sur through Avenida La Serena was a manifestation of 'planning without a plan', as it illustrates an awareness of a plan's range of impacts, but an unwillingness to address them comprehensively from the outset.

As the construction started, the project's effect on the entire neighbour-hood began to emerge through a series of what would later be termed by the MOP as 'unanticipated impacts'. At one level, basic construction mitigation measures such as dust and noise control were ignored or poorly supervised by the MOP. The most serious impacts, however, were triggered by a flaw in the tunnel's design, which called for the highway's north and southbound lanes to be accommodated entirely within the approximately thirty-metre width of Avenida La Serena.

Although the MOP and the state agency that permitted the project acknowledged the tunnel would fit very tightly within the right of way (COREMA 1999), the excavation of the trench through Avenida La Serena proved to be too close to homes facing the avenue. The project's contrac-tors broke a 1.5-metre buffer mandated in the project's RCA to protect sev-eral hundred homes from the excavation (COREMA 1999), and significant structural damage was caused to homes all along the construction site. In addition, residents complained about being blocked into their own homes, the dangers of having a large precipice right in front of their doorsteps and a loss of business for those who worked from home. Soon after excavation of the trench began, residents and neighbours living along Avenida La Ser-ena demanded that the MOP not only recognize the impact of the project's design and construction method, but also compensate the newly impacted properties.

As residents along the tunnel route mobilized to secure compensation for construction damages, the MOP's need to improvise was triggered. Techni-cally, the MOP and the highway franchise would have to determine how to continue construction without causing further damage to the homes along Avenida La Serena. Politically, the Ministry would have to engineer a response that achieved several goals at once: minimize the number of new compensation packets and expropriations, explain the initial logic of its plans and approach to development in the neighbourhood and limit the discussion about compensations to specific households and properties, not the entire neighbourhood (Silva 2008).[7]

The factor that started to fan the flames of protests in La Granja and La Pintana was not the project's overall impact on households along its route per se, but the MOP's improvised and divisive approach to project impacts on households *after* construction was initiated and damages were incurred by residents. As Avenida La Serena residents would quickly highlight regarding the MOP's approach to human settlements and expropriations, the planning challenge was not just identifying who counted as a household, but deter-mining *which* households and properties should be considered eligible for compensation packages. The issue was thus not 'what was planned and how', but 'what was *not* planned and *why*'.[8]

In the early months of 2004, residents on the La Granja side of the pro-posed Acceso Sur tunnel organized and formed a registered non-governmen-tal organization called Comité Ecológico Territorio (Committee on Ecology and Territory, CET). Despite some differences among group members that were both ideological (anti-market vs. anti-state) and personal (newcomers to area vs. long-time residents and descendants of squatter settlement lead-ers), CET's primary goal was to act as the mouthpiece for residents in La Granja and La Pintana who felt that their living conditions and safety had not only been ignored, but were jeopardized by the construction of the Acceso Sur. Specifically, the residents claimed that the excavation and construction of the tunnel were impacting an area much larger than the one contemplated by the project's environmental impact report. From the residents' perspective, the state-sanctioned right of way for the tunnel project was inadequate and irresponsible. They argued that with more thorough and socially conscious planning, the damage caused by the tunnel construction could have been avoided.

To avoid a costly and lengthy expropriation process, the MOP's response was to approach individual households and offer them variations on the vouchers given to some of the original 465 property owners identified in the 1999 environmental impact report. One variation was a time-specific rental voucher for non-property owners to rent a home for an eighteen-month pe-riod, the time the MOP estimated it would take to complete the tunnel. After the eighteen months, residents could return to their rental home on Ave-nida La Serena. Since the MOP would not expropriate the newly impacted properties, households were not obligated to accept the vouchers in any of the forms proposed by the Ministry. Ultimately, the nature of the voucher presented by the MOP to local residents depended on who was living in the impacted property at the time (owners or renters), as well as the degree to which the household representative could negotiate a satisfactory compensa-tion packet.

Despite the variation in tenancy along the construction site and the need to negotiate on a household-by-household basis, the vouchers were seen by the MOP as a speedy and flexible way to lure as many people out of their homes as quickly as possible, temporarily or permanently. Although this ad hoc approach to compensations for construction impacts included mecha-nisms that were formalized in the project's environmental impact report and the RCA, the MOP's case-by-case use of the vouchers and negotiations with households that *were not originally* considered in the environmental impact report were subsequently challenged by area residents as manipulative and illegal (Alvarez 2005).

Indeed, some CET members attacked the vouchers, claiming the govern-ment could not absolve itself of its responsibility for proper treatment of citizens and good planning *entirely* by paying residents off with vouchers. These residents were not rejecting the vouchers as much as they were seeking something that was more permanent than money, namely formal recognition of governmental indifference and ineptitude. Other CET members, aware that the MOP could not force them out of their homes without engaging in a costly expropriation process, sensed a singular opportunity to extract compensation packages above the market price for properties or rents in the area and aggressively negotiated the terms of the voucher packets offered to them by the Ministry.

These differences began to show the divisions among property owners, specifically around their relationship to housing. For some, housing and property were embraced as hard-earned rights that could not be negotiated lightly. For others, the home was an investment, a source of capital and profit. Regardless, to be effective in their claims against the MOP, these differences had to be surmounted by the residents. To some residents and observers of the Acceso Sur conflict, the wedge driven into the community by the MOP's improvised and individualized mitigation approach risked undermining claims that the project's flaws were affecting an entire community, not just individual households.

For residents of La Granja and La Pintana, this meant that the conflict over the highway had to transcend the issues specific to La Serena Avenue in two ways. First, it had to be linked to a larger structural problem in Chile. Second, the residents would need the help and resources of people outside of the immediate community. By the end of 2004, one CET leader contacted the Observatorio Latinoamericano de Conflictos Ambientales (OLCA), a Chilean NGO that promotes environmental sustainability by monitoring government and private sector compliance with national and international environmental standards and laws. OLCA's environmental watchdog role is exercised primarily via legal and technical counsel, often provided pro bono, to communities fighting public and private sector initiatives seen as damaging to the local environment.

Once the CET leader managed to bring the head of the environmental watchdog NGO to visit the construction site, she convinced him that the Acceso Sur was a case ripe for monitoring. Specifically, the local leader argued successfully that CET could benefit from legal advice and strategic planning on how to hold the MOP accountable for its failure to comply with the required construction mitigation measures. OLCA would prove an invaluable ally for CET, especially as it was faced with two major challenges: (1) deciphering and navigating the legal framework of Chile's environmental protection and review system; and (2) mounting a campaign that would galvanize public scrutiny and pressure on the MOP. It would thus be via OLCA and its expertise in linking local environmental conflicts to the larger debate on government accountability in Chile and abroad that CET sought to take the fight over the Acceso Sur beyond the confines of Avenida La Serena.

With OLCA's support, CET began to articulate a legal argument against the MOP, namely that it had breached the RCA-mandated 1.5-metre buffer meant to protect immediate abutters from the construction site. If the MOP was found to be in violation of the RCA, the Ministry should not only be subject to legal sanctions (fines), but it should also be obligated to submit a new EIR. The latter, as CET and OLCA argued publicly and in meetings with the National Commission on the Environment and the Regional Government of Santiago (*Intendencia*), would be required by virtue of the admission that the original project and its EIR were flawed and that there were unforeseen project impacts that still needed to be formally addressed (OLCA N.d.; Toro N.d.). Interviews with CET and OLCA suggested that the MOP had opened the door for scrutiny and the possibility of being forced to submit a new EIR precisely at the moment it admitted that there were unforeseen project impacts.

Nevertheless, at that time, Chile's environmental legislation did not specify what steps needed to be taken to redress a project's *unforeseen* impacts. In the case of the Acceso Sur, the head of the MOP's unit responsible for concessions projects, Carlos Uribe, argued on national television that the appropriate redress was not expropriations, but the use of vouchers (Megavisión 2004; Televisión Nacional 2004). OLCA, on the other hand, argued that the logical step would be to revisit the project design and draft more comprehensive and realistic plans for the urban portion of the highway. To do so would then require the MOP to submit a new EIR.

By pursuing this legal strategy, CET and OLCA were aiming to trigger several interrelated outcomes. By claiming that the project's environmental resolution (RCA) was violated, the MOP's performance would have to be reviewed and scrutinized by a third party, the Regional Office of the National Commission of the Environment. Although the MOP is a member of the National Commission of the Environment's governing body and its Regional Office formally falls under the direction of this body (Republic of Chile 1994, 1997–2001), the Regional Office's participation in the local conflict was still considered crucial by CET. For CET, bringing in the Regional Office to review the damages and improvised mitigation measures meant that the MOP could not directly control the nature and management of the conflict as it had been doing since the impacts of the tunnel construction became evident and the residents' complaints grew louder and more public.

Indeed, if CET's claims were accepted by the COREMA, the MOP would be subject to state-imposed sanctions as dictated by Law 19.300. These sanctions would formalize the Ministry's accountability beyond any of the promises that had been made thus far by the MOP to the residents: vouchers, landscaping and new lighting. Moreover, for OLCA, the sanctions opened up the possibility of strengthening Chile's environmental protection framework by creating a precedent for forcing project proponents to resubmit EIRs when flawed planning became evident and unanticipated impacts emerged.

To this end, CET documented the MOP's failure to properly regulate and enforce the mitigation measures it had proposed for the project. The most salient of these claims was the violation of the 1.5-metre buffer intended to keep the neighbours safe from the construction project. Furthermore, the individualized voucher approach, while attractive and immediate in the sense that it was a concrete example of compensation, was criticized for doing little to actually correct the environmental and social damage caused by a poorly planned project. CET was thus not rejecting the rental voucher proposal so much as it was saying that it was neither enough of a mea culpa nor an appropriate environmental mitigation measure.

This strategic choice – between accepting the vouchers as a final settlement and pursuing more far-reaching legal sanctions including a new EIR – would prove to be a major challenge to the cohesion of CET. The pursuit of a legal avenue to redress the impacts of the project was abstract, uncertain and time consuming. Even in the best-case scenario of a swift decision to sanction the MOP, there were no guarantees that the sanction would produce anything close to what the MOP had been promising in the form of the rental vouchers. Moreover, the spectre of a new EIR to account for the true impacts of the project failed to impress many local residents, since the review process would further delay any action by the government. The precedent of holding a ministry accountable for poor planning and regulation was not sufficient or immediate enough for residents whose houses and livelihoods were already damaged. It was certainly not attractive to those residents of La Granja and La Pintana who saw an opportunity to shame or strong-arm the Ministry into dispensing payments in the form of rental vouchers.

Residents and CET members who did not want to pursue a legal strategy against the MOP's flawed planning process chose tactics that included marches, picketing the construction site and sabotaging construction material. In addition, they attempted to pry open negotiations and deals with the MOP by pulling on political contacts within the municipal and central governments, as well as threatening to mobilize more residents against the government in ways reminiscent of the protests against the Pinochet regime.

The existence of these two camps within the neighbourhood and CET generated ambiguities about local leadership and representation, which ultimately stalled any significant response to the damage that had been and continued to be incurred by residents near the construction site. The divisions, especially within CET, were largely settled by September of 2005: there would be one organization, but two approaches.[9] One camp would continue to press for state sanctions against the MOP pursuant to Law 19.300, which would trigger a revision of the project and a definitive proposal from the MOP to compensate the families and households that had already been impacted by the project and those who could be affected reasonably by the remainder of the construction phase of the project. The other camp would continue to pursue compensation packages on a household-by-household basis by leveraging the spectre of public protests and other tactics that would physically disrupt the construction of the tunnel and stall its inauguration.

In 2003, approximately three years after the Acceso Sur's environmental impact report was approved, Chile's main daily newspaper, *El Mercurio,* announced that the Acceso Sur was well on its way towards completion and that the project's primary hurdles, the expropriation of homes, had been settled (Suárez 2003). It was estimated at the time that up to $50 million USD had been spent on expropriations for the project. The newspaper's announcement of imminent completion proved to be premature; the project only became fully operational in the first quarter of 2010. As a result of the tug of war between the MOP and the CET, for at least six years the project turned into a bridge that stopped in the middle of the river, a situation that literally left everybody hanging.

The Challenging Production of Citizenship under Regimes of Deliberate Improvisation

Chile's infrastructure planning process outpaced its government's capacity, and perhaps the will of its political leaders, to understand and manage the political and territorial dimensions of its public works projects. The country's market-driven model of public works delivers infrastructure that ensures Chile's place in global networks of production. Yet, seeking certainty in the economic sphere fostered uncertainty in the political sphere. As exemplified by protracted conflicts around highway development in Santiago, the economics and politics of planning in the city were not synchronized, nor could they be since the MOP's approach to development was to plan for the former and improvise with the latter. The insistence of the political class to give economic time more value than political time reinforced counterproductive forms of political and technical improvisation. The end result has been an uneven trail of physical and political interventions, as well as confused and combative residents, planners and political leaders. Deliberately improvised planning can deliver, but *what* and *how* it delivers generates ever more controversy and uncertainty.

For theorists and practitioners, the broader themes and issues that emerge from the Acceso Sur case include the legacy of territorialized struggles; whether and how these struggles can scale up to a movement; and the role of the state in framing the processes of citizenship formation. With regard to legacy, how should we frame and assess the short- and long-term effects of political struggles around citizenship and participation in the policy-making process, especially ones like the Acceso Sur, that are about both short-term needs *and* larger political tensions around governmental accountability and representation? The residents of La Granja and La Pintana stalled a major project and challenged the state, but the highway was ultimately built and inaugurated; the struggle is now part of academic analysis, people's lives have moved on, cars are running along the highway and those responsible for the infrastructure concessions program are out of power. All the while, the fundamental structure of the concessions system has been left largely intact, despite efforts by the Bachelet government (2006–2010) to reform key aspects of the program.[10] The practice of citizenship in this case is decidedly insurgent, but it is not clearly transformative, much less progressive.

Related to the issue of legacy is the challenge of scaling protests and grievances up into larger movements that can effect change in standards of accountability and representation across territorial scales (global, national, regional, urban, neighbourhood). The Acceso Sur was an emblematic case of urban highway protests, but it was only one of many in Santiago. Despite evidence of metropolitan and even global networks of support, along with the emergence of a discourse of rights to the city along Avenida La Serena, it was difficult for the Acceso Sur battle to scale up in any significant way. This condition generates other questions: Is a territorialized victory (however short lived) a victory for more than the people grounded in the case? How much time do we need to assess whether micro-struggles and micro-victories add up to more?

At the time research for this chapter was conducted (2005–2008), there were fledgling signs of solidarity among neighbourhoods challenging the MOP and other large-scale developments. Of note was the launch of the Coordinadora Pro Derechos Urbanos (Urban Rights Coordinating Committee), which was a loose attempt by a non-governmental organization called *Ciudad Viva* to organize the disparate urban struggles into a movement on urban rights and sustainability. Ciudad Viva has its roots in an earlier struggle against the Costanera Norte highway concession, but the strength and staying power of the broader Coordinadora Pro Derechos Urbanos were questionable. One explanation for the precarious launch of this civic umbrella group could be the capacity of discourses of private property and homeownership to both galvanize and unsettle collective action. As suggested by Francisco Sabatini (1998), the gains in homeownership made in the earlier struggles for land and housing in neighbourhoods like La Pintana and La Granja have planted seeds of individualism and self-interest that could defy not only the MOP's plans for franchised projects, but also the communities' own efforts to make collective demands against a government that appeared indifferent to their plight.

Finally, the state is a central actor in the Acceso Sur story, as it is in most experiences of citizenship and environmental management (Merlinsky and Latta, this volume). The Acceso Sur illuminates the power and logic of the state apparatus and the Chilean political elite to determine the state of exception, deciding what public works can be privatized, what counts as public debate, when and for whom. The term *deliberate improvisation* situates the Acceso Sur case in its broadest political context. While the Acceso Sur might be interesting as a case-study of local neighbourhood mobilization and the ways in which Chile's propertied poor can leverage home ownership and the country's environmental laws to their advantage, the case is still ultimately about the power of the state and the political elite to shape cities and public debate. The Acceso Sur really starts in the proverbial boardroom, not in the streets of La Granja, which emphasizes the position and capacity of non-state actors relative to public agencies.

The implementation of Chile's concessions system has been bittersweet. As seen through the Acceso Sur, public negotiation over accountability and representation leaves few indifferent because it has been triggered in large part by the success and strength of the Chilean state to deliver economic and political stability, regulation and order. This success of state capacity in a region better known for state failures is sweet. The reasons for bitterness, however, are more complex, as they stem from fresh memories of political violence and indifference, the spectre of instability and economic stagnation, as well as governmental perceptions of ingratitude and frustration over the fruits of success. To date, Chileans have not arrived at a participatory-democratic policy-making model such as the one that has repeatedly been described in political discourses since the end of the Pinochet regime. For the communities affected by large state projects, this might mean that there is no participation in policy unless it is through informal political pressure; what we might continue to see is participation through force and coercion, not discussion, collaboration or deliberation.

Notes

1. The *Costanera Norte* (CN) highway crosses the Santiago Metropolitan Region from East to West through several of the city's wealthier neighbourhoods. The anti-CN campaign sought to stop the highway on environmental and democratic principles: the CN would ruin Santiago's already precarious environment; protestors challenged the very need for a highway to improve mobility; and the MOP's technocratic and secretive planning process was held up as a blatant contradiction of the government's commitment to democratize the country's political and decision-making processes. The anti-CN protests did not stop the highway, but they did force a radical redesign of the project.
2. The analysis of Chile's concessions system, specifically its genesis, presented in this chapter is based on original doctoral research conducted by the author between 2004 and 2007.

The presentation of the government's approach towards the design and implementation of the system is based on recorded, open-ended interviews of the ministers, government staff, and industry representatives directly involved in the launch of Chile's concessions system. Most of the interviews were conducted in 2005. The analysis of the CET and protests in southern Santiago is based on extensive non-participant observations of the neighbourhood and residents' efforts to challenge the MOP (Silva 2008).

3. The principal source for Silva (2011) and these statements come from an extended interview conducted by the author with the former minister of public works and primary designer of the Concessions System, Carlos Hurtado, conducted on 10 August 2005.

4. The principal sources for this analysis are extended interviews conducted by the author in 2005 with senior staff members of the MOP and its Concessions sub-unit, as well as former Minister Hurtado.

5. Refer to Silva (2008, chaps. 1–3) for quotes and interview material supporting these claims and the analysis of the genesis of the concessions system.

6. Law 19.300, Title II, Article 10, for highways; Article 11, for human settlements; Article 26, for public participation (Republic of Chile 1994). Based on several interviews with MOP officials, most highway projects were subject to environmental review for reasons other than being a highway. In Chile, the terms *carretera* and *autopista* can be used interchangeably to mean high-speed road. Legally, however, it is only an 'autopista' that is subject to environmental review. Under Article II, Section E of the Regulatory Framework for Law 19.300 (Republic of Chile 1997–2001), an 'autopista' is defined, in part, as a road designed for vehicle flows greater than eight thousand trips per day, with four or more segregated, uni-directional lanes and controlled access into and out of the lanes. The MOP could determine that a high-speed road project was technically not an 'autopista' and thus avoid the environmental review process as long as the project did not trigger other review criteria.

7. The principal sources for this analysis are extended interviews conducted and recorded by the author in 2005 with senior and mid-level staff members of the MOP and its Concessions sub-unit.

8. Refer to Observatorio Latinoamericano de Conflictos Ambientales (n.d.) and Toro (n.d.) for two publicly disseminated representations of the residents' arguments.

9. In late 2005, the CET leader pursuing the expansive legal solution splintered off from CET to lead a group called Environmental Commission, Dignity and Rights.

10. Refer to http://www.concesiones.cl/acercadelacoordinacion/Paginas/default.aspx for a history of the Bachelet government's attempts to reform the concessions system.

References

Álvarez, V. (2005) 'Vecinos de la Granja furiosos con el MOP, por presiones indebidas' in *Observatorio Latinoamericano de Conflictos Ambientales (OLCA)*, online report, http://www.olca.cl/oca/chile/regionmp/accesosur02.htm (accessed 15 July 2011).

COREMA. (1999) 'Environmental Resolution No. 380,' *Santiago, Chile: Comisión Regional del Medio Ambiente*, 2 September.

Cruz, L. C. (1999) *Colaborar con la Tierra: La Asociación público-privada en el desarrollo de la infraestructura de Chile*. Santiago, Chile: Ministerio de Obras Públicas.

Foucault, M. (1991) 'Governmentality, Lecture at the College de France, February 1978,' in G. Burchell, C. Gordon and P. Miller (eds), *The Foucault Effect: Studies in Governmentality*. Chicago: University of Chicago Press, pp. 87–103.

Garretón, M. A. (2003) *Incomplete Democracy: Political Democratization in Chile and Latin America*. Chapel Hill: Chapel Hill Press.

Gómez-Lobo, A., and S. Hinojosa. (2000) *Broad Roads in a Thin Country: Infrastructure Concessions in Chile*. Washington, DC: World Bank Institute.

Holston, J. (2008) *Insurgent Citizenship: Disjunctions of Democracy and Modernity in Brazil*. Princeton: Princeton University Press.

Irizarri, A. (1997) *Construir con la Gente: Participación de la Comunidad en la Elaboración de los Proyectos Concesionados de la Ruta 5*. Santiago, Chile: Ministerio de Obras Públicas.

Lefebvre, H. (1996) *Writings on Cities*. E. Kofman and E. Labas (trans.). Malden: Blackwell Publishing.

Megavisión. (2004) Morning news interview, 2 November.

Miraftab, F. (2009) 'Insurgent planning: Situating radical planning in the Global South,' *Planning Theory*, Vol. 8, No. 1, pp. 32–50.

MOP. (1997) *Guía Para Conocer el Programa de Concesiones y Sus Proyectos*. Santiago, Chile: Gran Vía Prensa.

———. (1999) 'Estudio de Impacto Ambiental del Proyecto "Acceso Sur a Santiago",' Ministerio de Obras Públicas, 19 January.

Observatorio Latinoamericano de Conflictos Ambientales (OLCA). (N.d.) *Es fácil ser cara dura con los pobres*, online report, http://www.olca.cl/oca/chile/regionmp/lagranja.htm (accessed 15 July 2011).

Ong, A. (1999) *Flexible Citizenship: The Cultural Logics of Transnationality*. Durham: Duke University Press.

———. (2006) *Neoliberalism as Exception: Mutations in Citizenship and Sovereignty*. Durham: Duke University Press.

Republic of Chile. (1994) 'Ley 19.300: Bases Generales del Medio Ambiente.' Santiago, Chile.

———. (1997–2001) 'Decreto Supremo No. 95 del Ministerio Secretaría General de la Presidencia, Reglamento del Sistema de Evaluación de Impacto Ambiental.' Santiago, Chile.

Roberts, B., and A. Portes. (2006) 'Coping with the Free Market City: Collective Action in Six Latin American Cities at the End of the Twentieth Century,' *Latin American Research Review*, Vol. 41, No. 2, pp. 57–83.

Roy, A. (2005) 'Urban Informality: Toward an Epistemology of Planning,' *Journal of the American Planning Association*, Vol. 71, No. 2, pp. 147–158.

Rufián, D. M. (1999) *Manual de Concesiones de Obras Públicas*. Santiago, Fondo de Cultura Económica.

Sabatini, F. (1998) 'Local Environmental Conflicts in Latin America: Changing State-Civil Society Relations in Chile,' in M. Douglass and J. Friedmann (eds), *Cities for Citizens: Planning and the Rise of Civil Society in a Global Age*. Hoboken: Wiley, pp. 139–160.

Servicio de Evaluación Ambiental. (1999). *Ficha del Proyecto: Acceso Sur a Santiago, Estudio de Impacto Ambiental*. http://www.e-seia.cl/seia-web/ficha/fichaPrincipal.php?id_expediente =1629&idExpediente=1629 (accessed 24 June 2011).

Silva, E. R. (2008) 'Deliberate Improvisation: the Governance of Highway Franchises in Santiago, Chile 1990–2005,' PhD dissertation, University of California Berkeley.

———. (2011) 'Deliberate Improvisation: Planning Highway Franchises in Santiago, Chile,' *Planning Theory*, Vol. 10, No. 1, pp. 35–52.

Suárez, M. R. (2003) 'Futura autopista en la capital: acceso sur en la recta final,' *El Mercurio*, 24 August, A1.

Televisión Nacional. (2004) Morning news interview, 2 November.

Toro, A. (N.d.) '¿Progreso para quienes y a costa de quienes?' in *Observatorio Latinoamericano de Conflictos Ambientales (OLCA)*, online opinion piece, http://www.olca.cl/oca/chile/ regionmp/accesosur.htm (accessed 15 July 2011).

Zunino, H. M. (2006) 'Power Relations in Urban Decision-Making: Neo-Liberalism, "Techno-Politicians" and Authoritarian Redevelopment in Santiago, Chile,' *Urban Studies*, Vol. 43, No. 10, pp. 1825–1846.

Environmental Collective Action, Justice and Institutional Change in Argentina

María Gabriela Merlinsky and Alex Latta

As mobilization around social-environmental issues in Argentina reached new highs over the last decade, two cases are of particular significance: first, the prolonged protest by residents of a small community on the shores of the Uruguay River against the installation of pulp mills on the Uruguayan side of the watercourse; and second, the legal actions initiated by a group of residents in the Matanza-Riachuelo river basin, in Buenos Aires, claiming damages for environmental contamination of the waterway.[1] The pulp mill conflict gave a new profile to environmental issues in Argentina, and points to new modes of popular organizing in response to these issues, especially at the local scale. It also raises important links between the national-level definition of environmental rights, citizen action on transboundary environmental conflicts and the growing importance of international legal norms to such disputes. The case of the Matanza-Riachuelo similarly illuminates new modes of citizen action on environmental issues, but is particularly noteworthy because it represents the first significant attempt by the Argentinean judiciary to interpret constitutionally protected rights to a healthy environment. The legal judgments have had significant implications for relationships between the judicial and the legislative branches of the state, as well as for the shape of public institutions operating at various scales and across different jurisdictions. Together, the two cases reveal a general realignment of socio-political interaction between publics and government authorities in Argentina. At the heart of this realignment is a new lexicon of citizens' rights, revolving around a set of laws and legal instruments rooted in a 1994 constitutional reform.

In this chapter we focus our analytical lens on the political 'productivity' of environmental conflicts in terms of their contribution to the construction of emergent environmental rights and also of the subjectivities of citizens who hold or pursue such rights. With respect to this transformative expansion of citizenship rights, the formal register of citizenship (as national belonging and as a formal entitlement to rights) is in constant dialectical tension with citizenship's substantive content (citizenship practice stemming from insurgent processes) (Holston 2008). This tension speaks to the way that legal, political and economic spheres come together in concrete power relations, manifested both in the socio-ecological processes governing the appropriation and distribution of natural resources in each community or region, and in the differential exposure to environmental harms that result from the activities of economic development. In this way, the expansion of citizenship rights is related to the way that social actors raise demands and mobilize around questions of justice in an ongoing push towards the further elaboration of autonomous, state-sanctioned spaces for citizen-subjects in different spheres (political, civil, social, cultural and, more recently, environmental) (Delamata 2009).

Our focus draws particular attention to the three-way links between (a) the struggle for justice, (b) the redefinition of citizenship and (c) apertures towards institutional change, including the expansion of the available repertoire of legal instruments, the redefinition of inter-institutional relationships at various scales and the definition of an environmental governance agenda. How have particular conflicts become productive sites for the staging of new modes of citizenly conduct by different kinds of actors? What has been the capacity and importance of various actors in terms of raising new kinds of political claims, constructing a sphere of public debate in which such claims become legible and exerting political pressure on state institutions capable of translating these claims into new governance practices? In light of the transformative conflicts we examine, can we speak of the emergence of an 'environmental citizenship' in the sense of citizens' internalization of environmental norms as integral components of their political subjectivity, mirrored by the rise of a 'green' public sphere?

To this set of questions we propose several hypotheses. First, following Maristella Svampa (2008), we affirm that contemporary mobilization around environmental issues in Argentina has given rise to the formation of multisectoral collectives or networks. These networks draw on participants from a variety of social classes and cultural or ethnic backgrounds. As such, they take shape in a context of deliberation, within which a range of issues related to resource use, land ownership and environmental contamination are being reconfigured, increasingly via the language of rights. The emergence in Argentina of grassroots 'citizens' assemblies' has provided an important space of articulation for these deliberations. Meanwhile, certain state institutions, such as the National Ombudsperson, have facilitated and legitimized these new modes of political organization in defence of environmental rights. The species of environmentalism that results represents a shift away from the traditional principles and ideals commonly associated with the late-twentieth-century green movement in North America and Europe, characterized by Manuel Castells (1997, 110) as the 'greening of the self'. Rather than personal transformation around the uptake of new ecological values, in Argentina we see a broad array of actors seeking to defend local livelihoods and wellbeing. If specifically ecological issues have become increasingly central to such well-being, societal concern for the environment simultaneously opens up new ways to channel a range of related issues into the political sphere (Keck and Sikkink 1998, 121; see also Ferrero, this volume). Argentina's new environmentalism is notably more inclusive than the elite activism of the Global North's 'green' consumers. Nevertheless, we will see that it can also serve to perpetuate certain kinds of entrenched social exclusions.

Second, we argue that a significant dimension of the political productivity of these new kinds of mobilization rests in the way they have catalyzed an 'actualization of the law'. Both cases examined here point to an increasing importance for the legal dimensions of socio-ecological conflict. The conflict over paper mills on the Uruguay River eventually led to an international legal battle and a highly instructive 2010 decision by the International Court of Justice. Meanwhile, the struggle over the cleanup of the Matanza-Riachuelo has rested on legal resources that have been available in Argentina since 1994 but were never previously invoked. This 'juridification' of environmental conflict—whereby law attains socio-ecological relevance—rests upon the uptake of these resources by new social actors, and hence cannot be considered in isolation from broader changes in the political culture around environmental questions, as well as the specific experiences of socio-ecological conflict in different territorial contexts. In this process of juridification, legal experts become crucial actors, given that they serve as translators between citizen experiences and demands, on the one hand, and an array of juridical rules and relations, on the other (Melé 2003; Azuela 2006).

The third key hypothesis we propose is that the political impact of new citizen mobilizations, along with the processes of juridification to which they are linked, must be understood in relation to the politics of ecological knowledge (see Taddei, this volume, for a Brazilian comparison). The language of rights anchors environmental politics in the harm suffered by specific citizens and citizen collectives—literally *polluted bodies* in the case of the Matanza-Riachuelo. As such, measuring local environmental conditions is fundamental both for rights-claiming citizens and for the institutions that respond to these claims in judicial, legislative and administrative domains. In this context, we would like to highlight the importance of counter-expert knowledge. Popular actors increasingly seek to participate in the construction of environmental problems in reference to dominant scientific and technological cognitive frames. Indeed, this has become one of the ways that citizen groups can participate in legal proceedings over environmental disputes. What is important to recognize is that debates over 'the facts' are simultaneously key discursive and symbolic battlegrounds. As citizens interrogate the expertise around current or future ecological consequences of different forms of economic development, their inquiries potentially contribute to a reconfiguration of the issues, especially challenging the boundary between technical and social domains. In doing so, they generate a space of indeterminacy with respect to the balance of different forms of agency and open up technical debates to a plurality of perspectives, demands and potential ways forward (Callon, Lascoumes and Barthe 2001, 47). Conflicts are constituted, in this way, as 'collective learning and exploration mechanisms' (50).

Because of its overarching importance to the analysis, we begin by treating in more detail the legal and institutional basis for the recent juridification of environmental conflict in Argentina. Having established that basic framework, we then turn to a more extended consideration of the two emblematic cases that we touched on at the outset: resistance to pulp mills on the Uruguay River and the struggle to secure decontamination of the Matanza-Riachuelo river basin. The cases then become the basis for further reflections on the three hypotheses posed above, and on the overall implications of these new kinds of conflict for the shape of environmentally articulated citizenship rights and practices in Argentina.

The Juridification of the Environmental Question

Contemporary environmental politics in Argentina are increasingly shaped by new rights set out in the country's 1994 constitutional reform, which addressed the failings of a legal order that focused exclusively on individual rights and offered few tools to protect the public interest more generally. Article 41 of the 1994 reform declares citizens' right to a healthy environment (Constitución Nacional de Argentina 1994). In itself this reform represented an innovative expansion of citizenship rights; even more interesting is the way the right is framed as a collective rather than individual right. Arising from this distinction, Article 43 indicates that any party (i.e. not simply those directly harmed) may take legal action to protect collective rights. This opens the way for NGOs to litigate on behalf of the public interest in the pursuit of environmental protection. The reforms also created an important new institutional actor, which has come to play a crucial role in environmental governance: the Defensor del Pueblo de la Nación (National Ombudsperson). In the case of the Matanza-Riachuelo, we will see that the office of the Ombudsperson has been central in bringing constitutional claims forward and in monitoring the translation of legal precedent into government policy. Finally, the 1994 constitution enables the federal government to impinge on provincial areas of authority to establish minimum levels of protection for the environment. Under this enabling provision, referred to as *presupuestos mínimos* (minimum standards), the Ley General del Ambiente (Law 25.675) was passed by the National Congress in 2002. The law establishes 'minimum

requirements for the achievement of an adequate and sustainable management of the environment, the preservation and protection of biological diversity and the implementation of sustainable development' (Ley General
2002, Art. 1).

Legal change alone is not equivalent to substantively new modes of environmental governance and new practices of citizenly engagement. It is
only when legal rules come into play in actual disputes, where their content
and meaning is debated and applied to concrete instances, that law becomes
transformed into social practice. As environmental questions are increasingly
treated through the application of laws and regulations we might say that
environmental politics have become 'juridified'. The concept of juridification
is multifaceted and has been put to use in different ways by other scholars.
Lars Blichner and Anders Molander (2008, 39) present what we find a useful
definition, outlining five dimensions of juridification, including: (1) constitutive juridification, pertaining to the reform of a political order by adding
degrees of competence to the legal sphere; (2) the application of legal norms
to a growing range of issues; (3) increasing recourse to law in order to resolve
disputes; (4) increasing power of the courts and the legal profession; and (5)
'legal framing', by which citizens increasingly come to conceive of themselves
as subjects within a legal order. The cases we examine here can be seen to operate in several of these dimensions. In particular we are interested in the way
legal norms relevant to environmental questions are increasingly picked up
by citizens as tools for holding public authorities accountable, supplementing
political struggle with legal contest as a mode of resolving conflicts around
environmental questions. At the same time, we note that legal actors themselves have contributed to the increasing relevance of law to environmental
disputes. Finally, it is important to note that the conversion of abstract norms
into concrete legal practice can also lead actors to increasingly conceive of
their subjectivity in legal terms, invoking the language of rights in ways that
are of equal measure instrumental *and* symbolic.

Much of the scholarship on juridification is critical of the impact of expanding legal influence on social and political life (for example, Habermas
1986; Teubner and Firenze 1987). While this is not the primary orientation
of our analysis, the cases explored here do demonstrate that legal remedies to
environmental conflicts suffer from significant limitations and can have impacts on the shape of environmental politics that are not necessarily positive.
One key difficulty is that environmental litigation often calls upon courts not
merely to rule on matters of law but also to make judgments about the merits
of scientific data and opinion. In their analysis of the science–law interface in
environmental decision making in the North American context, Larry Reynolds and Steve Hrudey (2006) identify a range of issues, three of which are
particularly related to the judicial sphere, as follows: (1) courts have a difficult
time insuring the quality and objectivity of expert witnesses; (2) there are

often difficulties with the communication and comprehension of knowledge between different players in judicial processes; and (3) uncertainty is handled very differently in scientific and legal domains. In particular we would like to highlight the last of these issues. Where science aims to pursue ever-better understandings of the world by weighing competing interpretations of data and leaving questions open to new information and new theories, courts exist to close questions on the basis of thresholds of reasonable certainty (Reynolds and Hrudey 2006, 41–42). Where the diversity of scientific opinion meets with the clash of competing interests in adversarial judicial processes, differences over methodologies and competing interpretations of data become highly charged debates. Due to their lack of expertise, courts are poorly placed to establish appropriate thresholds of certainty in their interpretation of scientific data and adjudicate between duelling expert opinions about the meaning of that data.

Gordon Silverstein (2009, 2010) highlights another nest of difficulties associated with processes of juridification, drawing our attention to the implications of law for political life and the potential disadvantages of law displacing politics as a mode of conflict resolution. In particular, law may short-circuit the deliberative function of politics, perhaps leading to circumstances where changing rules does not equate with changing minds. As we will see in the case of Matanza-Riachuelo, this can create stumbling blocks when it comes to the actual implementation of new environmental policies. There are also reasons to be concerned about the way that the legal sphere elevates expertise over opinion, potentially heightening the degree to which ordinary citizens are excluded from environmental decision-making processes.

In Argentina, there remains a significant gap between the formal recognition of rights and their implementation in substantive practice, but popular movements increasingly invoke environmental rights in their public discourses and in so doing have actively politicized this gap between formal and substantive rights. What is the role of citizens in bridging the formal recognition of environmental rights with their effective implementation as legal precedent? To what extent does the process of activating new rights within an expanding order of environmental law allow for the generation of new ways of exercising citizenship, and does this turn towards law constrain citizenship in other ways? These questions lie at the heart of the two case studies that follow.

'No More Paper Mills': The Conflict over Pulp Mills on the Uruguay River

Between the years 2002 and 2005, the government of Uruguay announced the construction of several large pulp mills on a stretch of the Uruguay River opposite the Argentinean frontier. Two of these plants were to be built near Fray Bentos, across the river from the town of Gualeguaychú in Argentina, one by the Finnish transnational Metsä-Botnia, and one by a local subsidiary of the Energía y Celulosa (ENCE) group of Spain called Celulosa de M´bopicuá. While construction of the M´bopicuá plant was eventually relocated, the Metsä-Botnia plant went ahead to completion, becoming a major focus of public concern about contamination in the shared waters of the river. Meanwhile, in 2009 a controlling share in the venture was bought by another Finnish transnational, United Paper Mills (UPM); hereafter we refer to the plant as Botnia-UPM.

From the beginning, the transboundary nature of the mills' potential ecological impacts shaped the field of political mobilization and contest. Stirrings of a movement against the projects first appeared in 2003, when Uruguayan environmental organizations alerted various citizen groups in Gualeguaychú about the planned developments (Aboud and Musseri 2007; Merlinsky 2008). By 2005, when construction of the Botnia-UPM plant began, Argentinean resistance had grown in importance, its most noticeable and enduring manifestation consisting of a road block on the international bridge between Gualeguaychú and Frey Bentos, which began in 2006 and was only definitively lifted in 2010. The protestors demanded compliance with the 1975 Uruguay River Treaty, which prescribes a consultation process between the two countries for projects that potentially impact the shared waterway. The government of Uruguay refused to negotiate while the roadblocks remained in place, and rather than seek the removal of the protestors the Argentinean government launched a lawsuit against Uruguay in 2006, through the International Court of Justice (ICJ) in The Hague. When the court issued its decision on 20 April 2010, ruling that Uruguay had violated the consultation and negotiation requirements set out in the Uruguay River Treaty (International Court 2010), the roadblocks finally ended. By that time, however, the Botnia-UPM plant had been constructed and was already in operation.

Argentinean popular mobilization against the mills was anchored by an Environmental Citizens' Assembly, which was founded as a platform for publicizing concerns and channelling demands to the Argentinean Government. The assembly includes a wide range of local organizations under its umbrella but is anchored in local economic interests articulated by small producers, professionals, businesspeople and entrepreneurs in the tourism industry. These sectors had pre-existing working relationships within the Corporación para el Desarrollo de Gualeguaychú (Gualeguaychú Development Corporation), an association of local businesses responsible for coordinating an annual event of crucial importance in attracting visitors to the city: the Gualeguaychú Carnival. Despite being grounded in a particular set of local economic interests, the Citizens' Assembly achieved a broad degree of legitimacy in the Gualeguaychú community as the principal site for mobilization among diverse groups. Indeed, it became a space of popular deliberation, where key decisions about the direction of the anti-mill campaign were reached through mechanisms of direct democracy (Vara 2007; Delamata 2009). Perhaps reflecting the diversity of its base, but also embodying a novel kind of political strategy, the Citizens' Assembly seeks to work closely with government even as it cooperates with environmental NGOs that are more oriented to a confrontational politics of protest and direct action. As a symbolic affirmation of this orientation, the honorary president of the Assembly is the Mayor of Gualeguaychú.

These features make the Gualeguaychú Citizens' Assembly a new species of actor in the sphere of environmental politics in Argentina. Its inclusive profile and broad legitimacy within a territorially defined community, along with the key strategic resources that its diverse membership has been able to provide (especially political connections and professional expertise) have given it a kind of authority in the public sphere that environmental NGOs, which are often viewed as idealistic or extreme in their politics, typically lack. As such, during the mobilizations against the pulp mills it succeeded in bringing all levels of government into the debate. Moreover, it continued to be involved in the debate as it moved into the sphere of transnational litigation. Doctors, lawyers, engineers and university researchers affiliated with the Assembly played important roles in the technical teams that elaborated the arguments presented in the ICJ to support Argentina's case against Uruguay.

To the disappointment of the members of the Citizens' Assembly, the Court's April 2010 decision ruled that it was not possible to identify substantial impacts of the Botnia-UPM pulp mill on water quality in the river (International Court 2010). With this decision the mill's decommissioning and relocation is clearly off the agenda, and the Citizens' Assembly has switched gears to press for transparent monitoring of effluent discharge through the Administrative Commission of the River Uruguay, a bi-national body that oversees coordination between the two nations for ongoing implementation of the 1975 treaty. The Commission's role has been significantly strengthened by the ICJ's judgment, which sets an obligation on both parties to cooperate through the Commission in ongoing monitoring of water quality in the river (International Court 2010, 266). After lengthy negotiations, a bi-national scientific committee initiated its monitoring activities in May of 2011.[2]

The mobilization of citizens in Gualeguaychú to protect the ecological and economic values of water quality along their shores presents a turning point in the history of socio-environmental conflict in Argentina (Giarraca and Petz 2007; Vara 2007; Delamata 2009). The locally rooted and broadly inclusive nature of the Citizen's Assembly set a new mould for popular organization on environmental issues. This feature is combined with the Assembly's ability to participate in different modes of agency in conjunction with various kinds of actors and across a range of scales from local to international. Together, these features allowed the Assembly to open new spaces of debate over environmental questions and also to change the character of that debate, linking environment to livelihood and collective well-being. Finally, although national environmental legislation was less important to this debate, the mobilization in Gualeguaychú rested heavily on a discourse of 'collective environmental harm'. As we will see in the following case of Matanza-Riachuelo, this is a concept embedded in the Argentinean constitution since 1994, which has only recently been mobilized as a key fulcrum for citizens' efforts to protect their local environments.

The Gualeguaychú citizen movement also had impacts beyond national boundaries. The struggle over the pulp mills has stirred broader debates over the need for improved institutional and legal frameworks to regulate the impacts of economic activities in the shared ecological territory of the countries that border the Uruguay River basin (Brazil, Uruguay and Argentina) (Gautreau and Merlinsky 2008; Gorosito Zuluaga 2008; Merlinsky and Gautreau 2010). Beyond regional concerns for management of shared waterways, the conflict also stimulated important advances in international environmental legal norms. According to Owen McIntyre (2011), the ICJ decision made significant steps towards solidifying certain duties under international law, including the duty to notify and the duty to conduct an environmental impact assessment taking into account transboundary dimensions of major development projects. In addition, it contributed an important precedent with respect to delineating the relationships between procedural and substantive norms in international environmental law. In this way, the citizen mobilization in Gualeguaychú set in train a series of legal events which have in turn reshaped the terrain for future political mobilization around similar issues. In particular, the ICJ's decision has meant that the Administrative Commission of the River Uruguay has become a more powerful point of leverage for citizens' groups on both sides of the river frontier.

'Justice for the Riachuelo': The Conflict over Cleanup of the Matanza-Riachuelo Basin in Buenos Aires

Coincident with the increasing politicization of environmental issues through the citizen mobilization in Gualeguaychú, in 2006 the Argentinean Supreme Court made legal history by declaring its jurisdiction in the 'Beatriz Mendoza' case, a lawsuit filed in 2003 on behalf of residents of Villa Inflamable (Flammable Town), a marginal settlement in a particularly contaminated zone of the Cuenca Matanza-Riachuelo (Matanza-Riachuelo River Basin, hereafter CMR) in the heart of the Buenos Aires Metropolitan Region. Where constitutional rights were only rhetorically invoked in the case of Gualeguaychú, they became the central point of articulation between social and political actors in the case of the Matanza-Riachuelo.

Since the end of the nineteenth century, the watersheds that empty at the southern shore of the mouth of the Río de la Plata have served as the largest site of growing urban settlement in Argentina. In the absence of meaningful regulation, this urban expansion has had grave consequences for the ecology of these waterways (Di Pace 1992; Herzer and Gurevich 1996; Clichevsky 2002). The Matanza-Riachuelo is the largest of these watersheds, stretching into fourteen distinct municipal districts and becoming a prominent landscape feature by the time it reaches its mouth at the southern border of the Federal District. It has also become the most notoriously degraded urban waterway in the metropolitan region of Buenos Aires. The pollution of the CMR is a product of poor infrastructure, regulatory neglect and the externalities of economic development, its waters receiving effluents as a result of incomplete or malfunctioning sanitation systems, open garbage dumps and a host of petrochemical and other toxic industries that populate its banks. Despite periodic rhetoric about cleaning up the river basin, concern over the waterway only emerged decisively in local politics and began to receive consistent media attention over the past decade (Auyero and Swistun 2009; Merlinsky 2009). The Beatriz Mendoza lawsuit set in train a series of events that have turned that growing concern into novel kinds of judicial and political action.

Lawyers for residents of Villa Inflamable, supported by a group of environmental NGOs and the National Ombudsperson, launched their lawsuit on the basis of articles 41 and 43 of the 1994 constitution. The residents made claims against corporations and all levels of government for environmental damages, on the basis of medical reports indicating their exposure to lead poisoning, along with evidence that various nearby industries were discharging untreated waste into the river. In particular, they denounced the government for its failure to establish and enforce adequate norms to protect the local environment (Corte Suprema 2006). The claimants sought individual compensation, but they also demanded reparation for collective damages, as spelled out in the constitution and the 2002 Ley General del Ambiente. Setting aside the individual claims as outside its jurisdiction, the Supreme Court nevertheless took up the issue of collective damages and, as per the stipulations of the law, set about considering the necessary steps to ensure environmental cleanup, prevention of future damages and compensation for the collective damages already suffered. Moreover, drawing for the first time on the new constitutional principles of legal standing for the defence of collective rights, the Supreme Court's 2006 declaration of jurisdiction granted the Ombudsperson and the supporting environmental NGOs *amicus curiae* status in the case.[3] In its 2006 preliminary judgment, the Supreme Court required the riverside industries to account for the content and treatment of their effluents, and called on all levels of government with jurisdiction in the CMR to present an integrated plan for the watershed contemplating zoning of land use, control of human activities with impacts on the ecosystem, an environmental impact study on the effects of effluents from the industries named in the case, a program of environmental education and the ongoing monitoring of environmental quality with public access to the results of such monitoring.

The federal government responded to the court ruling by creating a new jurisdictional authority for the basin, Autoridad de la Cuenca Matanza-Riachuelo (ACUMAR), which draws together federal, provincial and municipal agencies to put into action the measures required by the court. In 2007 and 2008 the Supreme Court emitted further judgments in the case, updating the requirements it had placed on public authorities. Its 2008 sentence finalized the requirements for repairing the environmental integrity of the waterway, as well as the stipulations for preventing further damage; the case remains open with respect to compensation for the collective damage already suffered. The 2008 sentence also delegated authority over execution of the ruling to a lower federal court, including the authority to assign sanctions against ACUMAR and the various levels of government should they fail to carry out the Court's instructions. Meanwhile, the Court named the Ombudsperson and the NGOs involved in the case to conform a 'collegiate body' of the court with authority to act as a monitoring commission overseeing the implementation of the ruling and insuring citizen involvement in the process.

Unfortunately, ACUMAR has been plagued by the same jurisdictional battles that have hampered environmental management on the river for decades, undergoing two reorganizations during its first two years of operation and generally failing to implement the measures mandated by the court. Indeed, in late 2010 the president of ACUMAR was fined for the organization's violation of the cleanup timeline established by the court. More recently, the lower-court judge named the minister of the environment and the fourteen *Intendentes* (Mayors) of the municipalities in the CMR in a ruling requiring immediate action to move ahead with the long overdue work of clearing the waterway of obstructions, including unauthorized dwellings, improvised garbage dumps and the carcasses of long-abandoned vessels. Inaction after the stipulated date of completion for the cleanup is to be met with personal fines for all the named authorities ('El Juez Armella' 2011). In this way, the judiciary continues to drive forward this experiment in inter-jurisdictional and inter-institutional coordination to develop new tools for environmental governance in urban watersheds.

Taking Stock: New Actors, Juridification and the Politics of Knowledge

Environmental politics in Argentina is clearly in the midst of a transformative period. While it is premature to speak of a clearly delineated 'environmental citizenship', it is evident that environmental concerns are the object of new modes of collective mobilization and citizen engagement with political and judicial processes. This shift is in part enabled by a new language of environmental rights, but the drivers and implications of this new rights discourse are complex and multifaceted. To bring the fundamental features of the transformations described here into sharper relief, we return now to the three hypotheses laid out at the start of the chapter, examining each in light of the specific lessons to be learned from these two cases.

First we turn to the dimension of citizen mobilization. In both cases new forms of organization for collective action have been crucial to laying rights claims and advancing new governance agendas. Each case, however, reflects a very different basis for collective action. In the conflict over the paper mills, the Citizens' Assembly came together out of a constellation of interests associated with the local business and professional classes in Gualeguaychú. This largely middle-class constituency perceived that its lifestyle and economic interests were being threatened, and conceptualized its appeal to environmental rights in terms of a defence of place. The assembly has proved to be a durable feature in the local political landscape, attaining something like an institutionalization of citizens' abilities to monitor local environmental quality, keep tabs on important decision-making processes and bring collective voices to bear on key issues. In the case of Matanza-Riachuelo, on the other hand, the claimants in the case brought before the Supreme Court were from socio-economically marginal neighbourhoods, and the discourse of environmental rights was explicitly linked to their own immediate physical well-being – the defence of place became simultaneously the defence of injured bodies. Oddly enough, the citizens of Villa Inflamable, whose bodies form the basis for the claim of violated environmental rights in Matanza-Riachuelo, have remained largely silent in both the court proceedings and the political mobilization around the cause. Instead, it has been NGOs and professional activists, articulated with the office of the Ombudsperson, that have constructed the voice of 'the public interest'.

There are obvious problems with a scenario where marginalized communities become pawns in political and legal struggles where their own voices are left out. One of the most progressive outcomes associated with environmental justice struggles in North America has been the link between justice claims and the possibilities for more participatory citizenship, where subaltern subjects speaking about the plight of their local environments have gained recognition as political actors from their fellow citizens within the broader public sphere (Schlosberg 2004; Latta 2008). In the case of Villa Inflamable, this dynamic connection does not exist. In their ethnographic study of the settlement over a three-year period leading up to the 2006 Supreme Court ruling, Javier Auyero and Débora Swistun (2009) describe a community whose collective psychology has been shaped by submission to the chronic uncertainty generated in equal parts by their long-term exposure to a plethora of environmental contaminants and by the ambivalent and capricious attention they receive from government authorities, corporations, the media, doctors, lawyers and other external social actors. Ayuero and Swistun argue that through the 'social production of toxic uncertainty' (140), residents of Villa Inflamable have lost faith in the possibilities for collective action and have simply resigned themselves to a tyranny of waiting. They wait for government assistance, for medical attention, for compensation and for the elusive promise of relocation. To these citizens, the antics of the courts, NGOs and ACUMAR are simply another chapter in a story where they are the objects of concern but not major protagonists.

In comparison, the case of the mobilization in Gualeguaychú would seem to be more hopeful. Nevertheless, despite their claim to speak for the broader collective, the organizations comprising the Gualeguaychú Citizens' Assembly have not attempted to significantly articulate their demands with those of other regional and national groups arguing more generally for better environmental regulation. As such, their opposition to the pulp mills has not extended to questioning the economic system of production that presupposes the expansion of an agro-industrial model based on eucalyptus monocultures to feed the burgeoning pulp industry in both Uruguay and Argentina (Böhm 2009). Hence, even though their protests have raised national consciousness about environmental rights, it is possible that they have simultaneously increased environmental risks for less affluent communities with fewer political resources, whose backyards might in the future be more attractive sites for large industrial installations. Clearly, despite their innovative character and political efficacy, the new modes of collective action emerging in the landscape of environmental conflict in Argentina currently point to an uneven implementation of the environmental rights enshrined in the constitution.

To better understand both the promise and limitations of emerging forms of citizen action, it is necessary to look more closely at the interaction between citizens and institutions. This takes us into the domain of our second hypothesis about the significance of the juridification of environmental conflict, since the courts have been key interlocutors between citizens and public authorities in the two cases examined here. At the same time, we find that addressing the legal dimension of these cases almost immediately draws us into consideration of our third hypothesis about the increasing role of a politics of knowledge. In both of the cases, the ability of various actors to mobilize knowledge about environmental quality was crucial to their participation in judicial processes. Such participation involved submitting contentious and competing truth claims to legal judgment, hence abstracting environmental knowledge from both the social and the scientific contexts in which it is produced.

Dealing with conflicting scientific opinion was a major element of the ICJ's deliberations over Argentina's claims that Uruguay had violated the terms of the 1975 Uruguay River Treaty. Indeed, it was ultimately the ICJ's determination with respect to the science, not its decision regarding violation of the procedural obligations of the 1975 treaty, which determined the outcome of the conflict. Although it found that Uruguay had engaged in 'wrongful conduct' with respect to its obligations under the treaty, it ruled that such wrongful actions had now concluded, rendering them irrelevant to the ongoing operation of the Botnia-UPM paper mill. Argentina claimed that such wrongful conduct should be considered ongoing if impacts associated with that conduct (pollution due to operation of the plant) were also ongoing. So the court was obliged to make an objective decision as to whether there was good evidence that the paper mill had harmed the shared river ecosystem.

The court was presented with evidence generated by experts on both sides, addressing dissolved oxygen content in the water, as well as the prevalence of key pollutants such as phosphorus, phenolic substances, nonylphenols, nonylphenolethoxylates, dioxins and furans (International Court 2010). It reached conclusions about whether levels of these various substances fell outside normal concentrations for the ecosystem and whether there were any demonstrated links between contamination by these substances and changes in the biodiversity of the river. In addition, it made a determination as to whether or not a 2009 algae bloom event was caused by the operation of the Botnia-UPM plant and whether air quality in the region had deteriorated. McIntyre (2011, 132) notes that the opposing parties expressed significant reservations about each others' scientific data, questioning 'the independence of authors, the comprehensiveness and accuracy of data used, and the clarity and coherence of conclusions drawn.' Surprisingly, the court refused to comment on what kinds of standards should be considered in order to evaluate scientific claims, indicating simply that 'the Court will principally weigh and evaluate the data, rather than the conflicting interpretations given to it by the Parties or their experts and consultants' (International Court 2010, 236). The Court's professed attention to 'data' clearly diverged from the conviction of all parties involved in the conflict that the conduct of science around the dispute was heavily steeped in the political struggle. Here we see the limits of counter-expertise.

As Luc Boltanski (2011) observes, the authority of counter-experts rests precisely on their acceptance of the dominant principles, or 'ways of encoding reality', within which expertise itself is constructed; they are confined to challenging expert knowledge only on the fidelity of its application of those principles (137). He notes a similar relationship between social critique and legal frameworks, where the legitimacy of critique (expressed, for instance, as strikes or protests) rests on its ability to express itself within the bounds of existing legal norms. When we combine the judicial and scientific spheres the effect is in a sense multiplied: counter-experts who have sought to challenge experts on their own terrain are faced with a judicial authority that elevates scientific fact even beyond the status it normally holds. In such a scenario, the politics of truth escapes the grasp of democratic deliberation and debate.

In the case of the Matanza-Riachuelo, the constitutional guarantee of rights to a healthy environment was *the* point of leverage for radically transforming the terms of political struggle over the fate of the waterway. As such, we see here a concrete example of the way that juridification, in this case driven in no small part by legal professionals themselves, can reshape the political landscape. In responding to the claims that citizens' collective rights to a healthy environment had been violated by polluting industries and the government that failed to regulate them, the Supreme Court made bold use of its new powers. Drawing on its authority to direct the executive branch of government, which was conferred to it through the mechanism of minimum standards in the 2002 Ley General del Ambiente, the Court set in motion the involvement of diverse actors in a dramatic process of public policy innovation. Under the lights of intense media scrutiny, the Court's decision transformed the Matanza-Riachuelo conflict into a key site in which new norms of environmental governance are being put to the test.

As important as the Court's role has been, however, it would not have had the opportunity to engage in this innovative interpretation of the new body of environmental law if the case had not been brought forward by a novel coalition of social actors. Here the role of counter-experts was fundamental. Prior to the case there was almost a complete lack of environmental monitoring in the river basin. The protagonism of the Ombudsperson was central in addressing this vacuum by bringing together key NGOs, which between them shared a great deal of scientific and legal expertise, in order to document the environmental state of health in the watershed. These activities culminated in the 2003 publication of a scientific report (Defensor 2003), which effectively set the stage for the court challenge and the public debate that followed. The report's publication became crucial to the crystallization of publicly shared knowledge about the drastically degraded state of the river. The Ombudsperson followed up on the report with a series of recommendations and finally another report in 2006, denouncing the lack of action by public authorities. In fact, those very recommendations ended up comprising the substance of the Supreme Court's direction to state authorities in its various rulings. In this way the work of counter-experts, embedded in institutionalized social actors, has been fundamental in transforming an essentially 'lost' waterway into a perceived site of socio-ecological injury, while simultaneously providing the scientific and technical knowledge for a judicial ruling to correct that injury.

Final Reflections: Uneven Environmental Citizenships

Both of these cases suggest that the new nexus for environmental conflict in Argentina lies at the intersection of law and the politics of knowledge, and is animated by shifting multi-sectoral relationships between publics, citizen organizations and state institutions. While these are the shared features of contemporary environmental politics in Argentina, we follow Walter Pengue (2008) in arguing that the fundamental drivers of conflict are issues of ecological distribution rooted in the increasing territorial penetration of global capital, which seeks to generate profit from a range of natural resources while externalizing environmental and social costs wherever possible. In a place like Gualeguaychú we can see the fresh footprints of this process on local environments; in the Matanza-Riachuelo the abuses of current socio-ecological exploitation are layered on top of a century or more of similar practices.

The language of rights is becoming ever more central to these ecological distribution conflicts. Rights claims constitute new tools by which citizens can challenge established power hierarchies and render 'normal' practices illegitimate (Unger 2004). Such claims are undoubtedly strengthened by the rise of counter-experts, who are able to substantiate and authoritatively denounce the violation of rights. At the same time, there are key limitations to these new modes of contestation. For instance, we have seen that counter-expertise can lead to new kinds of exclusions, since many citizens are not equipped with the knowledge and skills to assemble scientific data and manoeuvre their way through complex legal processes. Moreover, even for citizens and citizen organizations that are able to mobilize counter-expertise, the politics of science, especially when refracted through a legal prism, promises sometimes ambiguous returns.

An increased reliance on rights claims and other legal tools can also have potentially troubling implications for the scope of public deliberation and the ultimate resolution of socio-environmental conflict. Examining the U.S. context, Silverstein (2009, 2010) argues that the deliberative benefits of politics can become displaced by processes of juridification. In the case of the

Matanza-Riachuelo, the institutions put in place according to the Supreme Court's order for a cleanup have continued to delay key steps in the implementation of the recovery plan for the river. Is it possible that, by forcing rapid action through the courts, a requisite level of socio-cultural change among politicians and administrators has been foregone, leading to dysfunctional institutions that push back against the legal authority? Or must we instead conclude that an even more profound process of political change – not just in values but in broad relationships of socio-economic power – must take place for ecological distribution conflicts to be resolved and meaningful protection of citizen rights to become a reality?

To be sure, rights-based claims founded on the notion of environmental injury (whether local injury of individual bodies or trans-border injury of socio-economic interests) have won crucial progress towards a substantially more open public sphere for debate about environmental concerns. In the case of the Uruguay River, the judgment of the ICJ means that citizens in both countries are now able to demand greater accountability from the bi-national Administrative Commission and can rely on a more transparent and rigorous scientific process of monitoring. All the same, the Botnia-UPM plant continues to operate. In the case of the Matanza-Riachuelo, rights claims under the previously unused section of the 1994 constitution revealed the complete disfunctionality of the institutional frameworks for environmental management in the watershed and have brought the matter of the river's future into sustained public debate. Nevertheless, if this disfunctionality persists there are far-reaching issues at stake in the gap between law and reality. As environmental laws are passed but only partially implemented, a widespread lack of confidence in government agencies grows; politicians and state officials are perceived to be quite simply unaccountable to public judgment. In this context, we might well conclude that the right to a healthy environment really belongs only to those Argentinean citizens who have the wealth and political power to insulate themselves from the externalities of industrial development.

Notes

1. The chapter is based on research conducted by the principal author between 2005 and 2008, comprising analysis of press coverage and extensive consultation with a range of other forms of documentation, as well as extensive ethnographic interviews with legal, political, economic and civil society actors in each of the two conflicts. Unless otherwise stated, the statements of fact herein are based on data collected during that ethnographic research.
2. Updates on the monitoring process are available on CARU's website: http://www.caru.org .uy/.
3. The NGOs names were: Asociación Ciudadana por los Derechos Humanos (ACDH), Asociación de Vecinos La Boca (AVLB), Centro de Estudios Legales y Sociales (CELS), Fundación Ambiente y Recursos Naturales (FARN) and Greenpeace Argentina.

References

Aboud, L., and A. Musseri. (2007) 'En caída libre: Del diferendo al conflicto,' in V. Palermo and C. Reboratti (eds), *Del Otro Lado del Río: Ambientalismo y Política Entre Uruguayos y Argentinos*. Buenos Aires: EDHASA, pp. 15–56.

Auyero, J., and D. Swistun. (2009) *Flammable: Environmental Suffering in an Argentine Shantytown*. Oxford: Oxford.

Azuela, A. (2006) *Visionarios y Pragmáticos: Una Aproximación Sociológica al Derecho Ambiental*. México DF: UNAM, Instituto de Investigaciones Sociales.

Blichner, L. C., and A. Molander. (2008) 'Mapping Juridification,' *European Law Journal*, Vol. 14, No. 3, pp. 36–54.

Böhm, S. (2009) 'Clean Conscience Mechanism: A Case From Uruguay,' in S. Böhm and S. Dabhi (eds), *Upsetting the Offset: The Political Economy of Carbon Markets*. London: MayFlyBooks, pp. 119–128.

Boltanski, L. (2011) *On Critique: A Sociology of Emancipation*. Cambridge: Polity.

Callon, M., P. Lascoumes and Y. Barthe. (2001) *Agir dans un Monde Incertain: Essai sur la Démocratie Technique*. París: Seuil.

Castells, M. (1997) *The Power of Identity*. Oxford: Blackwell.

Clichevsky, N. (2002) *Pobreza y políticas urbano-ambientales en la Argentina*. Santiago de Chile: CEPAL-ECLAC. División de Medio Ambiente y Asentamientos Humanos, Document N.49.

Constitución Nacional de Argentina. (1994) Online document, http://www.senado.gov.ar/web/interes/constitucion/cuerpo1.php (accessed June 2011).

Corte Suprema de Justicia de la Nación Argentina [CSJN]. (2006) *M. 1569. XL. ORIGINARIO. Mendoza, Beatriz Silvia y otros c/ Estado Nacional y otros s/ daños y perjuicios (daños derivados de la contaminación ambiental del Río Matanza - Riachuelo)*, online document, http://www.acumar.gov.ar/ACUsentencias/CausaMendoza/Fallos/cortesuprema2006.pdf (accessed July 2011).

Defensor del Pueblo de la Nación. (2003) *Informe Especial Sobre la Cuenca Matanza-Riachuelo*, online report, http://www.dpn.gob.ar/riachuelo/r-info1.htm (accessed June 2011).

Delamata, G. (2009) 'Introducción,' in G. Delamata (ed.), *Movilizaciones Sociales: ¿Nuevas Ciudadanías?* Buenos Aires: Biblos, pp. 13–28.

Di Pace, M. (ed.). (1992) *Las Utopías del Medio Ambiente. Desarrollo Sustentable en Argentina*. Buenos Aires: CEAL.

'El Juez Armella Ordenó Sanear el Riachuelo Antes del 1 de Julio.' (2011) *InfoRegión: Diario del Área Metropolitana de Buenos Aires*, online report, http://www.inforegion.com.ar/vernota.php?id=228013&dis=1&sec=1 (accessed June 2011).

Gautreau, P., and G. Merlinsky. (2008) 'Mouvements locaux, Etat et modèles de développement dans le conflit des usines de pâte à papier du fleuve Uruguay,' *Problèmes d'Amérique Latine*, Dossier Amérique latine, conflits et environnement, No. 70, pp. 61–80.

Giarracca, N., and I. Petz. (2007) 'La Asamblea de Gualeguaychú: su lógica de nuevo movimiento social y el sentido binacional "artiguista" de sus acciones,' *Revista Realidad Económica*, No. 226, pp. 101–126.

Gorosito Zuluaga, R. (2008) 'Tratado sobre recursos compartidos y los conflictos ambientales.' Paper delivered at a colloquia titled Pasteras en el Río Uruguay y la problemática de la deslocalización de las industrias contaminantes, Facultad de Ciencias Jurídicas y Sociales, Universidad Nacional del Litoral, Santa Fé, online report, http://www.idea.org.py/espanol/comunicados.php (accessed July 2011).

Habermas, J. (1986) 'Law as Medium and Law as Institution,' in G. Teubner (ed.), *Dilemmas of Law in the Welfare State*. New York: Gruyter, pp. 203–220.

Herzer, H., and R. Gurevich. (1996) 'Construyendo el riesgo ambiental en la ciudad,' *Desastres y Sociedad*, Vol. 4, No. 7, pp. 8–15.

Holston, J. (2008) *Insurgent Citizenship: Disjunctions of Democracy and Modernity in Brazil.* Princeton: Princeton University Press.

International Court of Justice [ICJ]. (2010) *Judgment: Case Concerning Pulp Mills on the River Uruguay (Argentina v. Uruguay)*, online document, http://www.icj-cij.org/docket/files/135/15877.pdf (accessed June 2011).

Keck, M. E., and K. Sikkink. (1998) *Activists Beyond Borders: Advocacy Networks in International Politics.* Cornell: Cornell University Press.

Latta, A. (2008) 'The Ecological Citizen,' in E. F. Isin (ed.), *Recasting the Social in Citizenship.* Toronto: University of Toronto Press, pp. 239–260.

Ley General del Ambiente [Law 25675]. (2002) Online document, http://www.ambiente.gov .ar/ (accessed June 2011).

McIntyre, O. (2011) 'The World Court's Ongoing Contribution to International Water Law: The Pulp Mills Case Between Argentina and Uruguay,' *Water Alternatives*, Vol. 4, No. 2, pp. 124–144.

Melé, P. (2003) 'Conflits Urbains pour la Protection de la Nature dans une Métropole Mexicaine,' in P. Melé, C. Larrue and M. Rosemberg (eds), *Conflits et Territoires.* Tours: Presses Universitaires François Rabelais, pp. 103–117.

Merlinsky, G. (2008) 'Nuevos Repertorios de Acción Colectiva y Conflicto Ambiental: una Cronología del Conflicto por la Instalación de las Plantas de Celulosa en el Río Uruguay,' *Revista Nuevo Mundo Mundos Nuevos*, online article, http://nuevomundo.revues.org/index16412 .html.

———. (2009) *Atravesando el Río: La Construcción Social y Política de la Cuestión Ambiental en Argentina. Dos Estudios de Caso en Torno al Conflicto por las Plantas de Celulosa en el Río Uruguay y al Conflicto por el Saneamiento de la Cuenca Matanza-Riachuelo.* Doctoral thesis, Faculty of Social Sciences, Department of Geography, University of Buenos Aires/Universidad Paris VIII, Buenos Aires: Mimeo.

Merlinsky, G., and P. Gautreau. (2010) 'Vers la Fin du Conflit Diplomatique Entre l'Uruguay et l'Argentine?' *Rue 89*, online report, http://www.rue89.com/2010/04/21/vers-la-fin-du-conflit-diplomatique-entre-luruguay-et-largentine-148302 (accessed July 2011).

Pengue, W. (ed.). (2008) *La Apropiación y el Saqueo de la Naturaleza: Conflictos Ecológicos Distributivos en la Argentina del Bicentenario.* Buenos Aires: Fundación Heinrich Böll, GEPAMA, Lugar Editorial.

Reynolds, L. A., and S. E. Hrudey. (2006) 'Managing Uncertainty in Environmental Decision-Making: the Risky Business of Establishing a Relationship Between Science and Law,' *International Journal of Risk Assessment and Management*, Vol. 6, No. 1–3, pp. 1–249.

Schlosberg, D. (2004) 'Reconceiving Environmental Justice: Global Movements and Political Theories,' *Environmental Politics*, Vol. 13, No. 3, pp. 517–540.

Silverstein, G. (2009) *Law's Allure: How Law Shapes, Constrains, Saves, and Kills Politics.* New York: Cambridge University Press.

———. (2010) 'Law's Allure in American Politics and Policy: What It Is, What It is Not, and What It Might Yet Be,' *Law & Social Inquiry*, Vol. 35, No. 4, pp. 1077–1097.

Svampa, M. (2008) *Cambio de Época: Movimientos Sociales y Poder Político.* Buenos Aires: Siglo XXI.

Teubner, G., and B. Firenze. (1987) 'Juridification: Concepts, Aspects, Limits, Solution,' in G. Teubner (ed.), *Juridification of Social Spheres: A Comparative Analysis in the Areas of Labor, Corporate, Antitrust and Social Welfare Law.* Berlin and New York: De Gruyter, pp. 3–48.

Unger, R. M. (2004 [1987]) *False Necessity: Anti-Necessitarian Social Theory in the Service of Radical Democracy.* London and New York: Verso.

Vara, A. (2007) 'Sí a la Vida, No a las Papeleras: en Torno a una Controversia Ambiental Inédita en América Latina,' *Redes*, Buenos Aires, Vol. 12, No. 25, pp. 15–49.

12

Environmentalism as an Arena for Political Participation in Northern Argentina

Brián Ferrero

In late 2006, sixty-two families occupied lands of the Yabotí Biosphere Reserve in the province of Misiones, in northeastern Argentina. They carved plots for each family out of the forest and constructed makeshift dwellings with scrap wood and plastic bags. The illegal settlers had previously inhabited lands near the reserve for more than a decade, developing an economy based on small-scale cultivation of plots averaging twenty-five hectares per family, combining industrial crops like tobacco and *yerba mate* with subsistence production (Bartolome 1991; Baranger and Schiavoni 2005). The occupied lands were part of the buffer area of the reserve, privately owned and dedicated to forestry.[1]

Three days after the occupation started, park rangers arrived to demand the squatters' immediate eviction, but the *colonos* (settlers) refused. One of them expressed the reasons for the occupation as follows: 'We came with the objective of having a small farm, occupying a piece of land for the sustenance of our children, to have a place to plant. Because we don't have land and we need a place to plant. We are thinking in the future of our children, since we can't send them to study' (quoted in Palma 2008, 12). The occupants requested an audience with authorities from the Provincial Ministry of Ecology, with whom they would discuss their departure from the reserve in exchange for access to development projects, as well as services such as roads, schools and electrical power. Besides making these demands, they also made a pointed declaration, that only small and medium rural producers such as themselves can properly 'take care of the forest, engaging in sustainable modes of cultivation and protect the environment. This forest is the lungs of the world and the *colonos* have to be the guardians of the forest' (Palma 2008, 20).

Contemporaneous to this conflict and several others like it, indigenous communities in the region were engaged in their own struggles with private property holders and state authorities. A 2008 manifesto presented by the gathered Mbya-Guaraní *caciques* of the region explains the origins of their struggle by remarking that 'we see the logging trucks daily carrying away the forest, and with it the water and our future; it seems that their wealth [of the forest companies] will be our death, as a people and a culture' (3º Manifiesto 2008). As with the unauthorized settlers in the Biosphere Reserve, we see here demands for social justice interlaced with claims to speak from a place of intimate human-ecological relationship.

While in the past such challenges to property rights and state authority have habitually been treated through recourse to penal justice, in these recent conflicts a new pattern of engagement and dialogue has emerged. In the case of the Yabotí *colonos*, the provincial government agreed to allow the Ministry of Ecology to negotiate with the squatters. These negotiations led to their withdrawal from the reserve in return for a package of state development assistance including credit, improved roads, connection to the electrical grid and the construction of schools. A few months after the conclusion of the negotiations a *mesa de diálogo* (roundtable) was created to insure a long-term basis for cooperation around regional development and conservation objectives. Similarly, over the past decade the Guaraní communities within the reserve have increased their political participation in dialogue with both the state and environmental organizations over the management of the territory. In 2006, negotiations led the state to designate ten thousand hectares of land around the Guaraní communities as off-limits to logging, and also to launch a process seeking the institutionalization of indigenous communities' participation in ongoing dialogue about conservation and development issues in the region.

These conflicts over land, and the emerging new relationships to which they have given rise, occur in the context of accelerating exploitation of forest resources in Misiones. At the same time, they correspond to a shift in the politics of conservation, where exclusionary models of nature protection have shifted towards approaches that aim to tie conservation with development, integrating local communities into the planning and management of preserved areas. These changes in conservation policies parallel those in other parts of the world, and indeed we might note that this new approach has arrived with some delay in Misiones (Redford, Robinson and Adams 2006; Adams 2004; West, Igoe and Brockington 2006; Brosius and Hitchner 2010). As in other conservation hotspots of the world, the language of environmentalism has come to permeate local language and speech, providing the discursive context for community-based conservation projects that link together nature protection with land rights, while incorporating a concern for local identities, social organization, livelihood and resource management (Li 2005, 431). These kinds of projects bring local peoples closer to the state, a shift which serves alternately as a form of more direct democracy and as a vehicle for intensifying state control over communities and populations (Li 2005, 440).

In this chapter, I analyse this changing relationship between state and local peoples in the province of Misiones, exploring the way that settler and indigenous communities reshape their political agency through participation in what I call an 'environmental arena', a discursive and territorial space in which environmental management systems and identities are collectively negotiated and substantively transformed. Here I propose that participation in this arena involves a key tension for local communities, which in part create new social identities for themselves and in part have new identities imposed upon them by conservation agencies (Scott 1998; Agrawal and Gibson 1999; MacDonald, 2003; Brockington 2004; Brosius 2006). This tension involves a fraught relationship between acts of submission to state authority, for instance by accepting the imposition of certain forms of group organization, and acts of defiance against the state in order to claim rights to a particular territorial space (Agrawal 2005). For *colonos* and indigenous peoples alike, negotiating this tension involves the uptake of new subjectivities and identities, particularly around the notion of being 'conservationists'.

In Misiones a diverse set of actors – government agencies, national and international NGOs, bilateral aid agencies – are engaged in the process of constructing a unified institutional framework around the emergent environmental arena. Despite the apparent homogeneity of the framework, distinctions between the way outside actors engage with *colonos* and Guaraní are not to be minimized. There are important differences in the kinds of struggles and demands that are presented by each of these populations, the ways that various actors respond to them and the shape of the multi-actor dialogues that result.

The analysis that follows is based on fieldwork realized during several visits to the region over fourteen months between 2002 and 2004. New fieldwork, including interviews with *colonos* involved in the 2006 occupation of the biosphere reserve, was conducted between 2006 and 2008. A final stage of fieldwork involved interviews with leaders of the Mbya-Guaraní communities in the reserve between 2007 and 2009. During the various fieldwork cycles interviews were also conducted with government officials in a range of agencies, as well as with representatives of key NGOs operating in the region.

The chapter begins with an exploration of theoretical concepts around development, conservation and socio-cultural subjectivity. Second, I offer a characterization of the economic processes that led to the deepening marginalization of rural populations in Misiones, fomenting the conflicts described at the outset of the chapter and also attracting the attention of development agencies. At the heart of the chapter is an examination of the formation of an environmental arena, including new ecologically oriented significations of territory and constructions of social subjectivity. The analysis concludes with a reflection on what the emergence of an environmental arena ultimately means for the inhabitants of the region, particularly with respect to the institutionalization of their struggles to secure land and livelihood.

Territories, Communities and Conservation

My analysis rests on the fundamental assertion that practices of nature conservation constitute new forms of management and control of spaces and populations (Igoe and Brockington 2007; Fletcher 2010). These practices can in part be understood as extensions of the administrative logic of the modern state (Scott 1998). At the same time, with the onset of new environmental governance practices based on markets and multi-actor networks, it has become clear that the state is not unique in its tendency to alternately reify/efface elements of the socio-ecological landscape in order to make populations and territories legible to a calculating logic (Chapin 2004).

More participatory models of conservation certainly seem to promise an improvement on the exclusionary modes of conservation that have had such widely noted impacts on indigenous peoples (Colchester 2003). At the same time, diverse observers have argued that these new conservation models veil equally new forms of subjection for local populations (Brockington 2004; MacDonald 2003; Ferguson 2006; West, Igoe and Brockington 2006; Fletcher 2010). In particular, participatory conservation initiatives have often been linked to the advance of neoliberal models of governance, where the diminished power of the state is simply the counterpoint to increasing power for vested economic interests (Igoe and Brockington 2007).

Within shifting models of conservations there is a tremendous tension between meaningful political participation and top-down manipulation for the purpose of legitimating certain entrenched paths of development. From the latter perspective 'participation' represents a regimen of civility that aims to constrain and domesticate dissent (Brosius and Russell 2003, 41). Peter Brosius (2006) suggests that the decentralization of resource management has become a key government tactic to forestall the political organization of subject populations. In this sense, the turn towards participatory conservation practices might actually augment the control of the state (Turner 2006). As such, from the perspective of popular concerns for social and environmental justice, community resource management can be no substitute for continued organizing to seek deeper political reforms.

As other contributors to this volume also observe, new practices of conservation must also be understood in terms of the multi-scalar relationships of power that they embody (see Baldwin and Meltzer, and de Castro, this volume). New forms of conservation are based on extensive networks comprised by corporate actors, international conservation organizations and states (Ferguson 2006). Conservation organizations have played a particularly important role in the emergence of these transnational actor networks, establishing global standards and best practices around the design and implementation of protected areas. Kenneth MacDonald (2003) describes this as part of a kind of recolonization process, where concern over a 'global environment' is the ideology that justifies new relationships of subjection to distant authority. Following Brosius (1999), we might see this process in terms of the spread of environmental discourse comprised of certain topologies. These topologies provide the scenario within which the state of the planet and of particular regions is problematized, actors are recognized and assumptions about the relationships between distinct subjectivities and their environments are formed.

Along these lines, Ferguson (2006) argues that transnational conservation networks effect a reterritorialization of conserved landscapes and the people who inhabit them. At one level, they are incorporated into the legal and administrative frameworks for conservation and resource management carried out by national states. At the same time, they become inserted into transnationalized spaces within global circuits of conservation and capital. Paradoxically, such transnationalization often depends on a particularly acute performance of 'the local', in the shape of traditional customs and quaint livelihood practices. Meanwhile, although conservation initiatives are often presented as beneficial for local populations, protected areas are in fact incorporated into modes of regulation that revalorize them for the extraction of new kinds of commodities benefitting outside interests, such as tourism agencies, resort developers and elite ecotourism operators. It is unclear how many benefits trickle back to local peoples.

Institutions are key points of articulation for this multi-scalar reterritorialization of the local. In Misiones, institution building, such as the formation of multi-stakeholder dialogues, has played a key role in defining who 'counts' in exercises of local citizenship around matters of conservation and development (see Sundberg, this volume, for a similar analysis in Guatemala). Such institutions also become central to demarcating the ground rules for dialogue – what will be discussed and in what terms. This kind of demarcation of political space has an impact on how local citizens imagine themselves in terms of their relationships to other actors, resulting in the reconfiguration of individual and collective subjectivities and identities (Agrawal 2005; Brosius 2006). In the administrative sphere, as state and conservation institutions grapple with phenomena such as the land conflicts in Misiones they seek to render such problems legible to dominant categories of analysis and intervention, particularly those that are proper to practices of conservation and rural development (Scott 1998; Brosius and Russell 2003; Li 2005). This leads to interventions such as the state-led formation of production cooperatives, which engage citizens in economic processes that fundamentally reshape rural social relations.

At the same time, local actors are not merely passive objects of manipulation by external actors; as local communities are constituted, transformed and co-opted in different ways, they simultaneously resist change and find ways to make new demands on external actors (Agrawal and Gibson 1999; Li 2005). In part, such responses can be facilitated by the contradictions inherent in the dominant models of conservation and development (Li 2007), born of the way in which modern forms of government turn their attention towards optimizing an array of specific finalities embedded in the interstices of social life (Foucault 2001). When power is constituted in local sites, local actors sometimes find themselves in circumstances where new and unanticipated forms of agency may become available. As Tania Li (2007, 26) argues, 'The multiplicity of power, the many ways that practices position people, the various modes "playing across one another" produce gaps and contradictions. Subjects formed in these matrices ... encounter inconsistencies that provide grist for critical insights.' In a similar way, James Scott (1985) imagines the weapons of the weak to arise where cracks in the administrative logic of the state allows space for resistance to gain hold.

Along these lines, observers such as Mac Chapin (2004) and Nicholas Winer (2003) have argued that protected areas in Latin America have offered indigenous peoples important new ways of struggling to protect their traditional territories. According to Arturo Escobar (1999), contemporary conservation practices imply new forms of colonization of the biophysical and human landscape, but also contribute to the creation of new political possibilities for local communities, suggesting that, ultimately, outcomes depend 'on the degree to which local communities are able to appropriate and use the new significations to achieve their own objectives, by bringing them into relationship with other identities, circuits of knowledge and political projects' (218). The search for popular agency is not simply about existing social groups finding new forms of agency, but also about the constitution of new social actors. Following Li (2007) we can assert that one of the unanticipated effects of multi-scalar processes of reterritorialization is the production of circumstances where new local affinities emerge from a diversity of previously disparate social subjectivities, organized around common experiences of development or conservation initiatives brought to them by actors at other scales.

Drawing together these insights, I considerer that the emerging environmental arena in Misiones generates new forms of social inclusion coinciding with the transformation of subjectivities. As such, if new forms of action appear they must be understood as linked to the networks and relations that produce the local spaces of conservation and development. Here there is a tension between an instrumental dimension of pragmatic participation and the progressive transformation of subjectivities, but these two tendencies are mutually conditioning rather than being simply contradictory. The processes by which the two sides of this equation interact are shaped and cemented by different kinds of social relations and institutions. As such, if new forms of action appear they do so in a manner linked to the networks and relations that produce this space.

Participation in the environmental arena is linked to the framing of problems in environmental terms, and to the fact that local populations are seen as having rights only to the extent that they are indentified as manifesting ecological qualities or potentials. In this context, the practice of citizenship is solidified through these new forms of local, 'ecological' identities. In this sense, the institutionalization that enables collective action also restrains it, delimiting the form and terms of participation while limiting the inclusion of actors who do not fit the mould of such identities. Citizenship, as both a formal and symbolic precipitate of these networks and relations, is co-constituted with the revaluation of territory.

A Marginal Space Becomes an Environmental Territory

The province of Misiones historically held a marginal place in the development of Argentina's agro-livestock sector. During the nineteenth century, when national borders were being defined, Misiones was considered a disputed territory by Argentina, Brazil and Paraguay. During the twentieth century, Misiones came to serve as an agrarian frontier, a space perceived as essentially vacant (despite its occupation by indigenous peoples) and attractive to populations in search of opportunities for improved social standing. Within the dominant model of agricultural production, the Paraná rainforest was considered to be an impediment to progress, in need of transformation and improvement if its potential productivity was to be realized. This outlook led to the promotion of logging activities and to colonial policies directed at small and medium rural producers. The principal social actor who mobilized the expansion of the agrarian frontier was the *colono*, usually a descendent of European migrants – principally Polish, German, Ukrainian and Spanish – who arrived in the region during the first half of the twentieth century. *Colonos* pursued their livelihoods organizing production around family labour and the cultivation of perennials (mainly *yerba mate* and tea) as well as annuals (tobacco). As *colono* populations arrived, indigenous populations in the region suffered encroachment on their territories, while being incorporated into the lower strata of rural production, working as temporary farmhands or generating income through the sale of artisanal products.

Expansion of the agrarian frontier came to an end in the 1990s, when there were no more available unclaimed lands. In this period, neoliberal politics were intensified, which brought about the elimination of barriers to external trade and the withdrawal of the State from the regulation of markets and in the provision of credit. In this way, a process of capital concentration was intensified in the stages of harvesting and manufacturing agricultural products, affecting above all the small and medium sized farmers and leading to the marginalization and impoverishment of rural families (Schvorer 2003). In response to the declining fortunes of rural smallholders, rural development programs were implemented throughout the region, through both official organizations and NGOs, with the objective of contributing to the subsistence of rural families (Baranger and Schiavoni 2005). The main strategy of these development agencies was to promote subsistence production in conjunction with a limited degree of local marketing. As conservation organizations began to work alongside development agencies, sustainable and agro-ecological development was increasingly promoted, spurring awareness-raising activities on the conservation of natural resources. For the most impoverished farmers, these programs have constituted one of the main sources of economic resources available for productive enterprises, family subsistence and marketing, making possible the creation of agricultural cooperatives and the installation of open markets where the locals can sell their products tax-free. Yet these programs are largely piecemeal and not integrated within a larger, strategic development program.

The marginalization of small- and medium-sized rural producers during the last decade of the twentieth century went hand in hand with a significant expansion of the industrial forestry sector in Misiones. Thanks to state initiatives, this sector came to serve as the main driver of the provincial economy, with 49 per cent of the sown area of Misiones used for forestation by 2002, representing 36 per cent of all forest plantations in Argentina (INDEC 2002). The expansion of the logging industry has also contributed to the process of land concentration. The logging of more than five thousand hectares has left 35 per cent of the provincial land area deforested, with only 11 per cent of the territory being occupied by logging projects smaller than twenty-five hectares, to the point that one single company possesses 8 per cent of the provincial land area (INTA 2003). The expansion of the forest industry has put new pressures on rural social relations. The development of the forestry industry in tandem with declining returns for family farms due to neoliberal policies has led many small farmers to either sell their lands to logging companies or convert their parcels into tree farms (Schvorer 2003). Similarly, the tensions between logging companies and indigenous communities have grown stronger as a result of the encroachment of logging operations into hunting and gathering areas. In various cases, with the consent of provincial officials, Chiefs have allowed exploitation of native forest on designated indigenous land, which has often become a source of internal community conflict.

The Environmental Arena of Misiones and the Construction of an Ecological Territory

At the beginning of the twenty-first century, Misiones contained the last unbroken remnant of the Paraná rainforest, which at the beginning of the twentieth century had occupied the whole eastern side of Paraguay and the southern states of Brazil, covering almost half a million square kilometres. By 2003 only 7.8 per cent of the Paraná rainforest was still standing (Di Bitetti, Placci and Dietz 2003), and the only portion left with the potential of reproducing wild species of flora and fauna was in Misiones. The province contains 1,123,000 hectares of forest, which represents 20 per cent of the existing Paraná rainforest (Di Bitetti, Placci and Dietz 2003). This situation is due to the fact that the Brazilian and Paraguayan portions of this environment were rapidly transformed into fields for cultivation, serving a similar economic function to the Pampas region in Argentina.

In the 1980s, conservation-related institutions and organizations started working in the province. The major actors included the NGO Vida Silvestre Argentina (FVSA), local representatives of the WWF and the Provincial Ministry of Ecology, all working to prevent the expansion of the agrarian frontier into the remaining native rainforest by creating a system of natural reserves. Their objectives brought them into conflict with agrarian users in a scramble over the fate of the last portions of unoccupied, state-owned lands. In this context conservationists sought to reconstruct the identity of Misiones around the remnant rainforest located there. In official slogans Misiones came to be described as 'wildly green' while on a global level it was presented as the 'green bastion of the planet'. The province ceased to be a territory defined by developmentalist ideas promoting agro-industrial development, and instead became a space where the logging industry, agriculture and conservationist causes would need to coexist.

In response to the conservationist agenda, from 1988 onwards, the Provincial Ministry of Ecology promoted a notable expansion of the province's nature reserves. Between the years 1988 and 2004, six protected areas grew to seventy, while the area under conservation went from 2.9 to 26 per cent (Ministry of Ecology 2008). At that point the dominant model of Protected Areas was one of strict preservation, in some cases leading to the expulsion of *colono* communities. With respect to indigenous communities, a historic tendency to render them invisible led much of their territory to be designated 'uninhabited'; in other cases such communities were actively removed to make way for conservation. In general, the *colonos* have considered the authorities of the Protected Areas to be repressive, leading them to pursue strategies of avoidance and to hide prohibited farming practices. Also, there have been more than a few incidents of direct violence, with an extreme case involving a firearms attack on a ranger.

Towards the end of the 1990s this emerging environmental arena began to undergo a dramatic reorientation, with the emergence of initiatives to integrate the local population in conservation practices. Environmental and development agencies began to disseminate materials on nature protection and sustainable development. Working in this vein were provincial and national agencies such as the National Parks Administration, the Secretary of Agriculture and the Provincial Ministry of Ecology, as well as NGOs like FVSA and international development agencies such as AECI and JICA (the Spanish and Japanese international cooperation agencies, respectively). In conjunction with refocusing the thrust of conservation policies, this collection of actors has problematized the agro-industrial model for regional economic development. To differing degrees, they have been critical of the concentration of land and wealth, and have sought to foment agricultural production by strengthening organizations of small producers and improving their access to markets. A vision of sustainable family farming, particularly involving the empowerment of women, has become pervasive. In line with this new vision of rural production, the main aim of conservation strategies has ceased to be about the quantity of protected area and instead depends increasingly on the establishment of ties between conservation and agricultural production. A host of new practices were introduced as part of this realignment, such as the implementation of agro-forestry projects, reforestation, demarcation of Indigenous lands, harvesting and marketing of products from the rainforest, application of selective forestry techniques, biodiversity prospecting and ecotourism. Pursuing different interests related to conservation, participants in this evolving arena created a political space of new alliances formed around the realigned development and conservation objectives. As a result of these changes, the legitimacy of nature protection has expanded within the *colono* and indigenous settlements.

The new conservation paradigm focuses on promoting 'participatory' processes of community building, given that 'top-down' interventions have been found to entail many obstacles and challenges for conservation (Brosius and Russell 2003; Colchester 2003). This has led to the reimagining of the protected areas as integrated with their surroundings, considering that they are directly affected by social and economic processes that take place beyond park boundaries. Community participation in decision making around territorial zoning and management practices is actively solicited as part of this new vision of conservation. Yet despite the good intentions, consensus is often elusive, given the many groups with a stake in the shape of the development model unfolding in the region. It is in this context that the conflicts around the Yabotí Biosphere Reserve outlined at the outset of the chapter have sparked new efforts at engagement and dialogue.

The Creation of a New *Colono* Identity and the Role of Place in Environmental Territory

While the state's sustainable development programs have not resulted in generalized improvements for producers, they have had other unanticipated results. The diffusion of sustainable development perspectives, discourses and practices has given rural inhabitants narrative elements that help them construct a new identity, or a new space of legitimacy from which to mount socio-political action, generating a type of citizenship that is bound to the occupation of a place in a specific territory. The category of '*colono*' is redefined in this context; if it previously indicated a mode of land tenure it has come instead to signify a legal standing and a new understanding of how to populate the rainforest and render it productive. With this reconfiguration of territory, being a *colono* implies a lifestyle linked to nature, the possession of knowledge about natural resources and the capacity to produce 'healthy', 'organic' and 'artisanal' products. This context highlights the productive qualities of small rural producers, characterized as they are by the development of small-scale operations based on family labour and the use of rudimentary technology, which are seen as more suitable for sustainable development than large-scale industrialized agricultural operations. This leads to the auto-'naturalization' of the *colonos,* who create their own version of an environmental territory.

Indigenous communities, on the other hand, generate an environmental identity by presenting themselves as possessing a lifestyle that can only prosper in the rainforest, thus implying that the preservation of the rainforest is necessary for the preservation of the Mbya-Guaraní. This identity construction is also framed in the struggle to regulate access to rainforest areas and to halt encroachment by logging companies. The manifestos of the *caciques* directed at the white authorities state that 'we are part of the forest not its owners like *kochi, pekari, venado, coati* and *paca* [forest animals]; without the forest not only our lives end but also the lives of all of them. It is the distinct lives of the forest that maintain its life, but we all depend on the trees; we ask the government that it order the suspension of all felling in the Yabotí Biosphere Reserve and in all the province' (3° Manifiesto 2008).

Both *colono* and Guaraní communities are finding new ways of positioning themselves in relation to the state, seeking to legitimize their rights as well as the potential that each group could have to conserve the rainforest. There is a noticeable difference, however, between the ways that the Guaraní and *colonos* organize. For the *colonos,* the legitimacy of the struggle is much more strongly linked to claiming rights in relation to levels of social service enjoyed by other citizens, such as schools, roads, access to markets and rural development programs. For the Guaraní communities, the rights demanded from the state have more to do with seeking the fulfilment or the improvement of legislation related to indigenous peoples, particularly regarding territorial rights. Without a doubt, the difference in how each of these groups positions itself towards national society is central. Not only do the *colonos* that live around protected areas already have standardized land tenure, but they further demand to be recognized as productive actors within a broader market economy. For the Mbya-Guaraní, on the other hand, the quest is to conserve a lifestyle linked to territory and to the rainforest; while they do participate in the dominant system of production, they generally do so as temporary farmhands or by selling artisanal products. Both *colonos* and Guaraní aim to exercise their citizenship by positioning themselves as agents with rights. Nevertheless, for the *colonos* this implies achieving equality in terms of living standards, whereas for the Guaraní this means maintaining their differences.

In the legitimization of the *colono* and Guaraní struggles, the definition of each sector in relation to territory plays a central role. The *colonos* take advantage of the valuation of the region as a unique environment that produces 'pure air for the planet', thus justifying the need to conserve it. From the onset of colonization the rainforest was thought of in relation to production, as an ideal source of agricultural lands. However, in the current phase of evolution in the environmental arena, the inhabitants have begun to think of themselves as a part of this environment instead of thinking of the rainforest as something that is foreign to them or that should be transformed. One consequence of this shift in thinking is that they see themselves as responsible for the rainforest's well-being. According to a small producer who lives in an area where there are conflicts taking place with a logging company:

> *Colonos* take care of the forest and care for the earth, because if we erode everything, then later we won't have anything left; we will not be able to find more land if we destroy where we live now. ... For this reason, we are obliged to take care of and protect the forest, the water, everything that we have, and all that ensures our livelihoods. If we were not here, the companies who claim these properties would have already cut down everything to plant pine trees. Because that's why they want to be the owners, to plant pine or to sell everything to Alto Paraná.[2]

Identity is constructed through oppositions and self-definitions. The image of the local inhabitants as possessing environmental capacities is elaborated in times of conflict, when it is necessary for them to distinguish themselves from others. Both for the Mbya-Guaraní and for the *colonos,* the forest industry is the primary social actor in opposition to which they construct their identities. While both see how the forestry industry encroaches upon the native forest, the *colonos* feel economic pressure because of limited access to markets for their agricultural products, leading many of them to reluctantly sell the trees on their properties (usually at low prices), and in the long term to sell their land to the logging companies. The Mbya-Guaraní communities, on the other hand, feel the pressure of seeing how the forests where they hunt and gather are progressively diminished.

Colonos construct their local identity in opposition to the way the rainforest is managed in neighbouring and First World countries. As one *colono* maintains: 'They have torn down their forests and now send scientists to study our rainforest.' One central element in the construction of this environmental identity relates to its nationalistic component. The province of Misiones is presented as a territory that contains the last remnant of the Paraná rainforest, in opposition to the highly fragmented state of the Brazilian and Paraguayan Atlantic rainforest ecosystems. This situation can be observed via satellite images that are publicized by environmentalists. Seeing these images, particularly the Brazilian countryside as an infinite expanse of monocultures, the *colonos'* opinions are often contradictory. On the one hand, they might admire industrial agricultural development, but on the other hand they understand how such development involves the degradation of the land, water and forests, as well as the expulsion of the small producers. In relation to Brazilians and Paraguayans, the *colonos* present themselves as conservationists defending their national and provincial patrimony. In turn, narratives are constructed in which the Misiones rainforest is positioned at the global level as being the 'lung of the planet', while the *colonos* acquire global responsibilities as guardians of the rainforest, given that their practices can determine 'climate change' or the future of the 'world's oxygen'. Brazilians and Paraguayans who venture into Misiones are described as 'predators' that don't 'respect nature, and when they step on a plot of land they destroy all of the vegetation'. In this way, elements of nationalism appear to reinforce the process of identity construction, given that migrants, based on their foreign origin, are seen as devaluing the local natural environment. Here nature is an element that constitutes the nation.

The *colonos'* environmental identity is also constructed through the meaning that they give to their own personal and group trajectories; as Joël Candau (2001) proposes, memory and identity are mutually constructed. Recurrent elements appear in the *colonos'* life-trajectory accounts. For example, in recalling the moment when they arrived at their farm settlements, the *colonos* often describe the area as paradise on earth, with abundant rainforest, wild animals, plants, rich red earth and the like. Since personal productive trajectories are described as having involved hard work, capitalization and development, a certain tone of innocence can be detected in the *colonos'* justification of natural-resource exploitation: 'Logging comes to us naturally: we see a standing tree and we cut it down, until we realize that things don't work that way, that the earth can't endure such treatment.' This period of intensive resource exploitation, in general, ends with stories of impoverishment in the settlements, where the land was left without its green cover, barren and cracked, and where forest clearings grew larger, water became contaminated and families suffered from low production levels and unequal marketing conditions. Stories of the *colonos'* current situation are often characterized by a certain loss of innocence, or by an eye-opening 'realization' of how 'traditional production' might degrade the health of the land, water and family.

At the same time, the *colonos* appear to naturalize themselves in relation to their accounts of land settlement, establishing strong ties with the environment and relating their personal trajectories to the history of the rainforest. In these accounts, the trees and the forest serve as turning points in personal, family and group histories. A reduction in forest areas seems to be an indicator of the passing of time or of distinct moments in a family's development. *Colonos* appropriate environmentalism's de-territorialized discourse and convert it into a re-territorialized mode of asserting natural/national identity, anchored in the rural spaces and places of Misiones.

New Institutionalization

The entrance of local inhabitants into the environmental arena has given way to processes of negotiation with state agencies, which has led to both the institutionalization of collective action and the formal regulation of participation. Two types of institutions are generated by this process: the *aty-guazú* in the case of the Guaraní and the *mesa de diálogo* in the case of the *colonos*.

In the case of the Mbya-Guaraní in the Yabotí reserve, land-use conflicts led to the recovery of a traditional form of collective deliberation called *aty-guazú*, a formal and ritualized space where leaders of various communities come together to form a unified position with respect to threats to their territory. Curiously, it has been the provincial State and the Catholic Church, rather than Guaraní leaders themselves, that promoted (and more importantly financed) the revival of this institution. The Provincial Ministry of Ecology considered that recovering this element of traditional forms of governance both contributed to the conservation of Guaraní culture and at the same time facilitated consultative and participatory measures undertaken by state agencies. The *aty-guazú* begins with a meeting exclusively between Guaraní leaders; when they have reached an agreement and a collective stance, they open the meeting to representatives of the state and other outsiders. Since there are no stipulations as to how long each *aty-guazú* will last, visitors (representatives of government, NGOs and universities) generally have to wait several days until being called to meet with the *caciques*. Via the mechanism of the *aty-guazú*, representatives of the Guaraní communities have a permanent place in the Reserve's Management Committee, where they discuss operations with state officials, landowners and environmental NGOs.

In the case of the *colonos,* formal interaction with the state has taken place through *mesas de diálogo,* spaces created to ameliorate conflicts and insure that a wider range of voices are included in decisions affecting local agricultural communities. The roundtable that resolved the original conflict over the illegal occupation of the Reserve included the Provincial Ministries of Ecology and of Agrarian Affairs, the Spanish NGO Petjades, the FVSA, AECI and JICA. Subsequent *mesas de diálogo* (between 2006 and 2010 there were five in total) have included only the *colonos* and the Ministry of Ecology. The space of dialogue offered by the *mesas* became the context for creation of an agricultural cooperative run by the *colonos.* While clearly giving voice to *colono* concerns, the *mesas* have also increased the degree to which state and non-state institutions steer the interests of local populations into a mould that fits with overarching conservation goals.

The construction of new institutions such as the *aty-guazú* and the *mesas de diálogo* is not simply about imposing forms of organization from above, but rather depends on the resignification of local discourse and practice. A kind of tacit pact is generated between local actors and state agencies, which permits the orderly governance of the territory and the reduction of conflict. A series of rules and norms are established to regulate collective action, thus privileging certain practices and limiting others. For example, just some *colono* demands were defined as acceptable or as suitable for negotiation, such as the creation of rural schools, the installation of water pumps and the implementation of sustainable development programs or horticultural projects for family consumption. In contrast, demands for lands and access to credit for purchasing machinery were left out continually until they eventually disappeared from the agenda of the participants in the more recent *mesas de diálogo.* In turn, other *colonos,* who maintained their demands for the redistribution of lands owned by logging companies or subsumed within protected areas were gradually excluded from dialogue. While many of these *colonos* had led the first phases of protests, when they began to negotiate with the state and nongovernmental agencies, they were progressively marginalized by the agencies' representatives as well as by their neighbours. The institutionalization of collective action leads to the development of privileges and exclusions, through which institutions mould the contours of discourses and practices over time, privileging certain forms of action and limiting others. In this sense, the environmental institutions, though partly providing new avenues for progressive change, are also new forms of intervention (Brosius 1999).

Final Considerations

The emergence of environmental ideas and discourses in *colono* and Indigenous people's struggles in Misiones perhaps begins with, but certainly comes to exceed, the search for legitimacy of political action. For these inhabitants, mobilizations through environmental initiatives do not merely represent an instrumental means of legitimizing old demands. Instead we witness the construction of new subjectivities, local identities and new forms of citizenship. This process is accompanied by the development of new territorial meanings as the inhabitants begin to describe the territory as a 'green' and 'ecological' place. The inhabitants also begin to critically evaluate how their productive practices and their forms of occupying space have shaped the environment. *Colonos* and Guaraní alike have also begun to develop a growing sense of reflexivity in regards to their own position in the territory, as well as the practices of others (including logging companies and inhabitants of neighbouring countries). By seeing themselves as builders of the environment, they take on responsibilities towards it. For this reason, a central element in understanding the local inhabitants' collective action can be found in the active positionality that they assume, which permits them to participate in the environmental arena and leads them to raise their problems in environmental terms. The transformation of subjectivities is generated by symbolic processes that are not simply imposed upon social groups but that instead emerge through social interactions. Thus, new subjectivities can be understood in terms of relations within the environmental arena, changes in environmental politics and new institutional arrangements (Agrawal 2005).

What direction will this incipient collective action take and what will local inhabitants' new role be? Will they attain greater and more profound democratization and citizenship? The answer is uncertain, but it is possible that discourses and institutions could become rigid over time, resulting in the formalization and bureaucratization of participation. Moreover, in the long term this process could be transformed into a new form of subjugation, this time with a green packaging. Among state agencies and environmental NGOs that work in the region, the participation of local populations is considered fundamental to conservation goals. At the same time, participation alone has proven to be an insufficient basis for environmental governance in the region, leading to the continued reliance on more conventional administrative practices and legal norms – such as the regime of private property. The participative paradigm arises in a determinate political and economic context, defined by the expanding reach and power of forestry companies, which in the last instance defines the character and limits of the aperture created by the new practices of governance. Ultimately, their interests subtly shape collective action, influencing which kinds of demands and forms of political mobilization are legitimate. In this sense, although we can see the emergence of newly empowered citizens, moved to defend and care for their territory, we must also take note of the ways that such empowerment becomes interwoven with new forms of marginalization.

Notes

1. The Yabotí Biosphere Reserve (YBR), in the province of Misiones, has a surface of 253,773 ha. The buffer area (215,955 ha., or 85 per cent of the total area) consists of private properties, owned by thirty-two forestry companies. The core area parks, property of the provincial state (20,658 ha., 8 per cent of the total area). The rest of the land is owned by different governmental institutions (Secretaría de Ambiente 2011).
2. The Chilean company Alto Paraná S.A. is the largest logging company in Argentina. The company's headquarters are located in Misiones.

References

3° Manifiesto de Pindo Poty. (2008) Unpublished document presented at tekoa Pindo Poty, 24–27 March, http://argentina.indymedia.org/news/2008/04/591892.php (accessed 22 June 2011).

Adams, W. (2004) *Against Extinction: The Story of Conservation.* London: Earthscan Publications.

Agrawal, A. (2005) 'Environmentality: Community, Intimate Government, and the Making of Environmental Subjects in Kumaon, India,' *Current Anthropology,* Vol. 46, pp. 161–351.

Agrawal, A., and C. C. Gibson. (1999) 'Enchantment and Disenchantment: The Role of Community in Natural Resource Management,' *World Development,* Vol. 27, No. 4, pp. 629–649.

Baranger, D., and G. Schiavoni. (2005) 'Censo de Ocupantes de Tierras,' *Estudios Regionales,* Vol. 28, No. 13, p. 32.

Bartolome, L. (1991) *The Colonos of Apóstoles: Adaptive Strategy and Ethnicity in a Polish-Ukrainian Settlement in Northeast Argentina.* New York: AMS Press, Inc.

Brockington, D. (2004) 'Community Conservation, Inequality, and Injustice: Myths of Power in Protected Area Management,' *Conservation and Society,* Vol. 2, No. 2, pp. 411–432.

Brosius, P. (1999) 'Analyses and Interventions: Anthropological Engagements with Environmentalism,' *Current Anthropology,* Vol. 40, No. 3, pp. 277–310.

———. (2006) 'Seeing Communities: Technologies of Visualization in Conservation,' in G. Creed (ed.), *The Seductions of Community: Emancipations, Oppressions, Quandaries.* Santa Fe: School of American Research Press, pp. 227–254.

Brosius, P., and S. Hitchner. (2010) 'Cultural Diversity and Conservation,' *International Sciences Journal,* Vol. 61, No. 199, pp. 141–168.

Brosius, P., and D. Russell. (2003) 'Conservation from Above: An Anthropological Perspective on Transboundary Protected Areas and Ecoregional Planning,' *Journal of Sustainable Forestry,* Vol. 17, No. 1/2, pp. 39–65.

Candau, J. (2001) *Memoria e Identidad.* Buenos Aires: Ediciones del Sol.

Chapin, M. (2004) 'A Challenge to Conservationists,' *Worldwatch Magazine,* November/December, pp. 17–31.

Colchester, M. (2003) *Salvaging Nature: Indigenous Peoples, Protected Areas and Biodiversity Conservation.* Moreton-in-Marsh, UK: World Rainforest Movement, Forest Peoples Programme.

Di Bitetti, M., G. Placci, and L. Dietz. (2003) *Una Visión de Biodiversidad para la Ecorregión del Bosque Atlántico del Alto Paraná: Diseño de un Paisaje para la Conservación de la Biodiversidad y Prioridades para las Acciones de Conservación.* Washington, D.C.: World Wildlife Fund.

Escobar, A. (1999) *El Final del salvaje. Naturaleza, cultura y política en la antropología contemporánea.* Santafé de Bogotá: CEREC/ICAN.

Ferguson, J. (2006) *Global Shadows: Africa in the Neoliberal World Order*. Durham: Duke University Press.

Fletcher, R. (2010) 'Neoliberal Environmentality: Towards a Post-Structuralist Political Ecology of the Conservation Debate,' *Conservation and Society*, Vol. 8, No. 3, pp. 171–181.

Foucault, M. (2001) *Defender la sociedad. Curso en el College de France (1975–1976)*. Buenos Aires: Fondo de Cultura Económica.

Igoe, J., and D. Brockington. (2007) 'Neoliberal Conservation: A Brief Introduction,' *Conservation and Society*, Vol. 5, No. 4, pp. 534–561.

INDEC. (2002) Censo Nacional Agropecuario, Buenos Aires, online report, http://www.indec.gov.ar (accessed 13 June 2011).

INTA Centro Regional Misiones. (2003) *Plan de tecnología regional (2001–2004)*. Buenos Aires: Ediciones INTA.

Li, T. (2005) 'Engaging Simplifications: Community-Based Natural Resource Management, Local Processes and State Agendas in Upland Southeast Asia,' in J. P. Brosius, A. Tsing and C. Zerner (eds), *Communities and Conservation: Histories and Politics of Community-Based Natural Resource Management*. Lanham: Altamira Press, pp. 427–448.

———. (2007) *The Will to Improve: Governmentality, Development, and the Practice of Politics*. Durham: Duke University Press.

MacDonald, K. I. (2003) 'Community-Based Conservation: A Reflection on History,' International Union for the Conservation of Nature, online report, http://cmsdata.iucn.org/downloads/cca_kmacdonald.pdf (accessed 25 June 2011).

Ministry of Ecology of Misiones. (2008) Online report, www.ecologia.misiones.gov.ar (accessed 1 March 2008).

Palma, M. (2008) *Importancia de la gestión en el rol del guardaparque para la resolución de conflictos en áreas naturales protegidas*. Trabajo Final Técnico Universitario Guardaparque. Universidad Nacional de Misiones.

Redford, K., J. G. Robinson and W. M. Adams. (2006) 'Parks as Shibboleths,' *Conservation Biology*, Vol. 20, No. 1, pp. 1–2.

Secretaría de Ambiente y Desarrollo Sustentable de la Nación. (2011) *Reserva de Biosfera Yabotí*, online report, http://www.ambiente.gov.ar/?idarticulo=2843 (accessed 22 June 2011).

Schvorer, E. (2003) *Etnografía de una Feria Franca. Estudio de un proyecto de desarrollo rural con productores familiares, Misiones, Argentina*. Master's thesis in Social Anthropology, Universidad Nacional de Misiones.

Scott, J. (1985) *Weapons of the Weak: Everyday Forms of Peasant Resistance*. New Haven: Yale University Press.

———. (1998) *Seeing Like a State: How Certain Schemes to Improve the Human Condition have Failed*. New Haven: Yale University Press.

Turner, M. (2006) 'Shifting Scales, Lines, and Lives: The Politics of Conservation Science and Development in the Sahel,' in K. Zimmerer (ed.), *Globalization and New Geographies of Conservation*. Chicago: University of Chicago Press, pp. 166–184.

West, P., J. Igoe and D. Brockington. (2006) 'Parks and Peoples: The Social Impact of Protected Areas,' *Annual Review of Anthropology*, Vol. 35, pp. 251–277.

Winer, N. (2003) 'Co-Management of Protected Areas, the Oil and Gas Industry and Indigenous Empowerment: The Experience of Bolivia's Kaa Iya del Gran Chaco,' *Policy Matters*, Vol. 12, pp. 181–191.

Legislating 'Rights for Nature' in Ecuador

The Mediated Social Construction of Human/Nature Dualisms

Juliet Pinto

On 28 September 2008, Ecuadorians overwhelmingly voted to approve a new constitution that made sweeping changes in various arenas, including reformulating political power structures, creating new social sectors in public programs and establishing an ambitious new set of environmental rights. With these reforms, and the referendum that passed them, President Rafael Correa made good on key promises that had helped him ride a wave of popular mobilizations into electoral victory in late 2006. As many news outlets observed, the resounding support for the constitutional proposals could be linked to widespread voter discontent with corruption and weak state regulation, as well as anger over a string of ecological disasters that many felt were wrought by multinational companies which promised to contribute to the country's development, but in various instances left little behind other than polluted areas stripped of natural resources (Romero 2007; Kendall 2008).

In theory, granting rights to nature may be viewed as a legal response to ongoing environmental degradation, as in Ecuador and elsewhere in Latin America, environmental systems are under stress. Many communities live with recurrent environmental crises – the results of rapid economic globalization that increased the pace of natural resource exploitation and carried benefits to metropolitan areas and developed countries, while exacerbating social and economic inequalities. Such instances have long histories in Ecuador. Multinational companies have utilized Ecuador's natural resources, but in many cases, local populations saw few benefits, economic or otherwise. For example, instead of building or improving roads or transport infrastructure, oil companies working in Ecuador used private transport networks; further, private security forces or the Ecuadorian military were employed to facilitate extractive activity or overcome local opposition (Clark 2002). But revenues from oil extraction and production have not, for the most part, trickled down to local populations: those living in zones of oil production are characterized as among the poorest in the country and also suffer effects from environmental contamination. For example, a high profile Chevron/Texaco case recently brought international attention to an unfolding class-action lawsuit against the multinational corporation by residents of contaminated lands (Clark 2002; Newell 2008).

For years, such disparities were largely ignored in policy making. Successive administrations adopted neoliberal economic policies with fervour, as part of development strategies promising national modernization and social progress, ending underdevelopment and poverty (Valdivia 2005). The state was rapidly transformed, but not necessarily reduced. As Suzana Sawyer (2004, 116) puts it, 'Economic globalization was not leading to the dissolution of the state in Ecuador. Rather, the state was being redefined such that it increasingly assumed the role of an administrative and calculating organ that facilitated the workings of transnational capitalism.'

Correa's election to the presidency in 2006 signified for many a significant public response to former administrations that had wholeheartedly adopted neoliberalism. As Correa assumed office, he faced a battle with a right-wing dominated congress that sought to block completion of the promises in his electoral platform, a deadlock that the new president succeeded in breaking by going back to the people with a proposal for a constituent assembly, which was approved by 82 per cent of voters (see El País 2007). This victory was followed by another landslide in the selection of members for the constituent assembly, with the majority of seats going to allies of the president and his party, the PAIS Alliance. The assembly convened over the constitutional issue in 2007 and by mid 2008 had approved a draft constitution, after much debate and not without controversy (Gudynas 2009). Two contested issues included the privatization of natural resources and water – which were excluded from the final draft, but with an exception that allowed the president to ask Congress for permission to do so – and the defeat of a proposal that would have forced the government to obtain consent from indigenous peoples living on land before extracting resources (Dosh and Kligerman 2009).

Among the issues most relevant to this chapter's exploration of the changing relations between state, society and nature was the creation of what Catherine Walsh (2010, 18) calls a 'new model of development' grounded in a 'triangular relationship ... among the rights of nature, *buen vivir*, and what is referred to as the "regimen of development"'. The constitution introduced an 'orienting concept' of *buen vivir*, which is translated as 'living well' or collective well-being. Walsh (2010, 18) argues that 'Buen vivir denotes, organizes, and constructs a system of knowledge and living based on the communion of humans and nature and on the spatial-temporal-harmonious totality of existence.' The concept, rooted in indigenous life philosophies, contrasts with hegemonic conceptualizations of development as the mechanism for progress. Rather, as Alberto Acosta (2008, 34), ex-president of the Ecuadorian Assembly and a champion of the introduction of *buen vivir* as a model of development, wrote: 'There is no conception of a linear process that establishes a past or future state. There is no vision of underdevelopment to be overcome. And neither a state of development to be reached. ... From the indigenous cosmovision, the social betterment – development? – is a category in permanent construction and reproduction.' The inclusion of *buen vivir* can be interpreted as a response to the prevailing conceptualization of the relation between nature and society as one where nature is inexhaustible and human progress and development depend upon its exploitation and subjugation (Byrne, Glover and Martinez 2002). This is to be realized, according to the 2008 Constitution, via a new regimen of development that entails improving the quality of life, protecting cultural diversity, promoting participation and in effect 'giving rights to nature'.[1] Walsh (2010) relates the concept of *buen vivir* to the emergence of an alternative development framework in Latin America, grounded in humanistic views of development and social capabilities. In this view, protection of natural resources forms an intrinsic component of a framework seeking to improve human capabilities in the present and provide for sustainable futures – in subsequent media representations in Ecuador, the two concepts (*buen vivir* and development) have been understood as interchangeable in documents detailing the project. Recent realizations and discourses of such frameworks may present opportunities to hybridize development models by 'humaniz[ing] capitalism and its neo-liberal project' (Walsh 2010, 20).

The shift towards new understandings and constitutional configurations of development and the relationship between societal well-being and natural systems required changes in the way natural resources were defined and regulated, entailing a shift from a legal emphasis on protecting property rights towards a regime that protects the resources themselves. In an effort to formalize sustainable development, the notion of nature as an object of rights held by citizens was displaced by the idea of nature as a subject that holds rights. The new constitution is designed to force state bodies to 'remedy damages' against violations of nature's rights, as a provision was created for citizens to legally sue on behalf of ecosystems in peril.

The articles awarding rights to nature were drafted with the counsel of the Community Environmental Legal Defense Fund (CELDF) – a Pennsylvania-based group that describes its mission as helping communities construct legal frameworks that enable sustainability.[2] The CELDF was brought into Ecuador's constitution drafting exercise by the San Francisco-based Pachamama Alliance – a group committed 'to develop tangible, real-life projects through which rainforests provide more direct economic benefit standing than cut' (Pachamama Alliance). According to the CELDF, they worked with delegates in the Assembly to draft language for the constitution regarding rights to nature.[3] The CELDF and other proponents insist that awarding rights to nature and natural systems is an innovative model for global leaders interested in protecting ecosystems from further damage and collapse. During debate surrounding this inclusion in the draft constitution, other actors considered it an 'eccentricity' (Gudynas 2009, 41). But positive international attention lent an important degree of legitimacy to the measure, including an article written by Uruguayan writer Eduardo Galeano (2008): 'The revindication of nature forms part of a process of recuperation of the oldest traditions of Ecuador and all of America. It proposes that the state recognize and guarantee the right to maintain and regenerate vital natural cycles, and it is not by accident that the Constitutional Assembly has begun with identifying its objectives of national rebirth with the ideal of life of sumak kawsay [*buen vivir*].'

Buen Vivir and Environmental Citizenship

Ecuador's 2008 reform potentially reshapes the constitutional relationship between citizens and the state. The measures shifted the constitutional paradigm from the human-centric, linear view of modernity and progress linked to the domination and mastery of nature, to that of a philosophy derived from traditionally subordinated and marginalized groups, where humans and nature are seen to live in an important degree of communion and notions of well-being are not linked to linear notions of progress. This philosophical reconfiguration leads to the possibility that in the context of concrete polities, humans and nature might be conceived of as constitutional equals. Rather than simply being the agent of their modernity, the state becomes responsible for fostering a kind of development that actively promotes citizenship as a 'form of personhood that links rights to agency', supplanting a limited concern for the legal formulation of rights with a broader preoccupation for the 'distributions of rights, resources and recognition' (Mukhopadhyay 2007, 263–264).

As Andrew Dobson and Derek Bell (2006a, 4) note, 'there is no determinate thing called "environmental citizenship".'[4] In scholarly research, this ambiguous concept has been approached in various ways: as the 'intersection where citizenship meets green politics' (Latta 2007b, 378); as a way of linking beliefs and attitudes to concrete behaviours, so that sustainability might arise from underlying commitments to ecological values (Benson 2003; Dobson 2003; Dobson and Bell 2006b); as a space for thinking through sustainability values and practices within the orbit of rights and environmental justice (Horton 2005); as shaped by ontologies based on competition, cooperation, development or domination (Lipschutz 2004); as a way to formulate suprastate, non-contractual obligations that address unjust distributions of costs and benefits associated with resource extraction and consumption (Dobson

2003); and as a sphere within which to link up legal and political rights with ethical practice in an age of politicized nature and ecological reason (Isin and Wood 1999).

Rather than trying to distil a single definition from this wide variety of perspectives, this chapter endeavours to probe the meanings of environmental citizenship by analysing the discourses around the constitutional changes in Ecuador. The approach I take is social constructionist in character. The idea of citizenship as learned, forgotten, socially developed, informed by ethics, values, opinions or expectations; or as stemming from socially developed or reinforced motivations and reasons, is echoed in the literature (see, for example, Smith 2005; Connelly 2006; Gough and Scott 2006; Nash and Lewis 2006; Latta 2007a, 2007b). Social construction, however, does not operate in a vacuum, but rather occurs within and around social institutions, contributing in turn to the evolution of these institutions, as well as reflecting discourses that maintain or challenge them. As Barbara Hobson, Marcus Carson and Rebecca Lawrence (2007, 444) note, citizenship as membership and inclusion 'reflects the role of institutions on the rights and obligations of citizenship ... [and is] bound up with cultural identities and group rights'. This analysis probes that relationship between elite social construction and institutional evolution by examining debates around Ecuador's constitutional changes, as viewed and mediated through the discourses employed in opinion articles and letters in Ecuadorian mainstream online news. How is citizenship conceived, via a set of social constructions that reflect identities, processes and relations: the relations of and among humans, nature, culture, individuals, communities and the nation?

Social constructions of nature are rife with power relations inherent within the societal context. I have already discussed how the dominant development paradigm values the exploitation of nature in the name of modernity and progress, a configuration that other authors in this volume have noted works towards excluding those whose belief systems favour different treatments and visions for nature and natural systems (see, in this volume, Grillo and Sharon; Henne and Gabrielson; Taddei). In this context, Ecuadorian citizenship has in part focused on reproducing this paradigm within understandings of citizen agency, particularly in the sphere of market relations. And yet the ability of some citizens to harness nature's capital has consistently undermined the socio-cultural agency of others. As Enrique Leff (2001, 28) notes, today's environmental degradation is associated with the 'disintegration of cultural values, identities and productive practices from "traditional societies"'. Building on this perspective, Ronnie Lipschutz (2004, 77) explains that the degradation of nature continues unabated because 'those in power legitimate and reproduce both their dominant positions and the social organization that authorizes their rule through normalized and naturalized actions and beliefs'. Nature is constructed as separate from and inferior to humans. As Thomas Berry (quoted in Hendry and Cramer 2005, 4–5) notes, the 'other-than-human is seen as "less than," as having no rights, and is thus vulnerable to exploitation'. Scholarship and citizen mobilization addressing what Judith Hendry and Janet Cramer (2005, 117) call the 'human/nature conceptual split that grounds the prevailing environmental discourse,' seek to contest dominant discourses and regimes that view nature as rightless, as property and as a raw material to be exploited in the name of modernity and progress. However, dominant narratives can prove tenacious, especially when the interests they protect are embedded in the publicly available means of collective communication.

Media reconstructions of the day's events and issues result in media discourses, built from expert quotes, elite interpretations, framing devices and other mechanisms to provide arenas, as Michael Gurevitch and Mark Levy (1985, 19) describe them, where 'various social groups, institutions, and ideologies struggle over the definition and construction of social reality'. The degree to which mass media grant or deny legitimacy, credibility or voice to a range of environmental perspectives, ideas and points of view may be powerful agenda-setting forces (Cracknell 1993; Neuzil 1996). If, as Peter Dahlgren (2009, 48) asserts, 'the fundamental role of journalism in democracy is to link citizens to political life,' then how media discuss environmental issues in content may have import for engagement in civic action, or in building identities as civic actors. In terms of debating inclusion of indigenous cosmovisions into constitutional guarantees, the question then becomes how do mediated opinions present different understandings of the relations among societies, natural systems and state institutional mechanisms?

Environment and Media Discourse in Latin America

Evaluating communication regarding environmental issues in media presents various analytical issues. One is the lack of comparative contexts: While much scholarly attention has focused on U.S. press and broadcast coverage, less has been done to understand other nation's articulations of the dimensions of environmental themes in mass media contexts. Another is the complexity of assigning causes to content outcomes. Variables operating at different levels have import for resulting publications, particularly when examined through a lens of press freedom and quality of public sphere debate for democratic governance. Previous research has explored factors steering coverage or audience comprehension in Latin America as including pressures of market economies and/or strong states on media organizations; volatility in political and economic systems; high levels of poverty and illiteracy, coupled with weak penetration of communications infrastructure; collusive relations between powerful political or economic actors with media executives and professionals; hostile legal environments for investigative reporting or, conversely, weak systems of investigation into attacks against journalists; organizational ideologies or agendas; levels of professionalization among media actors; access to databases, officials and other sources; and individual value systems and orientations, among other factors[5] (Waisbord 2000, 2008, 2009; Hughes and Lawson 2005; Hughes 2006; Nauman 2008).

Further, beat reporting may face particular pressures – specialized environmental journalism in Latin America, as elsewhere, is scarce. Environmental news often may not meet editorial muster in the 24/7 news cycle, as traditional tenets of immediacy, locality, novelty or drama may not be immediately apparent, and may not evoke the ratings of crime, scandal or corruption stories. Conversely, environmental stories tend to garner media attention if they deal with breaking news or ongoing narratives in the form of disasters or other dramatic events; if they are visually compelling; or if narratives dealing with environmental themes have become linked to political agendas (Anderson 1997).

Accordingly, scholarly examination of media and environmental issues in Latin America has also been rare, but what does exist points to publications that focus less on substantive material capable of fostering audience comprehension of complex environmental issues (Mariño 2009), and that can, in Silvio Waisbord's (2008) view, reflect varied degrees of civic, political and commercial principles of media organizations. Julieta Carabaza et al. (2007), for example, found that when environmental coverage did appear on Mexican television, it did so in a specialized manner emphasizing the aesthetics of nature, rather than any substantive theme; in another instance (2004) she describes print coverage in Saltillo, Mexico, as giving nature a 'low profile', or being poorly interpreted, with little contextualization or background. In a study of one Mexico City newspaper's coverage of climate change, Joye Gordon, Tina Deines and Jacqueline Havice (2010) found that ecology and science frames predominated, while conflict and technology frames were de-emphasized.

Analyses of environmental crises or events in Latin American news media found similar emphases pointing to these media-centric logics, rather than overarching concern for public comprehension of the complexities of issues. Honduran news media demonstrated event-centred reporting after Hurricane Mitch, focusing on the 'short-term crises at hand', rather than providing systematic context or background to heighten audience awareness of climatic events (Boykoff and Roberts 2007, 19). Marco Encalada (2001) found that the Ecuadorian mainland press heavily covered the Jessica Oil Spill in the Galápagos archipelago, using political frames to discuss fractious relations between territorial and national governments. But Encalada argues the conservation emphases perhaps came from the international prestige and visual and informative impact of themes associated with the Galápagos that made for dramatic visuals and copy.

Indeed, political and ideological overtones can figure broadly in media coverage of environmental issues. Walsh (2002, 68) noted that dominant groups in Ecuador have used the press to 'promote the notion that [indigenous peoples] are re-establishing ethnic division. ... But while they establish the difference, they also promote a liberal-multiculturalist vision of society based on tolerance and inclusion, thus promulgating the idea that indigenous people and their movements are the perpetrators of their own exclusion.' This study seeks to understand the presentation of the debate leading up to Ecuador's September 2008 constitutional referendum by examining the content of opinion articles in the elite national press as expressions of themes in arguments between elite sectors. Given that the impetus was from elite political actors seeking to transform institutions, what were the interpretations and responses from elite and non-elite actors in a mediated context? How were conceptualizations of citizenship presented in the context of constitutional reconfigurations of rights and obligations relating to nature and development? Which elements were challenged or upheld?

To evaluate mediated opinion discourse critically and understand not only socially constructed claims of nature and the environment but also the construction of the 'other', this chapter builds on Val Plumwood's (1993, 41) work delineating 'dualism, the construction of a devalued and sharply demarcated spheres of otherness'. Dualisms, in Plumwood's view, are a 'logic of colonisation' that operate according to dualistic pairs embedded in Western thought, including nature/culture, nature/reason, reason/emotion (nature), freedom/necessity, human/non-human, public/private, self/other and more (42–43). Such dichotomies are hierarchical, since in each case one term is dominant and subjugates or excludes the other term. This dichotomous rationality is fundamental to the way that Western society conceives of and relates to nature (Hendry and Cramer 2005). It is also useful when evaluating media accounts, as such discourse can be organized around conflict between constructed opposites, and therefore may reflect dualistic pairs.

Plumwood offers a framework by which to evaluate discourse for dualistic logics, including the use of backgrounding, radical exclusion, incorporation, instrumentalism and homogenization. Backgrounding deals with the locating of what is inferior in the background, de-emphasizing or particularizing its role, while foregrounding the dominant term as a universal truth. Radical exclusion refers to maximizing the distance between dichotomized poles via the denial of any possibility of shared qualities. Incorporation makes the subordinate a subset of the dominant object, while instrumentalism refers to the idea that the other is used as a means to the dominant's ends, as a resource with no moral value, only instrumentality. Finally, Plumwood (1993) argues that the dominant term must be seen as a homogenous category in order to maintain its superiority, while diversity is seen to undermine this standard.

Plumwood's framework is applied here to opinion articles published online during the year leading up to Ecuador's 2008 constitutional referendum, specifically focusing on the constitutional changes regarding the environment. Through this preliminary evaluation of three news websites linked to Ecuador's top general market newspapers, we can gain insight into how opinions regarding citizenship and the environment were presented in mediated spheres. Although internet use is low in Ecuador, at almost 13 per cent in 2009, according to SUPERTEL estimates (Internet World Stats 2010), online news articles from news sources can have national impact, particularly for middle and upper classes and younger news seekers. Rodrigo Jordán-Tobar and Allen Panchana-Macay (2009, 120–121) characterize Ecuador's press as 'the largest influence on public opinion' and cite the most-visited internet media sites as *El Universo, El Comercio, Hoy* and regional news source *La Hora*. Opinion articles and letters to the editor published online through 28 September 2008, the day of the referendum vote (as well as a few published in 2007 and 2009 that were directly relevant), were selected for content analysis, thereby providing an overview of the landscape of mainstream media news coverage on the environmental components of the constitutional changes. The articles were found via a search at each online news site, using combinations of the search words: *constitución, enmienda, natureleza, ambiente* (as well as versions of those words, such as *derechos a la naturaleza*).

The Social Construction of Dualisms

Thirty discrete opinion pieces and fourteen letters to the editor were found, with pieces running from 28 April 2008 to 20 January 2009. *El Universo* published the most content regarding the subject, with fourteen op-eds and nine letters to the editor, followed by *El Comercio,* with ten op-eds and four letters, then *Hoy,* with six opinion articles and one letter. Most opinion articles across the three outlets negatively characterized the idea of giving rights to nature[6] and reinforced the nature/human split, as well as the reason/nature split. At the same time, some opinion pieces were slightly more circumspect in their discussions of *buen vivir.* The idea of giving rights to nature was criticized for its insinuation that humans and nature are somehow equals. Columnists also suggested that legislators who supported the idea were 'fundamentalists' or 'extremists', evoking reason/nature and subject/object dualisms as columnists equated ecological concern with illogical thinking. For example:

But, for an elemental common sense, we cannot accept that there is a right for nature itself; to include such affirmation in the Constitution, our assembly have let themselves be influenced by those, who with a charge of intransigence and fanaticism, have adhered to environmentalism as if it were a religion. (*Hoy*, 30 April 2008)

If you, sceptical reader, have doubts regarding the goodness of the work and some of the assembly members' outlandish themes (like that of 'rights' to nature, for example), you run the risk of being characterized as having an 'anachronistic way of seeing the world'. (*Comercio*, 24 June 2008)

A constitutional text should be logical and precise, coherent and clear, and can't be the result of arrogance and sectarianism, volunteerism and ignorance. ... A system of law, and therefore, of rights and obligations, is a product of the necessities and intelligence of man. Man – subject of rights and obligations – is its foundation and end. Nature is not a subject of rights and obligations. How would it execute and complete them? (*Comercio*, 24 June 2008)

The issue of *buen vivir* also received a cool reception in the mainstream media, exposing undertones of the debate relating to citizenship and identity with respect to practices of inclusion and exclusion – cleavages that run deep in Ecuador and are directly related to issues of access to and management of natural resources. Sawyer (2004) describes how elite voices painted indigenous movement attempts to introduce components at odds with neoliberal conceptions of economic and political systems as divisive, anti-progress, anti-modernity and contrary to movement towards a 'modern' Ecuadorian society. As Gabriela Valdivia (2005, 288) notes, discourse painting indigenous practices or knowledge systems as backwards has a long history in Ecuador under modernization ideologies, buttressed by 'national policies [which] were instituted to erase cultural difference and to integrate the Amazonian Indian into civilization in the name of "national progress"'. In the context of these discourses seeking to derail the concept of *buen vivir* the instrumentalization of nature can be widely observed, as a perceived precondition for modernity, social progress and economic well-being. Various instances of the civilized/primitive were summoned here:

Soon the *sumak kawsai*, the concept of life in communion with nature that dominates the Constitution point to point will be the expressed official religion. ... The Constitution is openly hostile to the contemporary society. One thing is to respect and recognize the communities' manners of maintaining their ancestral customs. Another is to proclaim in the Constitution that in the Palaeolithic, life was better. (*Universo*, 27 July 2008)

Did the electorate of the Alianza PAIS realize that they were proposing to renounce progress and return to a pre-Colombian system of life? (*Universo*, 1 June 2008)

Other letters and columns discussed the measure and its corollaries, particularly references to Pachamama in the preamble and in the articles giving rights to nature. The mention of Pachamama in the preamble, using backgrounding, incorporation or hyper-separation techniques, served to deny non-Catholic, non-liberal views as essential or universal, discussed them only in terms of what they lack, maximizing existing cleavages in Ecuadorian society. Such mechanisms highlighted dualisms such as universal/particular or reason/emotion:

> It is incredible that in a democratic society, one particular form of perceiving life and the world, and the relation with nature, is imposed, and further, elevated to the constitutional realm. In a democratic society, as the Ecuadorian one still is, so many visions about the good life can potentially exist, so many citizens exist in that society, and it is the duty of the Constitution to guarantee that all citizens can coexist without one imposing over the other. So the *buen vivir* doesn't only present philosophical problems, like privilege of collective rights and communities over the individual. ... The problem is that the text subordinates explicitly the individual liberties to the general interest. ... Individual liberties are seen as sources of inequality and nothing more. (*Hoy*, 19 September 2008)

> To believe Earth is the giver or protector per se of life is to give it an interpretation that does not correspond. Objectively, the Constitution should say to the world that Ecuador is of Christ (I don't speak of a religion in particular, and I am not Catholic.) It would appear this is a religious argument, but it's not; it's a connotation beyond logic. (*Universo*, 7 September 2008)

> But a constitutional text should always be concrete, simple, general, comprehensible, because it is the basic document of the legal life of a society, and for this, also, it should reflect that in its totality. The allusion to Pachamama, adequate and comprehensible for Andean culture, doesn't have the same significance for Ecuadorians of other cultures, many of whom have never even heard the word. (*Universo*, 21 June 2008)

Nevertheless, coverage was not uniformly negative. All three news outlets also published opinions cautiously in favour of *buen vivir*, couching it as a measure to mitigate destructive climate change and protect the environment for future generations:

> It's about a positive text that makes nature a structural axis of all social, economic, political and cultural activity of our society. In an international context affected by climate change, pollution, natural resource deterioration, stronger and stronger natural disasters, just as changes in consumption toward those more environmentally conscious, it could be an economic, political and cultural answer from our society. (*Universo*, 18 August 2008)

Articles and letters sketched nuanced difficulties with reconciling the ideal with the real, the theoretical guarantees of the country's newest constitution with the realities of the actual reaches of rights and institutional limitations, as they had been experienced with previous regimes:

> Ecuador must be in first place among the countries that generate public obligations, and one of the last in enforcing them. It has been a champion in constructing rights of the most diverse nature, but at the same time it has been delinquent in attending to them. (*Comercio*, 18 September 2008)

> Acosta signalled to the BBC that he 'wanted to give justice to nature and recognize that if social justice was in the 20th century the axis of conflicts, environmental justice is going to be it in the 21st century.' This is just the beginning of a new development regime, according to Acosta. Nevertheless, the route to achieving it in Ecuador looks just as difficult as finding a healthy river in the mining zones, or a 100-year-old matapalo tree in the garden of a lumber magnate. (*Universo*, 1 February 2009)

Views expressed here looked beyond the hierarchy of dualisms in terms of overcoming their 'polarized understandings', to a limited degree. While not tacitly discussing the reorganization of the hierarchical dualism nature/human, discussions couched analysis in terms of sustainability as the desired end, thereby maintaining, to some degree, original parameters of development models, or as Walsh (2010, 20) notes, the 'universalization' of the sustainable human development model.

Mediated Opinions Around the 'Rights to Nature'

This chapter examined mediated opinions around the 'rights to nature' as presented in Ecuadorian online media in order to understand elite social constructions of identity and relations of humans with nature in the context of development and constitutional transformation. The resulting cultural expressions and justifications associated with the new model of development bounded by rights to nature, *buen vivir* and development regimes were responses to a discursive shift from an instrumental, anthropogenic view of 'natural capital' to an emancipation for nature grounded in ethics and values that reduce the modernity-induced distance between humans and nature (Acosta 2010).

However, separations and exclusions were also observed in the mediated discourse of opinion regarding the proposition. In terms of articulating membership, agency, power relations and communality, environmental opinions expressed in elite news outlets delineated and idealized social constructions of human relations with and perceptions of nature, creating dualisms and granting legitimacy to various dualistic poles in manners that reinforced elite and state discursive constructions that emphasized separations between indigenous views and 'mainstream' society. Membership and inclusion in the nation, as well as cultural identities and group rights were explicitly and implicitly evoked in these arguments. Plumwood's dualisms, however, were still observed, as opinions highlighted such splits as: human/nature, reason/ emotion (nature), self/other, subject/object, civilized/primitive or rationality/animality. Illogicality, irrationality, fundamentalism and anti-modernity were used to argue against reformulations of the human relation with nature. Such configurations echo other instances of Latin American political elites characterizing indigenous communities in rural areas as 'primitive', 'irrational', 'backward' or 'anti-modernity' (Grillo and Sharon; Taddei, this volume). Another common theme in discussing the viability of rights to natural systems was one of 'no rights without obligations', echoing Third Way formulations, where, as Dobson (2003, 47) puts it, 'Reciprocity is built into the normative understanding of the relationship [of citizenship] itself rather than driven by external threat of sanction.' A final theme evoked reason/emotion as a dualistic pair, where, as Plumwood (2002, 9) notes, 'Reason/emotion dualism divorces prudence from ethics, codes the former as rational, and sees the opposing sphere of ethical and ecological concern as dispensable, mere subjective sentiment.'

These dualisms were contrasted with several op-eds and letters cautiously in favour of the reforms. Here, the 'strategies of mastery ... between the mastering one and the dualised other' (Plumwood 1993, 191) were not observed, but the tendencies were not to embrace new perspectives of mutuality. Rather, authors cited sustainable development, benefits to future generations or international prestige as reasons to vote in favour of the referendum and tended to frame their comments in spirits of pessimism of the chance for any significant realization of such guarantees by the state.

This content analysis is largely descriptive, observing dualisms and logical structures employed in mediated opinions that criticize the proposed reform. However, several caveats in terms of this study's limitations are needed here. First, one cannot overlook the role of politics and interests in mediated content. Political overtones and special interests can infuse media content beyond philosophical and ideological organizational perspectives. A referendum generated from the electoral campaign of the president may be criticized in media circles for reasons other than conceptions of legitimate environmental cultures; rather, such dualisms may serve as little more than useful mechanisms that resound in public and elite sectors to mitigate political credibility or viability. In recent years, media-state relations in Ecuador have grown increasingly contentious, with increased state presence in media sectors, including increased regulation and restriction of industries and content and questioning of press credibility and legitimacy (Freedom House 2009; Jordán-Tobar and Panchana-Macay 2009). Various articles in the new constitution also directly impacted the media, including provisions for regulating content, access to information, anti-monopoly or oligopoly measures and ownership conditions (Jordán-Tobar and Panchana-Macay 2009). One cannot overlook possibilities of organizational interests in negating or supporting the proposed reforms' viability.

Second, to date, reality has not entirely reflected the ideals, in terms of norms expressed in the constitution. Contradictions within articles and in subsequent decisions have mitigated the potential for realizing the document's lofty ideals, including: allowing the president to ask Congress for permission to privatize natural resources, the failure to adopt a measure giving indigenous communities residing on land where outside entities wish to extract natural resources the power to deny such initiatives and the subsequent passage of legislation which would expand extractive activities, have served to dilute the efficacy of such measures and distance one-time supporters of Correa and his administration (Mychalejko 2008; Dosh and Kligerman 2009) Even before the September 2008 vote, and with the incorporation of indigenous knowledge systems and words, indigenous groups that had initially supported Correa and participated in the Constitutional Assembly distanced themselves from the project (Gudynas 2009). Some leaders of social movements said at the time of the vote that their vote should not be mistaken as a sign of support for Correa, and have since questioned the degree to which the measures reduce Ecuador's dependence on natural resources as a fundamental economic base (quoted in Dosh and Kligerman 2009).

However, mainstream opinion articles from elite outlets provide a view into mediated issues with the evolving legal and conceptual relationship between state, society and nature, a concept with profound implications for the region. For any successful implementation of state-guaranteed rights or broad fostering of green ethos in civil society, particularly when such rights cross social and cultural boundaries and normative understandings of 'living well' in a world of globalized capitalism, how the issues are articulated to audiences, fragmented as they may be, is of import. In Ecuador, these challenges were observed in mediated opinions that delineated the differing conceptual splits: that of the legitimacy of perspectives not rooted in neoliberal development models, conceptualizations of modernity or social bureaucracy, and tied to indigenous traditions, concepts and beliefs, which largely had been also subordinated. Future research would do well to explore the evolution and potential realization of such guarantees as events unfold and rights and obligations are called upon.

Notes

1. The articles in full may be accessed here: http://pdba.georgetown.edu/Constitutions/ Ecuador/ecuador08.html.
2. The CELDF mission statement is available at: http://celdf.org/section.php?id=220.
3. See the CELDF website at: http://celdf.org/article.php?list=type&type=142.
4. Here, the terms *environmental citizenship* and *ecological citizenship* are used interchangeably. See Dobson (2003) for his delineation of the two.
5. See also the country reports from Freedom House's press freedom indices: http://www .freedomhouse.org and Committee to Protect Journalists http://www.cpj.org/.
6. Voices in the global public sphere also painted the measure negatively. As Mychalejko (2008) noted, a *Los Angeles Times* article in 2008 said 'That sounds like a stunt by the San Francisco City Council.' Others, while cautiously praising the idea, criticized Ecuadorian President Rafael Correa's administration's 'extractive economic model of development' and failure to include tough enforcement measures as a prelude for loopholes around any constitutional measures.

References

Acosta, A. (2008) 'El Buen Vivir, Una Oportunidad por Construir,' *Revista Ecuador Debate*, Vol. 75, pp. 33–48. Online report, http://flacsoandes.org/dspace/handle/10469/1443.

———. (2010) 'Hacia la Declaración Universal de los Derechos de la Naturaleza [Toward a Universal Declaration of Rights for Nature],' *América Latina en Movimiento*, online report, http://alainet.org.

Anderson, A. (1997) *Media, Culture and the Environment*. New Brunswick: Rutgers University Press.

Benson, A. (2003) *Citizenship and the Environment*. Oxford: Oxford University Press.

Boykoff, M., and J. T. Roberts. (2007) *Media Coverage of Climate Change: Current Trends, Strengths, Weaknesses*. Human Development Report 2007, online report, http://hdr.undp .org.

Byrne, J., L. Glover and C. Martinez. (2002) 'The Production of Unequal Nature,' *Environmental Justice: Discourses in International Political Economy, Energy and Environmental Policy*. New Brunswick: Transaction Publishers, pp. 261–291.

Carabaza, J. (2004) 'La Temática Ambiental en la Prensa Escrita: El Caso de los Periódicos de Saltillo, Coahuila,' in B. Russi (ed.), *Anuario de Investigación 11*. Mexico City: UI-CONE-ICC, pp. 263–285.

Carabaza, J., et al. (2007) 'Cobertura Medioambiente en la Televisión Méxicana,' *Comunicación y Sociedad*, Vol. 7, pp. 45–76.

Clark, T. (2002) *Canadian Mining Companies in Latin America: Community Rights and Corporate Responsibility*. Toronto, Ontario, Canada: York University, Centre for Research on Latin America and the Caribbean at York University (CERLAC) and MiningWatch Canada.

Connelly, J. (2006) 'The Virtues of Environmental Citizenship,' in A. Dobson and D. Bell (eds), *Environmental Citizenship*. Cambridge, MA: MIT Press, pp. 49–73.

Cracknell, J. (1993) 'Issue Arenas, Pressure Groups and Environmental Agendas,' in A. Hansen (ed.), *The Mass Media and Environmental Issues*. Leicester: Leicester University Press, pp. 3–21.

Dahlgren, P. (2009) *Media and Political Engagement: Citizens, Communication, and Democracy*. Cambridge: Cambridge University Press.

Dobson, A. (2003) *Citizenship and the Environment*. Oxford: Oxford University Press.

Dobson, A., and D. Bell. (2006a) 'Introduction,' in A. Dobson and D. Bell (eds), *Environmental Citizenship*. Cambridge, MA: MIT Press, pp. 1–17.

———. (2006b). *Environmental Citizenship*. Cambridge, MA: MIT Press.

Dosh, P., and N. Kligerman. (2009) 'Correa vs. Social Movements: Showdown in Ecuador,' *Political Environments: Development, Dissent, and the New Extraction*, September/October 2009, NACLA Report on the Americas, Vol. 42, No. 5, online report, https://nacla .org/volumeissues?volume=042.

El País. (2007) 'Ecuador elegirá la nueva Asamblea Constituyente el 30 de septiembre,' online report, http://www.elmundo.es/elmundo/2007/04/25/internacional/1177453909 .html

Encalada, M. F. (2001) 'La Prensa y la Conservación en las Galápagos,' *Chasqui*, Vol. 74, online report, http://chasqui.comunica.org/encalada74.htm

Freedom House. (2009) 'Freedom of the Press: Ecuador,' online report, http://www.freedom house.org/.

Galeano, E. (2008) 'La Naturaleza no es Muda,' online report, http://www.rebelion.org/ noticias/2008/4/66335.pdf.

Gordon, J., T. Deines and J. Havice. (2010) 'Global Warming Coverage in the Media: Trends in a Mexico City Newspaper,' *Science Communication*, Vol. 32, No. 2, pp. 143–170.

Gough, S., and W. Scott. (2006) 'Promoting Environmental Citizenship Through Learning: Toward a Theory of Change,' in A. Dobson and D. Bell (eds), *Environmental Citizenship*. Cambridge, MA: MIT Press, pp. 263–285.

Gudynas, E. (2009) 'La Ecología Política del Giro Biocéntrico en la Nueva Constitución de Ecuador,' *Revista de Estudios Sociales*, Vol. 32, pp. 34–47.

Gurevitch, M., and M. Levy. (1985) 'Introduction,' in M. Gurevitch and M. Levy (eds), *Mass Communication Review Yearbook, Vol. 5*. Beverly Hills: SAGE, pp. 1–22.

Hendry, J., and J. Cramer. (2005) 'The Logic of Colonization in the "What Would Jesus Drive?" Anti-SUV Campaign,' in S. Senecah (ed.), *The Environmental Communication Yearbook, Vol. 2*. Mahwah: Lawrence Erlbaum Associates, pp. 115–131.

Hobson, B., M. Carson and R. Lawrence. (2007) 'Recognition Struggles in Transnational Arenas: Negotiating Identities and Framing Citizenship,' *Critical Review of International Social and Political Philosophy*, Vol. 10, No. 4, pp. 443–470.

Horton, D. (2005) 'Demonstrating Environmental Citizenship? A Study of Everyday Life Among Green Activists,' in A. Dobson and D. Bell (eds), *Environmental Citizenship*. Cambridge, MA: MIT Press, pp. 127–150.

Hughes, S. (2006) *Newsrooms in Conflict: Journalism and the Democratization of Mexico*. Pittsburgh: University of Pittsburgh Press.

Hughes, S., and C. Lawson. (2005) 'The Barriers to Media Opening in Latin America,' *Political Communication*, Vol. 22, No. 1, pp. 9–25.

Internet World Stats: Usage and Population Statistics. (2010) 'Ecuador: Usage and Market Report,' online report, http://www.internetworldstats.com/sa/ec.htm (accessed 10 September 2010).

Isin, E., and P. Wood. (1999) *Citizenship and Identity*. London: SAGE.

Jordán-Tobar, R., and A. Panchana-Macay. (2009) 'The Media in Ecuador,' in A. Albarrán (ed.), *The Handbook of Spanish Language Media*. New York: Routledge, pp. 103–135.

Kendall, Clare. (2008) 'A New Law of Nature,' *The Guardian Online*, 24 September, online report, www.guardian.co.uk.

Latta, A. (2007a) 'Citizenship and the Politics of Nature: The Case of Chile's Alto Bío Bío,' *Citizenship Studies*, Vol. 11, No. 3, pp. 229–246.

———. (2007b). 'Locating Democratic Politics in Ecological Citizenship,' *Environmental Politics*, Vol. 16, No. 3, pp. 377–393.

Leff, E. (2001) 'Espacio, Lugar y Tiempo: La Reapropiación Social de la Naturaleza y la Construcción Local de la Racionalidad Ambiental,' *Nueva Sociedad*, Vol. 175, pp. 28–42.

Lipschutz, R. (2004) *Global Environmental Politics: Power, Perspectives and Practice*. Washington, D.C.: CQ Press.

Mariño, M. V. (2009) 'Environmental Communication Research in Spanish,' *Media Development*, Vol. 3, pp. 33–38.

Mukhopadhyay, M. (2007) 'Situating Gender and Citizenship in Development Debates: Towards a Strategy,' in M. Mukhopadhyay and N. Singh, Zuban (eds), *Gender Justice, Citizenship, and Development*. New Delhi: IDRC.

Mychalejko, C. (2008). 'Ecuador's Constitution gives Rights to Nature,' Upsidedownworld.org Blog Post, 25 September, online report, http://upsidedownworld.org/main/ecuador.

Nash, N., and A. Lewis. (2006) 'Overcoming Obstacles to Ecological Citizenship,' in A. Dobson and D. Bell (eds), *Environmental Citizenship*. Cambridge, MA: MIT Press, pp. 153–184.

Nauman, T. (2008) 'From the Bottom Up: Mexican Environmental Journalists Improve Coverage,' *Americas IRC Online*, 25 August, online report, http://americas.irc-online.org/am/5494.

Neuzil, M. (1996) *Mass Media and Environmental Conflict*. Thousand Oaks: SAGE.

Newell, P. (2008) 'Contesting Trade Policies in the Americas: The Politics of Environmental Justice,' in D. Carruthers (ed.), *Environmental Justice in Latin America: Problems, Promise and Practice*. Boston: MIT Press, pp. 49–73.

Pachamama Alliance Website. (N.d.) 'A New Voice,' The Pachamama Alliance, online report, http://www.pachamama.org/content/view/2/4/.

Plumwood, V. (1993) *Feminism and the Mastery of Nature*. London: Routledge.

———. (2002) *Environmental Culture: The Ecological Crisis of Reason*. London: Routledge.

Romero, S. (2007). 'Ecuador appears likely to rewrite constitution,' *The New York Times*, 16 April, online report, nytimes.com.

Sawyer, S. (2004) *Crude Chronicles: Indigenous Politics, Multinational Oil, and Neoliberalsm in Ecuador*. Durham: Duke University Press.

Smith, M. J. (2005) 'Obligation and Ecological Citizenship,' *Environments Journal*, Vol. 33, No. 3, pp. 9–23.

Valdivia, G. (2005) 'On Indigeneity, Change, and Representation in the Northeastern Ecuadorian Amazon,' *Environment & Planning*, Vol. 37, No. 2, pp. 285–303.

Waisbord, S. (2000) *Watchdog Journalism in South America*. New York: Columbia University Press.

———. (2008) *Press and the Public Sphere in Contemporary Latin America*. Presented at the Harvard World Bank Workshop, 29–31 May, Cambridge, MA.

———. (2009) 'Can Civic Society Change Journalism? The Experience of Civic Advocacy Journalism in Latin America,' *Brazilian Journalism Research*, Vol. 5, No. 1, pp. 5–21.

Walsh, C. (2002) 'The (Re)Articulation of Political Subjectivities and Colonial Difference in Ecuador: Reflections on Capitalism and the Geopolitics of Knowledge,' *Nepantla: Views from the South*, Vol. 3, No. 1, pp. 61–97.

———. (2010) 'Development as *Buen Vivir*: Institutional Arrangements and (De)Colonial Entanglements,' *Development*, Vol. 53, No. 1, pp. 15–21.

Contributors

Andrew Baldwin is a lecturer in the Department of Geography at Durham University. His research interests include environmental politics, race, climate change and migration, and political and cultural theory. Andrew currently chairs COST Action IS1101: climate change and migration.

Fábio de Castro is an assistant professor in Human Ecology and Brazilian Studies at the Center for Latin American Research and Documentation (CEDLA). His research interests include protected areas, biofuel production, agroforestry and co-management in Latin America.

Brián Ferrero is a post-doctoral associate at the Center for Integrative Conservation Research (CICR) at the University of Georgia, and an associate researcher at the National Council of Scientific and Technological Research (CONICET), Argentina.

Teena Gabrielson is an associate professor of Political Science. She teaches political theory at the University of Wyoming. Her research focuses on questions of citizenship in both American and environmental political thought.

María Teresa Grillo is an assistant professor at the Department of Languages and Cultures of Mount Royal University in Calgary. She teaches Spanish and Spanish American literature and culture. Her research focuses on colonial and contemporary texts by Andean authors.

Adam Henne is an assistant professor of International Studies and Anthropology at the University of Wyoming. His research and teaching deal with the cultural politics of nature, informed by post-structuralism, political ecology and feminist theory.

Alex Latta is an associate professor in the Departments of Global Studies and Geography & Environmental Studies at Wilfrid Laurier University; he is also faculty in the Balsillie School of International Affairs. His research explores citizenship and socio-ecological conflict in Latin America, with a special focus on water, energy and environmental policy in Chile.

Judy Meltzer has a PhD in Political Science from Carleton University. She was previously senior analyst for the Andean Region at the Canadian Foundation for the Americas (FOCAL).

María Gabriela Merlinsky is a researcher at the National Council of Scientific and Technological Research (CONICET), Argentina. She is an associate at the Research Institute 'Gino Germani', and assistant professor in Research Methodology in Social Science at the University of Buenos Aires. Her specific research interests are environmental sociology, environmental conflicts and environmental policy.

Juliet Pinto is an associate professor in the Department of Journalism and Broadcasting, School of Journalism and Mass Communication, at Florida International University. Her major research interests include environmental journalism and media and democratization in Latin America.

Analiese Richard is an associate professor of Anthropology in the School of International Studies at the University of the Pacific. Her research concerns the role of the commons in democratic politics. Her current project examines the relationships between public science and grassroots organizing in struggles over biosecurity and traditional food systems in Mexico.

Tucker Sharon is a PhD candidate in History at the University of British Columbia and Liu Scholar at the Liu Institute for Global Issues. His current research focuses on road colonization and land tenure in the Peruvian Amazon.

Enrique R. Silva is an assistant professor and coordinator of the City Planning and Urban Affairs programs at Boston University, Boston, Massachusetts. His research and teaching foci are on urbanization and democratic governance in the Americas, as well as the formation of public sector planning institutions and practices. He is currently engaged in the institutionalization of planning policies in post-earthquake Haiti.

Juanita Sundberg is an associate professor in the Department of Geography at the University of British Columbia. Her work focuses on the cultural politics of nature conservation and is informed by feminist theory, critical race theory, post-humanism, political ecology and Latin American Studies.

Renzo Taddei is an anthropologist whose research in recent years has focused on environmental epistemologies and environmental politics. He earned his PhD in anthropology from Columbia University and is an assistant professor of Anthropology and Environment at the Federal University of São Paulo.

Jason Tockman holds a PhD in Political Science from the University of British Columbia and works as a sessional lecturer with UBC's Department of Political Science. His research and teaching explore Latin American state-society relations, indigenous politics, theories of citizenship and democracy, and natural resource policy.

Hannah Wittman is an associate professor of Food, Nutrition and Health in the Faculty of Land and Food Systems at the University of British Columbia. Her research interests include environmental sociology, food sovereignty, agrarian citizenship and agrarian social movements.

Index

Polo Campos, Augusto, 112, 126n
Potosí, Bolivia, 130
PRI. *See* Partido Revolucionario Institucional
   (PRI)
protected areas
   about, 55n2, 217–18
   in Brazil, 42–50, 52, 55n2
   See also Amazon rainforest;
   conservation; natural resources
protests. *See* campaigns and protests

Q'eqchí people, 101
Quijano, Aníbal, 112
quilombolas, 43, 45, 50, 51
Quixadá, Brazil, 85–86

race
   in Bolivia, 12, 134
   in Chile, 155, 156–57, 163–64
   dualism and, 239
   in Ecuador, 234
   in Guatemala, 11, 99, 103, 108n3,
      108n7
   imaginaries of place, 98
   in Peru, 115–17, 118–20, 121–26
Rainforest Action Network (RAN), 157–61
rain prophets, 78, 84–86, 88–89, 91
REDD programs, 8, 27, 30–33, 35, 36n5
Red en Defensa del Maíz Nativo (RDMN),
   60, 71
rights
   in Argentina, 190–93, 195, 198–200,
      202
   in Ecuador, 227–29
   frameworks of, 62, 78
   in Peru, 122
   See also land rights
road colonization, 117–20

Salinas, Carlos, 66
Sánchez de Lozada, Gonzalo, 136
San Geronimo, 103–5
Santiago, Chile, 13, 171–73, 177, 179, 186
scale, 4, 39–40, 54–55, 86, 149–50,
   155–57
science and technology
   authority of, 79–80, 157
   climate knowledge, 9–10, 78–79,
      80–86
   discourses of, 77–78, 79–80

in law, 194–95, 203–5, 205–6
in media, 233
See also knowledge; modernization
security
   biopolitical security, 11, 26–31
   climate security, 24, 26, 30–32, 36n2
   emergent risk, 25–26
   environmental citizenship, 24, 25–28,
      35
   framing of, 24
Serres, Michel, 15, 16
silver mining, 130–31
Sin Maíz No Hay País (SMNHP), 8, 60, 71,
   72, 73
social justice, 39, 43, 50
social movements
   in Argentina, 191–92, 196–98, 201
   in Bolivia, 130, 132, 140, 142
   in Brazil, 46, 51
   in Mexico, 59–60, 67
sovereignty
   food sovereignty, 8, 59–74
   of indigenous territory, 140, 143, 157,
      163
   of national state, 13, 24, 63, 68, 137,
      143, 173
   See also land rights
stewardship
   in Argentina, 216, 220–21
   environmental citizenship, 53
   See also the commons
Sumak Kawsay. *See buen vivir*
sustainable agrobiodiversity, 60–61, 63, 66,
   70–73
sustainable consumption, 39

technonature, 12, 149–51, 153
tin mining, 131
Tortilla Crisis, 59, 69–70
trade, 23, 61, 63, 66
traditional knowledge. *See* knowledge

Unión Nacional de Organizaciones
   Regionales Campesinas Autónomas
   (UNORCA), 65, 66, 67, 69
United Kingdom, 36n2
United States, 23, 28, 29, 30
El Universo, 235–38
urban contexts, 16–17
Uribe, Carlos, 183

Lightning Source UK Ltd.
Milton Keynes UK
UKOW07f2314080115

244127UK00009B/157/P